UPHEAVAL

LOU DOBBS

THRESHOLD EDITIONS

New York   London   Toronto   Sydney   New Delhi

Threshold Editions
A Division of Simon & Schuster, Inc.
1230 Avenue of the Americas
New York, NY 10020

First Threshold Editions hardcover edition January 2014

THRESHOLD EDITIONS and colophon are trademarks
of Simon & Schuster, Inc.

For information about special discounts for bulk purchases,
please contact Simon & Schuster Special Sales at 1-866-506-1949
or business@simonandschuster.com.

The Simon & Schuster Speakers Bureau can bring authors to your live event.
For more information or to book an event, contact the Simon & Schuster Speakers
Bureau at 1-866-248-3049 or visit our website at www.simonspeakers.com.

Designed by Akasha Archer

Manufactured in the United States of America

10   9   8   7   6   5   4   3   2   1

Library of Congress Cataloging-in-Publication Data

Dobbs, Lou.
  Upheaval / Lou Dobbs.
    pages   cm
  1. Social problems—United States.   2. United States—Social policy.
3. United States—Social conditions.   4. United States—Politics and
government.   I. Title.
  HN59.2.D63   2014
  306.0973—dc23
                                                                2013034055
  ISBN 978-1-4767-2885-8
  ISBN 978-1-4767-2887-2 (ebook)

CONTENTS

Author's Note • *vii*

Introduction • *1*

Chapter 1
CONSEQUENTIAL ELECTIONS 2014 • 15

Chapter 2
DIMINISHING, DISTANT DREAMS • 35

Chapter 3
BANKSHOT • 53

Chapter 4
BLESSED ARE THE CHILDREN • 69

Chapter 5
A TOUGH ENVIRONMENT • 89

Chapter 6
SPACE MYSTERIES AND MISADVENTURES • 111

CONTENTS

Chapter 7
FUNDAMENTAL FLAWS AND FAILINGS • 127

Chapter 8
DEMOGRAPHICS AND DESTINY DISTURBED • 149

Chapter 9
CHINA'S GOOD FORTUNE • 175

Chapter 10
THE SHARIA SPRING WE SPRUNG • 197

Chapter 11
OUT OF ONE, MANY • 221

Notes • 245

Acknowledgments • 255

Index • 257

AUTHOR'S NOTE

American history is filled with glory and victory, great achievements, a nation of stalwarts and heroes who discovered a new world, tamed wild frontiers, whose proud citizens won wars: fought, bought, bargained, and traded, and built the United States, the world's greatest constitutional republic, its freest society, its most expansive, productive, and wealthiest economy. Only Americans have set foot on the moon, and Americans have explored deeper in space than any other people.

But we haven't returned to the moon in four decades, and we have to catch rides with the Russians to get back to the International Space Station. We build less than we once did on our little patch of Earth. We're told by elites in business, media, and politics that we are too smart, too knowledgeable to do physical labor. We are told that manual-labor jobs are jobs that Americans won't do, that we have mysteriously acquired some inexplicable privilege not to sweat. But apparently, in acquiring the right not to sweat, many of us have been convinced to give up our right to secure our borders, to decide whom we will confer citizenship on from among all the citizens of the world. Our president and his acolytes in oh-so-dour words and tone tell us effectively that part-time work is good enough for Americans, high unemployment and slow economic growth are simply "the new Obama normal."

American is now a vast conundrum. There is festering frustration among the wealthy, the poor, and the middle class. The American dream has become more elusive as millions of Americans struggle to become middle class, and millions more struggle to hold their places in the middle class. Our elites seem knowingly intent on tearing up social contracts that have held our society together through decades of rapid social and economic change.

And what are the values that we share as a people? Those values were once thrift, efficiency, faith, community, ingenuity, straight talk, honesty, industriousness—all values that once defined us and the American way. But increasingly those values are eroding and being replaced by complacency, even hopelessness and indifference, as expanding, encroaching government influences and in some cases controls the lives of citizens under the guise of protecting and providing for them. Ours has become a dependent nation, whose society ever less frequently hears the words "independence" and "self-reliance." The broad social contract with which America has prospered and prevailed for two and a half centuries seems at times to have been discarded a bit at a time, without notice or discussion and perhaps, to never be restored. Relationships between government and the governed, between employers and the employed, between teachers and their citizens, are strained, disrupted, and in some instances ended altogether. Our aspirations as Americans are not just frustrated, but too often many of our fellow citizens no longer have faith in their ability to achieve educational, financial, political, and societal goals and ideals that were once shared broadly in our country. Of late, we frequently hear that if we will surrender just one more liberty, surrender one more element of our independence, we'll be secure from the forces from without, from the anger and hostility of radical Islamist terrorists who mean to destroy us, or in time the rising power of the People's Republic of China, or North Korea and Iran, Al Qaeda and the Taliban, or some combination of these. All of which represent challenges, threats, or potential threats to American lives or living standards, to one degree or another, whether as economic competitors or truly extant threats to the American nation.

America has experienced great upheaval and struggle throughout our history. The number of wars we've fought, the very construction of our government, prejudices most Americans to think of threats primarily as coming from nation-states, and our vulnerabilities to be primarily to external forces, handled by the Department of State, Department of Defense, our president, the commander-in-chief. But I believe our principal vulnerability, and the chief threats to the stability of our social order and economic well-being, indeed the very essence of our American way of life, go well beyond leagues of nation-states and ideologues who mean us harm. The greatest threat of upheaval is a combination of those nation-states, ideological extremists, religious zealots, and the confluence of internal forces that are weakening our notion of who we are, diminishing our confidence in the American dream itself, and leaving many of our citizens and many of our leaders questioning American exceptionalism, our way of life, and our relationship to one another and to the world itself. The very idea of America is under great stress, from within and without. The prospect of a great upheaval rises with each passing day that we decline to examine the consequences of the choices we are making as a people and as a nation. And these forces are allied, not in conspiracy, but in their contemporaneous array against us, our ideals, our values, and our nation's future.

It is no wonder that many Americans possess an enlarged sense of entitlement. We have prevailed in war, scientific and technological achievement, and economic success, and have created the freest and most prosperous society on the planet. We are far from perfect, and the truth is that we Americans tend to believe that the laws of cause and effect are sometimes suspended on our behalf. We've been careless in choosing those who will lead and represent us, and we've been careless in our disregard for the consequences of the public policy choices that Washington has made. We've elected in succession three presidents unencumbered by any significant knowledge of international relations or practice in foreign policy. We have permitted the outsourcing of millions of jobs and the offshoring of thousands upon thousands of factories and plants to cheaper markets without regard to jobs or capital lost to our home economy. And we have actually listened to our elites' rhetoric about the need for highly educated, highly skilled immigrants, which of course is true, but those same elites have spent their energy and more than a billion and a half dollars in lobbying money to bring in mostly unskilled and uneducated illegal immigrants. We've watched the Federal Reserve shore up our six largest commercial banks while those same banks have spent more than $100 billion on attorney and litigation fees and in settlements of improper lending and mortgage foreclosures since the 2008 financial crisis. And we hear hardly a word in our national liberal media about our students' poor performance in mathematics, science, engineering, and technology or the result of allowing as many as one third of our high school students to drop out. We have ignored too often the consequences of the public policy choices that contribute to such outcomes when what we must do is look at the facts and understand fully that the laws of cause and effect have not been rescinded in America and those facts are pretty good guideposts for all of us.

Perhaps that explains why one of the most popular segments on my show, *Lou Dobbs Tonight*, is what we call the Chalk Talk. Each weekday evening on the Fox Business Network I stand in front of an old-fashioned blackboard and spend three to five minutes scribbling and scrawling numbers and words all over that blackboard, talking about the critical issues that face us all. My audience loves the sweep of the subjects we take up, subjects that are often larger stories than the headlines of the day, more important to the well-being of our audience, more important to the country. And the blackboard I use may seem a little familiar. My producers went searching through the Fox News storage warehouse in an undisclosed location and discovered an old blackboard. They brushed off the cobwebs and blew off the dust and carried it back to Studio F, where we've put it to work. This ancient audiovisual artifact even has a legend, perhaps more a myth, that accompanies it. It is said that a fellow named Glenn Beck once used it. I don't know whether the legend or the stories are true, but no matter. I enjoy using the low-tech device each night, and we have a lot of fun with it. Sometimes serious fun. The blackboard helps prove each night that detail and facts and statistics don't have to be fancy to explain the core of any issue, and they certainly don't have to be dull. I have the advantage of having one of the smartest audiences in television, which makes these Chalk Talks fun for the audience and fun for me. There will be more than a few Chalk Talks in the pages ahead, as we focus on the nature of the potential upheaval we face as a nation, and the axis of forces and powers that seek to end the great American experiment and the American dream.

UPHEAVAL

INTRODUCTION

June 10, 1991

That's the date we celebrated our military's victory over Iraqi forces in Kuwait and Iraq. We celebrated with a ticker-tape parade in New York City. It was a thrilling sight, confetti and ribbons raining down upon our troops as they marched proudly through the Canyon of Heroes. My family and I were among the estimated four and a half million people who stood on the sidewalks of New York that day to cheer our troops and their leader, General Norman Schwarzkopf. There was lots of brass there that day, General Colin Powell, Secretary of Defense Cheney, the mayor, of course, David Dinkins, but like most New Yorkers, my intention was focused on our troops, our flag, and the hero general who had made short work of repulsing Saddam Hussein's invasion of Kuwait and driving his forces beyond Basra, back to Baghdad.

Americans had much to celebrate that day. A decisive military victory, courageous and brilliant leadership, the fact that America's leaders had chosen not to press a victorious campaign into a full-on invasion and occupation of Iraq. America's restraint was all the more remarkable because the only limits to our global power were imposed by our values, our judgment, and our leaders' understanding that power is often greatly magnified and leveraged by the careful application of that power. With the collapse of Marxism-Leninism and the Soviet Union, the United States stood as the world's only superpower. And, by God, we were acting like it.

But it has always been strange to me that we never threw a parade for those who fought and struggled to secure the biggest victory of all, the winning of the Cold War. It would have been quite something to have celebrated all that America and our allies accomplished over the course of almost a half century of cold war and military conflict from Korea to Vietnam, and ceaseless covert engagement throughout the world between the United States and the Soviet Union. At least we finally got around to honoring our Korean War veterans with a parade in New York two weeks after the Gulf War parade. Have we really become a people who no longer want to celebrate our military, the achievement of our national goals? Are we a people who don't want to be reminded of all we owe our military and our intelligence agencies, who protect our nation each and every day? Is there now something so overwhelmingly politically incorrect about patriotism that we can't celebrate our heroes, those who achieve, those who sacrifice and serve our great nation?

Many of us are old enough to remember when our military marched in Independence Day parades everywhere around the country each July 4. So when's the last time you stood on a curb or sidewalk and thrilled at the sight of our troops marching proudly with our flag down Main Street or Eighth Avenue, or whatever street is the center of your town, your city? We've moved quite a ways over the years from those parades. I don't really know why. Did somebody make a decision and forget to tell us? Is there some reason we would not want our youngsters to thrill at the sight of our men and women in uniform, to watch our flag held high as we stand together as citizens saluting all that it stands for? Who made that decision, and why have we let it stand?

And why are we moving away from singing the praises of God for His bountiful blessings upon us and our beautiful country? It's as if there's almost a national silence, an aversion to public expressions of love of God and country. Some consider them overly sentimental, too patriotic, overly religious for our times, too hackneyed, I suppose, and too nationalistic. We don't hear Lee Greenwood's "God Bless the USA" nearly as often as I'd like. I'm sure to a lot of people these days it sounds startlingly unsophisticated, maybe even corny, to acknowledge our national pride and our debt and duty to this nation. Has it become politically incorrect to be grateful for our immense natural resources, to express pride in the great advantages we Americans enjoy because of the land we're so privileged to live upon and the seas that surround us? Instead of thanking God, we seem to spend more time trying to crowd Him out of our public square to appease those atheists, agnostics, and others who are put upon by us rubes who dare still cling to our Bibles, guns, and quaint patriotism and outright devotion to this great nation.

Our riches are overwhelming, and the most natural of human emotions would seem to be humility, our most natural reflex to express gratitude for being such fortunate beneficiaries, whether of our natural resources or of the technologies we've innovated to accelerate and expand our capacity to calculate and communicate, from dramatically reducing greenhouse emissions, to landing on the moon and exploring Mars and beyond. Instead of the deep, profound gratitude and humility that we might expect of most Americans, increasingly our fellow citizens seem to be in the grip of a festering frustration that is palpable almost everywhere I go. A sense among our citizens that our leaders don't elevate our society, but rather subvert the character and the values that have characterized a great and proud nation and people for almost two and a half centuries. Many of us feel alienated in our private lives from the institutions that were once the bulwarks of life in America, providing both support and guidance in our daily lives, but that now often merely confuse and disappoint us. Our politics disappoint because neither of our major parties is very effective at creating solutions to our most intractable problems or resolving the issues and challenges of our day.

Our political parties understandably don't always succeed, but we should expect at least that Democrats and Republicans would possess the energy and the honesty to acknowledge their failures, to on occasion relent and try a broad experimentation with integrity: intellectual integrity, moral integrity, integrity in governance.

I don't know whether such integrity will ever descend on Washington, but such an event seems less likely under this president. Barack Obama won the presidency campaigning on Hope and Change, on both the implied and explicit promise that he would unite all Americans. His failure to fulfill that promise emphatically suggests that he was not sincere, and far too many voters simply saw and heard in Obama and his words what they wanted to see and what they wanted to hear. The result over five years has been a greater sense of helplessness among our citizenry and a country firmly divided between red and blue states, left and right, Republican and Democrat. Division is to be expected in a two-party system as robust as ours, but the nastiness, the corrosiveness of our politics is rising to alarming levels. I'm no sissy, and I love the arena, the bad bruises and hard falls that all of us take when we engage in the national debate and discussion, campaigns and contests of public life. But it seems to me that the ideas in this great arena of ours have grown smaller as venom and bile have become more toxic. Perhaps this is as President Obama wants it, because he has certainly contributed mightily to it. I've never seen a man less concerned about the truth of his words, less concerned about the consequences of his choices, a man who's seemingly committed to creating an ever-greater dependency on our government, all the while seeming to preside over Washington, D.C., as a celebrity rather than a president fulfilling his constitutional duty to preserve and protect our Constitution and serve the American people and the national interest.

The pioneers, the entrepreneurs who built this country, believed that, while America's streets were never paved with gold, our country offered everyone an opportunity to succeed—as long as they had the work ethic and grit and determination required. Today, that dream, cherished and achieved for so long by so many, seems to be slipping out of reach for most Americans. The institutions that we have traditionally turned to for strength and leadership are in upheaval. As are our traditional values. Thrift, ingenuity, faith, independence, self-reliance, plain-spokenness, a fierce love of God, country, and family—all that once defined "the American way." We are a changing people. Much of the change is not for the better, much that is different in American life is not even remarked upon by our national media or our academic social critics, and as the challenges that confront us become more dangerous there is less evidence that we as a society are willing to confront those issues, let alone expend the energy to prevail against them. Our values, many of our principles and standards, are subsumed by a government that is insatiable in its appetite for greater dominion over our lives. The American way was an expression of our ideals, our values, and the social contract that formed the understanding of the basic relationship between our citizens and our government since our founding. That is changing. Relationships between the government and the governed, between employers and employees, teachers and students, even friends and family, are being redefined, replaced, or simply rejected. The rending of America's social contract is one of many forces that confront the very idea of America, and challenge our future, our destiny, which many of us have always believed to be assured by providence. We face an axis of upheaval, powerful dynamics set in motion over the course of the last half century, forces that have become far more powerful with the passing of each decade. Unchecked, those forces will overwhelm this nation and culminate in the failure of the great American experiment. I firmly believe we remain equal to the tests we face, but we must understand that arrayed against us is an axis of upheaval intent upon the destruction of America, and all that this nation has represented to the world for so long. The axis of forces arrayed against us is powerful. Let's examine several that are already diminishing our strength and our power:

OUR POLITICIANS AND POLITICAL LEADERS ARE FAILING

It has become popular to talk about bipartisan dysfunction, the culture of corruption and cronyism that infuses all of Washington, D.C. Would our system of government even be recognizable to our founders? Government has grown so vast in reach and power and numbers that Jefferson, Madison, Adams, and Washington would likely struggle to discern their intended balance among the legislative, executive, and judicial branches, and the political counterweight of state governments. And Washington, D.C., now operates less like a constitutional republic than a royal court or totalitarian regime suffused with members of a ruling class, an ever-expanding political establishment, and a vast, dumb bureaucracy to do the bidding of the splendid elites.

Politicians in both parties, from the White House to Capitol Hill, give lip service to free markets and competition while spurring ever-greater, dangerous expansion of our central federal government. In the royal court of the federal government, few elites can match the influence of the corporatists who bring vast sums of money to guarantee their access and favorable reception for even their most vapid and self-serving propositions. Corporate welfare is not simply an expression, it is a political reality and an industry unto itself in Washington, D.C. The same free marketers and competitive capitalists seek federal largesse, support, and yes, welfare, for almost every imaginable aspect of their businesses and industries. Bankers who protest government regulation of their industry are also the first to seek the support of government when faced with competition, or the prospect of collapse. We've allowed government to reach into almost every corner of our economy, where it can choose winners and losers, attack industries that the ideological adherents of an administration determine to be irrelevant despite the protests of the marketplace. Reasonable arguments can be made ideologically that the government's insistence on supporting some of Wall Street's most irresponsible bankers and Detroit's anachronistic carmakers was effective policy, or plain stupid. Either way, it was a public policy choice that a free-enterprise capitalist economy should not expect of a constitutional republic. The ultimate consequence of ever-larger government is the necessity of spending ever more money, a government that seeks to find new ways in which to spend money, and money that will have to be repaid by our children, grandchildren, great-grandchildren . . . you get the idea. Enormous, unimaginable debt is the enduring legacy of all the presidents who have served since Dwight Eisenhower. Our elected leaders of both parties in the House, the Senate, and the White House pretend that amortizing the debt they have amassed over succeeding generations is almost as responsible and prudent as good public policy in the first place. If only our political leaders would spend as much time creating intelligent, effective policies as they do rationalizing their ill-considered decisions and trying to mitigate the damage and pain their public-policy choices cause.

OUR BUSINESS LEADERS ARE FAILING

Business throughout our history has produced great leaders who vigorously served the national interest as government officials and public servants. If there were ever a demonstration of true bipartisanship, it was the service of these leaders who were brought into government by presidential administrations because of their talent, resourcefulness, intellect, and experience, rather than their partisanship. Throughout history, ambassadorships have been awarded to those who support, politically and financially, presidential candidates. Now, electoral and financial support for the president has become a first consideration in almost every leadership post of any administration. As for business itself, most CEOs have given up their public voice to business associations like the Chamber of Commerce or the Business Roundtable, relieving the CEO of one of his or her most important responsibilities, which is to advocate in the national interest. The Chamber and Roundtable, however, also relieve the CEO of the sometimes intimidating repercussions that can follow any public comment that carries political and economic implications. It's a shame. It's the way it is. Only the CEOs themselves, their boards of directors, and investors can change what has become a retreat by most business leaders from the arena of public discussion and debate. Many CEOs won't speak truth to political power because their businesses are often inextricably intertwined with government. And few corporations can withstand a vengeful administration. Nearly all seek favors that accompany the public support of the CEO and the CEO's corporation. It's the best kind of cobranding by the rich and powerful. Corporate leaders like Jeffrey Immelt and even billionaire icons like Warren Buffett have cozied up to Obama administration officials over state dinners and "business task forces." Quite a tradeoff. Warren Buffett in the last presidential election gave Mr. Obama virtual political immunity for his antibusiness policies and attitude, while Jeffrey Immelt gave the president plausible deniability of the charge that he wasn't working effectively to create jobs or improve America's international competitiveness. As I said, quite a tradeoff.

Men and women used to come home from work with sweat on their brow and grease on their sleeves. The blue-collar worker is now an endangered species in America. The hard work of making and fixing things was once respected in America. Labor on our farms was praised. Physical labor of any kind is looked down upon by many of the elites in both parties as "work that Americans won't do." Those elites need a kick in the butt, and everyone in this country must regain and honor the work ethic that built this nation. And there should be no work that Americans won't do, no American should look down his or her nose at anyone who does that work, and our elected officials and lawmakers must understand that work in and of itself is a cherished opportunity. And all our leaders, governmental, business, and academic, must set aside as a priority the opportunity to work, and work for a living wage.

In the Obama view, innovation has frequently consisted of pumping billions of taxpayer dollars into politically chosen, ideologically helpful enterprises like Solyndra that create spectacular public failures. Three of the first five companies that received loan guarantees for their projects—Solyndra, Beacon Power, and Abound Solar—declared bankruptcy. Taxpayers lost more than $535 million dollars in the Solyndra debacle alone. We expanded the role of government in our society rapidly as we confronted the worst economic crisis since the Great Depression. Government's influence permeates almost every sector of our economy and almost every aspect of our daily lives, most of which are now altering, perhaps irretrievably, the American way of life. We are a people slowly coming to grips with new realities, most of which potentially threaten the American way of life. President Obama made it clear in the days leading up to his first inaugural that he intended the "fundamental transformation" of America. The outcome of the 2014 midterm elections may well determine whether he is ultimately successful in his ambition.

OUR NATIONAL MEDIA ARE FAILING

Most of our national media are no longer working in their traditional role as watchdogs over our vast, powerful federal government. The national media are performing basically more as lapdogs than watchdogs. Many of the country's leading political journalists are in fact coconspirators with this administration and the political left. Fox News reported that the Obama administration created what it called a "Behavioral Insights" team, modeled on a similar program in the U.K. What does the administration want to do? It wants to create ways for the so-called nudge squad to subtly influence people's behavior and, in effect, make it easier for the government to ensure that its citizens do what they're told, whether it's paying taxes, insulating their homes, or whatever else Big Brother decides is best for them. Almost all of the national media saw no reason for concern, no suggestion of mind control or more pervasive government influence over our lives.

Then there's the indifference of the national media to the stonewalling of the Benghazi investigation and the targeting of conservative groups by the Internal Revenue Service. These White House scandals are truly becoming as much of a scandal for the national media that refuses to hold the government and this White House accountable. This new era of media compliance with power, complicity of purpose with the Obama administration, augurs poorly for our constitutional republic, which depends upon an aggressive, even adversarial news media to ensure the public has full knowledge of what our government is doing and the effects of its policies.

A host of forces are aligned in support of the president and his transformational vision. I call these forces the axis of upheaval, because whether consciously, conspiratorially, or even as unintended consequence, they have the potential to further roll back the standard of living for all Americans, to make the lowest common denominator the standard for American education and media. These forces range from an aging population to flailing younger generations, to banks too large and powerful, to corporations that seek to dominate the public square, and to the efforts of many to drive religion from that public square. Even as we experience the onset of an extraordinary energy boom in this country, we face the prospect of other dwindling natural resources, including water and fertile, productive agricultural land. Our court system, once the beacon of justice in the Western world, has been politicized and corrupted. And while civil trials take years to adjudicate, criminal trials bear little resemblance to the constitutional rights of due process and speedy trials with juries made up of engaged citizens. This is a bloated court and legal system that lawyers themselves will not reform. And infusing all quarters of our society and economy is the paralyzing, numbing political correctness that has reduced communication and public discourse to a sticky gruel of vacuous words that a single-minded public orthodoxy is forced to consume. These are some of the threats, even extant dangers, to our nation from within, and are all within our power to meet and to overcome should we muster the courage to face them honestly and engage them energetically.

There are, of course, immense challenges, serious threats, and yes, extant dangers to America from without. There is little doubt that the United States will be contending with what is now a red storm rising in China. It is impossible to know beyond a doubt whether China will emerge as one of several powerful competitors to the United States for economic dominance by the mid-twenty-first century, or whether it will be an ideological and geopolitical threat to our global interests. Much of the outcome, of course, depends on the choices our leaders make in the next few decades. As we cut our military budgets, China is spending huge amounts of money to enlarge and improve the capabilities of its military forces. China's military budget has risen nearly 10 percent each year over the past decade while the United States, after cutting twelve combat brigades, will be able to field an army only a quarter the size of the People's Liberation Army. Chinese military spending is forecast to outpace U.S. military spending by about a third by midcentury. Russia's leadership seeks to restore its place atop what it hopes will be a multipolar geopolitical world, and soon. Its recent economic success may well augur a military and strategic capability that, while less than that of the Soviet era, will assure Russia of considerable influence over world affairs. India most certainly will be among the global leaders that will compete with the United States, China, and Russia economically on all geopolitical issues. India represents, I believe, a powerful economic competitor, but also a natural geopolitical ally and potentially an important countervailing influence to both China and Russia in the region. Brazil is the third-largest country in our hemisphere, the second-most populous, and without question its economy will dominate the South American market for the foreseeable future. It will become an increasingly important trading partner in the next few decades, a competitor, and an increasingly natural ally of both the United States and the European Union. I hope that U.S. and European leaders will vigorously pursue geopolitical alliances and ever-increasing trade ties with each of these countries.

The axis of upheaval includes nation-states with geopolitical, economic designs on our future, as well as transnational, ideologically driven forces, such as radical Islamists. Internally these forces include weakened border and port security, an inability to enforce and indifference to the enforcement of law, an electoral system that in many states is simply corrupt and in others is operated as a network of overwhelmed volunteers who understand neither the threats to the integrity of our electoral system nor our government nor the technology with which we've begun counting often unverifiable electronic votes. The internal elements of this axis of upheaval are championed by none other than President Obama, who has not relented in his dream of fundamentally transforming America. His dream is not ours, and for ours to prevail, we must commit our energies to nothing less than preserving our great constitutional republic and free-enterprise, capitalist economy.

CHAPTER I

CONSEQUENTIAL ELECTIONS 2014

So it has come to this. Barack Obama is a two-term president. A president who in his first term presided over one of the worst economies in American history, whose foreign policy was utterly incomprehensible, a leader who expressed contempt for the foundations of our free-enterprise, capitalist system now has three more years in which to either further America's decline under his stewardship or truly reverse direction in his policies, as many of us expected he would in his first term.

It's clear we can no longer truthfully say that each presidential election is the most important in our recent history. That would leave out some awfully important elections—midterm elections. Had not the Republicans won decisively in 2010, it is likely things would have been woefully different. Only the Tea Party in 2010 stood between this president and the full implementation of what I believe would have been disastrous consequences for the nation. Even though President Obama won a historic victory (yes, another one) in 2012, a Republican Congress also prevailed and has managed to blunt at least some of President Obama's initiatives to expand without limit the size and power of our federal government. And, of course, 2012 lived up to its billing as the most important election in our history, although at times it seems Governor Mitt Romney had no idea how important the election was to him and to our nation. It mattered a lot. Mr. Obama's victory put in place for the next four years:

- Obamacare
- A government hostile to business
- A government hostile to free enterprise and innovation
- A government hostile to state and local governance
- A government enormously hostile to individual rights

Obamacare is a Frankenstein creation of a statist, socialist administration intent on raising taxes—taxes increasing now on those with higher income levels as well as small business owners. The national debt is rising, even as our rivals and enemies take unfair strategic advantage of a president and administration that seemingly do not understand economics, domestic public policy, or how to effectively pursue our national interests in a difficult, complex, and dangerous world.

It may be comforting to Republicans to consider Mr. Obama's victory another "fluke." But his 2012 victory was no fluke. Nor was it a stolen election. Were the polls "skewed"? It seems only the losers' polls were skewed. Let's be clear. Only the losers had the numbers wrong. Think about this number:

65,915,796

That is how many Americans decided to re-elect this president—about 51 percent of those who cast ballots across the country.

Barack Obama was the first Democrat since FDR to win two popular majorities in a row. Mr. Obama won in places like Virginia and Florida, Nevada and Colorado, all critical swing states that might have gone for a Republican candidate. He dominated all of New England, and came closer than expected in Mississippi and South Carolina, where he won 43 percent and 44 percent of the vote respectively. The president won 71 percent of Hispanic voters, 93 percent of African-Americans, and 50 percent of Catholics. Adding insult to injury, Democrats picked up an improbable two seats in the United States Senate and eight seats in the House of Representatives.

The 2012 election wasn't all that close. There was a lot of talk about the "enthusiasm gap" favoring Republicans, and somehow the GOP did manage to nominate a candidate who received almost one million more votes than John McCain in 2008. Obama had three and a half million fewer votes than in 2008. Sadly for Republicans, whatever enthusiasm gap there was, wasn't sufficient to bridge the vote gap. Few in either party were enthusiastic about going to the polls and pulling the lever for their candidate. Given the mediocrity of the choices, who can blame them? What made the difference was a well-conceived, well-organized, well-managed campaign on one side and an unmitigated mess on the other.

Let's give credit where credit is due. And Republicans had better hope that their party does exactly that. President Obama, David Axelrod, and David Plouffe turned out to be every bit as smart as they told us they were. Their campaign outstrategized, outorganized, outworked, and outclassed the Republicans at every turn. That's the first unpleasant reality with which the Republicans have to come to terms. They need to grow their party. They need to get out the vote, and to do that, Washington Republicans had better get out of town as much as they can and get to know a lot of soon-to-be Republicans. This midterm will be all about hard work, reaching out to new GOP voters and getting them so excited they actually vote.

If Republicans haven't been looking for and recruiting a dozen David Axelrods by now, people who know how to energize a base and get out their vote, then Republicans will see the same devastating results in 2014, and in 2016, as they did in 2012. I'm reluctantly complimenting the Democrats and I'm hoping Republicans have the humility and street smarts to do the same. Because the GOP must emulate Democratic success if they are to win anytime soon. Repeating one's mistakes, one's own stupidity, and ignoring cause and effect, is a sure path to even greater Republican frustration and continued failure.

The 2012 election wasn't about the Democrats. It was supposed to be, of course. But it turned out to be about the Republicans and their failures of imagination and courage, and their reliance on an old-guard cadre of greedy strategists and fundraisers who filled their pockets as they floated more empty rhetoric and broke more Republican hearts. The Republicans did all this to themselves in 2012, and will soon find out if they've done it again in 2014. And so will America.

The country needs a loyal opposition to the Democratic Party, a countervailing political organization to the Democrats, one that will stand in the way of the Democrats' inexhaustible appetite for ever-bigger government, higher taxes, and less respect for the individual and his or her rights.

Republicans in Washington have often seemed to be as eager for tax hikes, bailouts, and corporate welfare as Democrats.

Herewith a short primer for Republicans who want to be something more than Democrat-lite coupled with lower taxes for corporations, lower taxes and fewer regulations for businesses:

RULE #1: REWARD SUCCESS, NOT FAILURE

In the private sector, if you run a business into the ground, you don't tend to get rewarded with another CEO job. But not so in the Republican Party. Many of the people guiding Mitt Romney to defeat were the same people who in 2008 had helped John McCain run one of the worst imaginable presidential campaigns ever. Many of them had helped George W. Bush leave office with the lowest approval rating of any president in our history. You might have thought that these geniuses would be run out of Washington on a rail. Instead they've shown up again and again in the Republican Party. Why? One can only assume that it suits the Republican power elite to keep fools around who will do their bidding and forswear intellectual energy, originality, and political independence and integrity.

The Republicans are particularly gifted when it comes to recycling. By "recycling" I mean recycling the same leaders, the same consultants, the same pollsters, the same media advisors, and the same fundraisers election cycle after election cycle. It's insanity. Pure insanity. A manager at your local 7-Eleven has a better track record of hiring responsible, competent people than some of these multimillion-dollar political campaigns.

Even the choice of Republican candidates presented to the GOP electorate was symptomatic of a lack of imagination. And what a study in recycling! Most of the candidates on the stage in 2012 had been in politics for years, some for decades. Yet the Republican Party struggled to convince voters that any of them was a candidate in the tradition of the Republican Party, or would prevail in the national contest with Barack Obama. And yet it was from this group of candidates that the party chose the one candidate who lost the last time to the guy who lost to Obama the first time. I realize that's a tortured way to say that the Republicans selected Mitt Romney to challenge Barack Obama after Barack Obama had beaten the daylights out of John McCain, who had easily beaten Romney in the race for the 2008 Republican nomination. Somehow Republicans convinced themselves that Romney was a really good idea.

Washington doesn't make a lot of sense to the rest of the country. But even by Washington standards, Republicans have to be considered particularly screwball. Going into the most important election in our history, which is always by definition the next election, how can it be that Senator Lindsey Graham and Senator John McCain appear on Sunday talk shows and cable news networks more than any other senators or congressmen? How is it that the Republicans who raised the most money in 2008 and lost were the ones who raised the most money in 2012, and yes, lost again? So I want to propose a rule for the Republicans to consider. Henceforth and forevermore Republicans will not invite back members of campaign teams, or candidates, who make careers out of losing. Is the Republican Party so agonizingly and pitifully bereft of talent that there is no one in their ranks who is original or fresh or new or deserving of the party's support? I can think of a dozen likely candidates right now. I may not agree with all that any one of these candidates has to offer, but there is no question that Senator Ted Cruz, Senator Rand Paul, Senator Marco Rubio, Congressman Trey Gowdy, Senator Kelly Ayotte, Congressman Bob Goodlatte, and Dr. Benjamin Carson are just a few names that the Republican Party should embrace.

RULE #2: IDEAS MATTER

Take a look at this number, this very big, Republican number:

$992,500,000

That is how much money Republican-affiliated groups raised for the 2012 election. I'm talking about the Romney campaign, the Republican Party, and Mitt Romney's Restore Our Future Super PAC combined. When you add in the numbers of the six largest Super PACs and outside funders, here's what you get.

American Crossroads	$91,115,000
Americans for Prosperity	$33,542,000
Crossroads GPS	$22,146,000
American Future Fund	$19,038,000
Winning Our Future	$17,008,000
Americans for Job Security	$15,223,000[1]
SUBTOTAL =	$198,072,000
PLUS	$992,500,000
TOTAL =	$1,190,572,000

More than a billion dollars—a number that defies comprehension. It is also incomprehensible how much of that money was simply wasted. Television ads telling you why you shouldn't vote for Barack Obama and why Mitt Romney was the bee's knees. Now this is what Republicans across the country received in return for all that investment of big money, and lots of television time:

0

All that money bought nothing. The 2012 Republican campaign seemed at times utterly mindless. The Romney campaign was about money, invective, fear, and almost no discussion of ideas. The Romney campaign, and all who were making so much money from his candidacy, was bereft of imagination, and of new ideas. Ideas still matter in politics. Romney and his strategists, tacticians, and fundraisers had none. Not a single new idea with which to capture the attention and the hopes of Republican voters. Romney's television ads, the Republican Party's commercials, were all about full immersion. But the candidate himself was not only not immersed in the politics and the contest, his interest at times seemed to amount to no more than an infrequent furtive glance at a body politic who would have eagerly responded to a candidate with bright ideas and better promises. Even Obama's tired rhetoric seemed to brighten when compared to Romney's tiresome clichés and his lack of passion.

The 2012 presidential campaign was one of the dirtiest in recent memory. It was also one of the most disappointing and least interesting campaigns. None of this bothers the strategists and media buyers and consultants running Republican campaigns. They made millions off this losing campaign, just as they did in 2008. They may have left Republicans with nothing to show for it but smoldering ruins where the GOP once stood, but they walked off with millions of dollars in their own pockets. Why should they bother with ideas to appeal to the electorate when they and their friends can just air boilerplate attack ads and walk off with hefty checks, regardless of whether they win or lose?

The Democratic Party is a functioning coalition. The Republican Party is a fund-raising organization. The Democratic Party has members, while the Republican Party has visitors. You take the money away from the Democrats and they still have a group of followers committed to a set of ideas. Terrible ideas, but still ideas. You take away money and the other functions of the Republican Party apparatus and you have an empty tent. The Republican Party doesn't stand for much because most of all, they are the party of big business, working hard to cut corporate taxes as they quietly collaborated with Democrats to raise income taxes and payroll taxes. They have caved on taxes. They have caved on spending. The Republican Party has sent Americans abroad to do nation-building when the party promised they would not. The Republicans will do no better in the 2014 midterm elections than they did in 2012 if they continue to merely oppose what Democrats stand for, oppose anything Barack Obama proposes. And Paul Ryan talking about budget deficits and corporate taxes will not win the day. It's time for a Republican vision, it's time for Republicans to talk about values, and to demonstrate that the Republican Party is smart, and bold, and the party to lead us to a bright American future, the party of the American dream. And to prevail, the GOP must be recognized by voters as the party of ideas, and ideals.

RULE #3: SOLUTIONS MUST BE
SMARTER THAN THE PROBLEMS

As Hurricane Sandy bore down on America's East Coast, a comedian wrote this headline on his website: "Romney Calls for Emergency Tax Cuts." It was funny because Romney and the Republicans had been talking about tax cuts as a solution to almost everything. The headline was almost believable. Republicans have been harping on a few simplistic approaches to most big issues. To spur economic growth, cut tax rates, cut regulations, cut unions, and trim government: prosperity to follow. I don't argue with those ideas. In most cases they are sound economic policy. But as a prescription for all that ails us, they're simply inadequate, insufficient, and hackneyed beyond tolerance.

Republicans need to first admit those ideas won't resolve or fix the complex challenges we face in this economy and society. If Republicans are to hold their majority in the House, or perhaps enlarge it, they will have to ask Paul Ryan to forgo his obvious delight in being both the "Budget Man" and the self-appointed arbiter of Republican values as he's become increasingly Republican-lite, suddenly eager it seems to appease and accommodate Democrats on a host of issues, including immigration. His early embrace of the Senate Gang of Eight immigration and border security sham could well have led to disaster for the Republican Party. Republicans, led by Congressman Bob Goodlatte, chairman of the House Judiciary Committee, Congressman Trey Gowdy, and the House leadership, all discovered in the summer of 2013 that they could seize national leadership and responsibility for any issue, including immigration, border security, and farm policy, and win.

One of the reasons that Republicans did so poorly in the 2012 presidential election is simple. Republicans of all stripes and kinds shared two qualities: there was a lack of enthusiasm for the nominee, and the only detectable energy in the entire campaign was that of those being paid obscenely to strategize and consult the various candidates and the nominee, and of those raising obscene amounts of money, much of which ended up in their own pockets, and as best I can tell, accomplished next to nothing on behalf of the party or the nominee.

RULE #4: BITE REALITY BEFORE REALITY BITES YOU

The 2014 midterm elections are an extraordinary opportunity for the Republican Party, and the last best chance to save this nation. President Obama has presented this opportunity on a political silver platter. And you and I both know that the Republican Party is altogether capable of absolutely missing the moment and blowing the opportunity. After losing the 2012 presidential election, the Republican National Committee studied their mistakes, in all fairness tried to overcome their penchant for denial of reality, and came out with a report that can best be described as a modest exercise in self-flagellation. They even referred to the report as "the autopsy." Publicly. Time and time again. "The autopsy" basically concluded that the Republican Party wasn't enough like the Democratic Party and therefore failed in the election. (If the GOP brings similar analytical skills and deductive ability to this year's elections, their postelection report this year will be titled "Autopsy II.")

One of the astonishing stories of election night 2012 was the display of disbelief by Republican pundits, exemplified by Karl Rove, that they could have been so wrong as they watched, through the evening, the vote overwhelm their nominee. Rove and other party savants, Republican true believers, insisted that leading up to the elections the polls were wildly skewed in favor of Democrats, that Obama wouldn't win the black vote as he had in 2008, that the "silent majority" would go to the polls in massive numbers and rescue Romney. And reality bit, and bit hard. And I suspect all of them carry the scars of those bites from that night. I hope so, and that those scars will remind them not to indulge in a favorite Republican pastime of the past several election cycles—namely, ignoring inconvenient truths and indulging in the farcical belief that big money raised is better than big numbers voting at the polls.

Republicans still have the opportunity to engage voters all over the country, and to get reacquainted with grassroots politics. Big money buys a lot, but the Republican Party has the opportunity to shape the political reality this year, with an energetic and expansive grassroots campaign. It has the opportunity to do so with compelling ideas, and with great energy exerted in the national interest, and to make certain, this time, that in this year's elections, the Republican reality bites the Democrats and the Obama White House.

RULE #5: REPUBLICANS MUST BE THE PARTY OF THE AMERICAN DREAM

I realize a lot of Republicans want to forget the 2012 election. But to win, the leaders of the Republican Party have got to recall vividly their mistakes and failures. And chief among those failures was permitting themselves to become the party of privilege, to favor corporatism over dynamic entrepreneurialism, and to all but ignore the needs and concerns of the middle class.

I told my audience at the outset of the 2012 campaign that the party that best communicated its concerns for middle America, that talked to them directly and honestly, would win the election. Good God, Mitt Romney didn't even try to be an aspirational candidate. Obama tried everything possible to win the election. Despite his policy failures and his failures of leadership, Obama did speak to the middle class. Obama even picked up some of my language, using a phrase I first wrote in my book *The War on the Middle Class*, back in 2006, in which I referred to "the middle class and those who aspire to join it." That phrase I've used relentlessly ever since. Maybe he read my material. More likely his political advisors and writers did. It's for sure the Republicans didn't. It was as if in 2012 the Republican Party lost all connection to the people who make this country work, day in and day out.

In some ways, Mitt Romney can't be blamed for the yawning gap between his campaign and the middle class. He had a successful career in finance, but he hadn't worked a day in his life alongside a blue-collar worker. He was far more at home in the cushy cliff-top mansions of La Jolla overlooking the Pacific than walking the floor of a steel mill in eastern Ohio or riding a tractor in rural Wisconsin. And it showed every time his campaign staged photo ops alongside factory workers and farmers.

Throughout the campaign, there wasn't a Republican running for a major statewide or national office who didn't shuffle his or her way, hand outstretched, along the Wall Street cocktail circuit. The checks amassed from a single event at a Plaza Hotel conference room full of private equity financiers and hedge fund gurus beat a year's worth of campaign events back home. And we wonder why Republicans vote for billion-dollar bailouts to the banking industry? If you don't know any middle-class people and don't spend any substantive time with them, except as props in a camera shot, how can you expect to speak to them? In return for massive contributions to campaign committees and PACs and Super PACs, politicians end up fashioning policies that transfer hundreds of billions of dollars of taxpayer money to these corporations in the form of subsidies, loan guarantees, and tax breaks.

Say what you will about Bill Clinton, one of his greatest accomplishments was reforming welfare. The example of the single mother with six kids collecting welfare checks in perpetuity always suffered from exaggeration, but to the extent welfare queens did exist, Bill Clinton and a Republican Congress kicked them off the rolls in 1996. What hasn't ended is our government's doling out billions of dollars in support to well-connected companies.

Throughout the campaign, Republicans made no effort to distance themselves from handouts to big business or recklessness on Wall Street. They attacked Obama boondoggles like loan guarantees to green energy company Solyndra, but said nothing about their favored giveaways to big businesses like rural broadband, the Overseas Private Investment Corporation, and the Export-Import Bank.

RULE #6: NO MESSAGE IS A MESSAGE

I don't know what the Republicans' message will be this year. If I did, I could probably tell you whether they will win or not, whether they will hold their majority in the House, whether they will take the Senate. Forecasting Republican ingenuity, innovation, boldness, and energy is a hazardous proposition, so I'll refrain. Instead I'll just cross my fingers and hope they come up with a message for these midterms. I do have a few message suggestions for the Republicans. While personally I love the Gadsden flag declaration "Don't tread on me," I realize we need something a little warmer, a little fuzzier, for these modern times. So how about "America Works," or "Building Dreams"?

Republican candidates all across the country need catchy slogans and strong messages. Remember what happened in the 2012 election campaign. Even those who didn't pay attention to the campaign could tell you what Obama's re-election slogan was. It was "Forward." What the Obama campaign left out was that a second term would push America forward to the edge of a financial cliff. But it was nonetheless an effective branding strategy. The Democratic convention had thousands of participants clutching light blue signs with "Forward" printed on them.

No one except for Romney's campaign spinmeisters can tell you what Mitt Romney's slogan was. He didn't have one. Nearly every attempt at messaging involved inverting and criticizing something catchy that Obama said. You couldn't watch a speech at the Republican National Convention without hearing some critique of the phrase "You didn't build that," which Obama infamously said about business owners who relied on government services and investments like police and roads. Obama's statement was among the more revealing things he said on the campaign trail, and he did deserve criticism for it, but criticism is not the same thing as fashioning a message. And while most voters remember even now Obama's "You didn't build that" and how it rankled, voters also have no memory of the Republican riposte because there wasn't one. I hope every Republican candidate this year has a banner with a big elephant that reads "Building America's Future."

RULE #7: DIVISION DOES NOT CONQUER

This is the year for Republicans to reach out, to branch out, and to shatter the stereotypes that Democratic attack ads have burned into the mind space of millions of voters. The party should seek greater ethnic and racial diversity, without question. But it should seek a broader diversity, a diversity of occupation, a diversity of educational backgrounds. I would urge Republicans to bring into the fold more carpenters, plumbers, electricians, city and state workers, teachers, and policemen. And to do so without pandering to any one of the groups, but to maintain intellectual integrity and political ideals, and to be the party of the highest possible standards of conduct, ethics, and morality. And by whatever measure, Republicans should achieve concurrently solidarity and unity among all party members in support of American ideals and interests. They should seek to unify the party, and never seek to divide the electorate. Leave division to Democrats, call it their thing.

Like the McCain campaign before it, and the Bush presidency before that, the Romney team decided that the way to win the election was to divide the electorate. To talk to only those groups of people who could get Romney to 50.1 percent. Republicans never used to think like that. Ronald Reagan didn't. He spoke to everyone. He didn't lead with numbers and percentages, but with ideas. Today's GOP has utterly lost its way.

Consider this number:

47 percent

That was the figure infamously cited by Mitt Romney in that private fundraiser where he basically wrote off half the country as beyond his reach. Ironically, it was also the percentage of the popular vote he received in 2012.

There was no reason for a candidate for the presidency to accuse 47 percent of Americans of being dependents on the federal government. There was no reason to think of military retirees, people who are temporarily out of a job, or senior citizens as parasites. They are not. For the most part, the American people want a hand up, not a handout. That statement betrayed a lack of judgment about the people Romney was asking to represent. There are those who are dependent on government support—senior citizens and the disabled, for example. But that doesn't mean they can't vote for the Republican candidate.

What the GOP leadership has to understand is that the party's current predicament is the direct result of its failure to advocate and explain its own ideals and what have been historically traditional American values—that a free-enterprise capitalist economy creates jobs and drives growth. Republican leaders cluck sanctimoniously at everyone else in a tone of superiority. Yet from the last Republican administration on to its present leadership, the party of Reagan has lost all intellectual integrity and the capacity to adhere to its own values. That's what Republicans must say and demonstrate if the Republican Party is going to regain its credibility with the electorate.

RULE #8: FACTS ARE FRIENDS

Facts are our friends. Even the hard facts, like a $17 trillion debt. Like most Americans, I hope that this year will see congressmen elected and re-elected who will fight for prudent, responsible government, and yes, efficient and imaginative government as well. But such a government requires a renaissance in our economy, a restoration of our national values, tradition, and vision, and a new age of intellectual and political integrity and a reverence on the part of Republicans for public debate on the principles and the facts as we find them, not as we wish them to be. This year we have an opportunity to elect those who can truly serve the nation by committing to solving great national issues, rather than just continuing the bipartisan political process of deferring real action. Instead of confronting challenges, respecting the facts as we find them, our political representatives spend far more precious time trying to avoid consequences rather than eliminating the causes that create those consequences.

The voting public is content to watch mind-numbing television ads and endless so-called debates filled with meaningless pabulum and poses. The emptiness of the campaign discussion of major issues showed, for example, in the insistence, in 2012, of both presidential candidates on talking about abortion, an issue over which the president has almost no influence. Democrats easily distract the Republican Party and its candidates with one word. They shout "abortion." And Republicans react with "If you're not pro-life, then you're not welcome in the party," and by so doing, dismiss millions of Americans as immoral human beings, and lose millions of people who otherwise would potentially be Republicans. I know there are hardcore religious conservatives who find my words particularly upsetting, but I hope they will listen to both reason and reality. Consider this number:

78 percent

That is the percentage of Americans who believe that abortion should be legal, at least in some circumstances.[2] That's more than three-quarters of the country who accept abortion whether as a matter of solid pro-choice principles or only in the cases of rape, incest, or to protect the health of the mother. It is clear that Republicans often insist on electoral suicide by taking on the wedge issue of abortion, over which they have no political influence, whether running for president or mayor.

To enlarge the party, Republicans have to accept that "Good Republicans" can differ on many subjects, and do. I'm pro-life, but I also understand the views and positions of those who are pro-choice. I believe it is an issue of conscience, personal belief, and religion, and I believe every American woman has the right to have absolute control over her body, her life, her right, her conscience. I don't believe it is a matter for government, federal or state. But no matter what, Republicans who, as a matter of their religious beliefs and their personal views, are determined to roll back the rights of abortion should do so with a campaign of education on the issue. But the Republican Party cannot afford to be, as a party, distracted by wedge issues such as abortion, or, for that matter, gay marriage.

Republicans are too often excited by gay people. I don't know why, when many American families have someone who's LGBT, or have friends or coworkers who are LGBT. Same for every neighborhood and every community.

4 percent

That's the percentage of Americans who are LGBT, according to most surveys. And that 4 percent has a disproportionate voice and political influence relative to the number of voters, so Republicans do have a pragmatic political motivation to just get over themselves on this issue. Again, I understand religious objection, matters of conscience, and individual preference. That's what makes America great. But I don't understand discrimination, and I don't think most Republicans do either. And we all understand equal rights. If you happen to be one of those people who believe that homosexual marriage is a threat to heterosexual marriage for whatever reason, then let's be really honest. You have a far different understanding of physics and biology than most of us. As the saying goes, "It just doesn't work that way." And it makes no sense on any level, especially when there are so many perceptible, demonstrable threats to marriage in our society. Among the leading causes of divorce are infidelity (that is, heterosexual-on-heterosexual infidelity), marrying too young, unequal responsibilities, abuse, and financial strains. You will notice that homosexual marriage is conspicuous by its absence on that list. I'm begging the Republican Party to put aside cultural, social, and religious issues in favor of focusing on the important, even determinate issues that will shape our national future, maintain our standard of living, and ensure our quality of life. I'm asking all Republicans and independents to think about what matters most to us. In my opinion, nearly every wedge issue is best left to the conscience of the individual and the community standard is always highest when we recognize and preserve the individual rights of all citizens.

This year is the great test for the Republican Party, which should be committed to the greatest registration effort in its history, and making certain that Republican voter turnout in the 2014 midterm elections is by far the largest in its history. That means Republicans have to understand, clearly and unequivocally, that wedge issues have consequences, and that if 2014 is to be a consequential election, in which the Republican Party holds power in the House and takes control of the Senate, then wedge issues must be set aside for the good of the party, and for the good of the nation.

CHAPTER 2

DIMINISHING, DISTANT DREAMS

Traditional American values are most manifest in the men and women who work hard to become and remain part of the great American middle class. To our credit as a nation, most Americans consider themselves to be middle class, whether they work for a minimum wage or make millions. I love that fact, and I love that about Americans. But our middle class is shrinking. Millions of middle-class jobs have been shipped overseas. And the Obama administration has for five years inured itself to prolonged high unemployment and the pain of millions who have been unemployed longer than at any other time since the Great Depression. There is now a political class in Washington that appears callously indifferent to the unemployed and to those working men and women whose wages have been effectively stagnant for decades. But of course, our nation's capital is the home of a growth industry: government, and lots of it. Washington is prospering, with low unemployment, and the housing market is booming.

How can our elected officials be so removed from the lives of those who elect them? Well, it begins with this number:

$174,000

That is how much members of Congress earn in salary today—more than *three* times the median income in the United States. And of course this total does not include the many, many perks allotted to them and to their staffs:

- A choice of top-of-the-line health-care options
- Federal matching funds for their retirement programs
- Spacious offices—sometimes more than one—on Capitol Hill
- Free reserved parking at Washington Reagan National Airport
- Free reserved parking on Capitol Hill
- Staff members who are paid by the taxpayers to drive them around town
- Generous pensions that for members of Congress vest after only five years of service
- Taxpayer-paid "fact-finding" trips (i.e., five-star vacations) across the globe

Congress's approval rating is at an all-time low. And one party has no advantage over the other in terms of popularity or policy. Most Americans have a negative view of Congress because Congress is in Washington working only about half the time. Of course, they have district business and campaigns to run, particularly representatives who have to get themselves elected every two years. The U.S. House has now whittled its workweeks down to a mere three days.

What other occupation gives you the power to decide how much of a raise you deserve? Members of Congress love to tell the rest of us that we're their bosses. But when was the last time your member of Congress asked you—the alleged boss—if he or she deserved more money? Since 1990, Congress has given itself a raise thirteen times. Even in years in which it hasn't solved our entitlement programs, balanced the budget, or even tried to pass a budget.

Congress not only doesn't take its job seriously enough to pass the most basic pieces of legislation, but when it does, it routinely passes laws and regulations from which its members are exempt. They include: the Freedom of Information Act, whistle-blower protection provisions in the 1989 Sarbanes-Oxley Act, record-keeping requirements for workplace injury, and dozens of others. In other words, Congress has absolutely no understanding of the burdens its laws and regulations place on actual businesses. No wonder businesses leave America to seek a more business-friendly climate elsewhere.

The double standard was actually worse than this until a reform-minded Congress came to power in 1994. Until then the laws Congress exempted itself from also included the Fair Labor Standards Act, Title VII of the Civil Rights Act, the Americans with Disabilities Act, the Family and Medical Leave Act, and many others. For decades, members of Congress also were allowed a privilege that would send people in the corporate world to jail. They were allowed to buy and sell stock based on nonpublic information, a practice also known as insider trading. And they have made themselves rich in the process.

During the financial crisis of 2008, for example, members of Congress were given an early heads-up about the disaster looming for the country by the Bush administration, and specifically by Treasury Secretary Hank Paulson. That gave congressmen plenty of time to adjust their personal stock portfolios so they could benefit.

Investigations by newspapers such as the *New York Times* and the *Washington Post* uncovered the horrific scope of these practices. Secretary Paulson, for example, made frequent visits and phone calls with now–Speaker of the House John Boehner, a Republican from Ohio. After one breakfast with Paulson in early 2008, Boehner transferred as much as $100,000 from one of his mutual funds into a safer investment. Gee, I wish Boehner had told the rest of us about that one.

Senator Ben Nelson, a Democrat from Nebraska, sold between $250,000 and $500,000 in Lehman Brothers certificates of deposit that had fortuitously just matured one day after a meeting with Secretary Paulson. Lehman Brothers, of course, went bankrupt that same year, costing shareholders and financial investors millions. Luckily for Ben Nelson, he wasn't one of them.

A *Washington Post* investigation found thirty-four members of Congress who, as the paper put it, "took steps during the financial crisis to recast their investment portfolios after phone calls or meetings with Paulson, his successor Timothy Geithner or Federal Reserve Chairman Ben Bernanke." The *Post* reported that these lawmakers, many of them in congressional leadership, made 166 trades within days of meeting with administration officials on the financial crisis. This was a bipartisan racket—the lawmakers included nineteen Democrats and fifteen Republicans. They scored while senior citizens, small-business owners, and regular old shareholders like you and me lost a bundle.

A university study by Alan J. Ziobrowski, James W. Boyd, Ping Cheng, and Brigette J. Ziobrowski examined stock trades by three hundred members of the U.S. House of Representatives between 1985 and 2001. They found that these members on average beat the stock market's performance by about 6 percent a year.[1] Senators did 12 percent better than the market on average, and first-term senators' stocks averaged an incredible 20 percent better. One of the study's researchers said, "We have every reason to believe they are trading on information that the rest of us don't have."[2] Really?

When this behavior was finally exposed in November 2011, Congress quickly changed the laws to block these insider-trading practices. Predictably, they patted themselves on the back as great exemplars of ethics, but last year Congress quietly repealed the part of the law requiring lawmakers and members of their staff to post their financial disclosure forms in an easily searched online database, making it more difficult for the public to access this information.

When our government was first formed, Congress used to be a part-time occupation. People had other jobs—farmers, lawyers, businessmen, printers. They would travel to Washington for only a limited time to do essential business for the nation, and then they went home. That's not how it is anymore. Washington now has a permanent class of politicians, staffers, consultants, and lobbyists who rotate places all the time. Seemingly no one leaves Washington. They just get different offices, a new job title. Many use their time in public service, in fact, to secure even more lucrative employment once their political careers are over.

In 2012 the *New York Times* profiled former representative William D. Delahunt of Massachusetts, "one of the leading liberals in Congress," who "started his own lobbying firm with an office on the 16th floor of a Boston skyscraper." The *Times* reported that one of his first clients was a small coastal town that paid him $15,000 per month for help on a wind energy project. What was unusual about this, the *Times* reported, was that Mr. Delahunt had personally steered $1.7 million to this same project while a member of Congress. That money is now helping pay his fees as a consultant.

The *New York Times* found other examples of Delahunt's curious financial arrangements since he left office.

- "The Mashpee Wampanoag tribe, for instance, paid the Delahunt Group at least $40,000 to lobby for approval of a casino. Mr. Delahunt had secured Congressional earmarks for the tribe totaling $400,000 in 2008 and 2009 for a substance abuse program and other projects, the records show."

- "The city of Quincy, Mass., meanwhile, brought on Mr. Delahunt last year to help deal with federal officials on a downtown redevelopment program. In 2008, Mr. Delahunt secured nearly $2.4 million in earmarks for the city on a separate tidal restoration project."

- "And a fishermen's group on the elbow of Cape Cod hired Mr. Delahunt to navigate regulatory issues; he had helped the group get a low-interest, $500,000 federal loan in 2010, records show. The group, which thanked Mr. Delahunt, then a congressman, for his help getting the loan, used the money to renovate a historic coastal home as its headquarters."

Consider this figure:

195

That's how many former members of Congress, like Mr. Delahunt, worked as influence peddlers in Washington, D.C., in 2011. Among the big names were former senator Christopher Dodd, a Democrat from Connecticut, who became head of the Motion Picture Association of America; former senator Evan Bayh, a Democrat from Indiana, who went to work for the U.S. Chamber of Commerce; and former senator Blanche Lincoln, a Democrat from Arkansas, who went on to become a lobbyist for Alston & Bird, a major Washington, D.C., law firm before starting her own lobbying group, the Lincoln Policy Group, with one of her former staffers. For many members of Congress, becoming a lobbyist has proved to be a lucrative career change.

1,452 percent

That, according to a study by the *Republic Report*, is the average— repeat: the average—pay raise a member of Congress receives once he or she becomes a Washington lobbyist. Often this money comes from posh positions in industries in which they wrote laws and regulations as a member of Congress.

$19,359,927

That was how much former representative Billy Tauzin, a Republican from Louisiana, made over four years as a lobbyist for pharmaceutical companies. As the magazine reported:

- "Tauzin retired from Congress in 2005, shortly after leading the passage of President Bush's prescription drug expansion. He was recruited to lead PhRMA, a lobbying association for Pfizer, Bayer, and other top drug companies. During the health reform debate, the former congressman helped his association block a proposal to allow Medicare to negotiate for drug prices, a major concession that extended the policies enacted in Tauzin's original Medicare drug-purchasing scheme. Tauzin left PhRMA in late 2010. He was paid over $11 million in his last year at the trade group. Comparing Tauzin's salary during his last year as congressman and his last year as head of PhRMA, his salary went up 7110 percent."

And there's more:

- "Former Congressman Cal Dooley (D-CA) has made at least $4,719,093 as a lobbyist for food manufacturers and the chemical industry from 2005 to 2009. Republic Report analyzed disclosures from the Grocery Manufacturers Association (GMA), an industry lobby—for companies like Kellogg—where Dooley worked following his retirement from Congress. We also added in Dooley's salary from the American Chemistry Council, where Dooley now works as the president. The Chemistry Council represents Dow Chemical, DuPont, and other chemical interests. Dooley's salary jumped 1357 percent between his last year in the House and his last reported salary for the Chemistry Council in 2009."

- "Former Senator Chris Dodd (D-CT) makes approximately $1.5 million a year as the chief lobbyist for the movie industry. Dodd, who retired from the Senate after 2010, was hired by the Motion Picture Association of America, the lobbying association that represents major studios like Warner Bros. and Universal Studios. Although the MPAA would not confirm with Republic Report Dodd's exact salary, media accounts point to $1.5 million, a slightly higher figure than the previous MPAA head, former Secretary of Agriculture Dan Glickman. Dodd received about a 762 percent raise after moving from public office to lobbying."

No wonder our elected representatives are so kind to these big corporations and big-time lobbyists—they know if they do a good enough job funneling taxpayer dollars to them while in Congress, the payoff could be enormous. And that applies not just to members, but also to their staffs, some of whom become multimillionaires from their time in public service.

These guys in Washington have created a cozy little system for themselves. So why mess it up by letting new guys get in? Congress has created a system that makes it harder and harder for outsiders to run and win seats in the legislature. For decades, Congress has had an approval rating that would embarrass parking meter attendants. And yet they keep getting re-elected over and over again.

Year	Re-election Rate
2012	90 percent
2010	85 percent
2008	94 percent
2006	94 percent
2004	98 percent
2002	96 percent

Why does this happen? In part because they've created districts in which one party has the advantage in every election. For another the average cost of elections keeps rising.

$1.4 million

That was the average amount of money spent to win a seat in the U.S. House of Representatives in 2010. That is an increase since 2000 of more than:

71 percent

The average price for winning a Senate seat reached nearly $10 million in that cycle. The high cost of running for federal office often puts newcomers at a substantial disadvantage. That's why many members of Congress are super-rich—few others can mount an effective race.

47 percent

Nearly half (47 percent) of all members of Congress are million-aires, according to a report by ABC News. "The vast majority of members of Congress are quite comfortable, financially, while many of their own constituents suffer from economic hardships," said Sheila Krumholz at the Center for Responsive Politics. "Few Americans enjoy the same financial cushions maintained by most members of Congress—or the same access to market-altering in-formation that could yield personal, financial gains." And some of these members are millionaires many times over.

$305,460,000

That's how much the wealthiest current member of Congress, Representative Michael McCaul of Texas, was worth in 2012. Closing out the top five were:

Rep. Darrell Issa (R-CA)	$140.55 million
Sen. Mark Warner (D-VA)	$85.81 million
Sen. Jay Rockefeller (D-WV)	$83.08 million
Sen. Richard Blumenthal (D-CT)	$79.11 million

You might assume that these are just a few outliers, but they're not. In 2010, the estimated median net worth of a U.S. sena-tor was:

$2.63 million

Less than two years earlier, the global economy had been rocked by recession, with tens of millions of Americans losing their jobs and even more losing a major fraction of their retirement portfolios. That crisis didn't put a dent in the wealth of members of Congress. In fact, from 2008 to 2010, their net worth actually *increased* by 25 percent.

Members of Congress have not only enriched themselves from the public teat. They've slowly turned the D.C. area into their own version of Versailles or, for want of a more contemporary example, the Capital City in *The Hunger Games*.

One study recently found that of stimulus grants and contracts awarded by Congress, the Washington, D.C., region received almost *ten times* more money per capita than the national average, including states hit hard by the recession, such as Michigan, Florida, and Ohio. Of the money the state of Virginia received, two-thirds—or $562 million—went to northern Virginia, which is home to many current and former members of Congress, lobbyists, and contractors. Of that, $115 million was sent to the posh D.C. suburb of Alexandria, Virginia, where many of these lobbyists and consultants have homes or offices.

5 to 1

According to a 2007 report by the Tax Foundation, for every one dollar in taxes Washington, D.C., sends to the federal government, it receives five dollars in return.[3] This arrangement has paid off handsomely for the D.C. area. While most of America has felt the pain of Washington's ineffective fiscal policies—high unemployment, coping with health-care costs, worrying about entitlements—the District of Columbia itself, like its most powerful inhabitants, is doing just fine, thank you. Marie Antoinette would be proud.

Just a few years ago, things weren't so great in the District of Columbia. Murder. Theft. Carjacking. The nation's capital was surrounded by a shockingly criminal city, beset by liberal policies and crooked local politicians. Washington's NBA team was even named after them, the Wizards. (The team's name used to be the Washington Bullets. You can guess why they changed it.) That's changed, thanks to you, the American taxpayer. Washington has become bigger and bloated and the center of American life. Today, D.C. is still the Promised Land for liberal policymakers, federal employees, consultants, fundraisers, and contractors. Consider:

5.5 percent

That was the unemployment rate in the Washington, D.C., region as of early 2012. The nation's capital had one of the lowest unemployment rates among the largest metropolitan areas in the entire nation.[4] As reliably liberal writer Jonathan Chait writes, "And for affluent people, there is essentially no recession. Unemployment for workers with a bachelor's degree is 4 percent—boom times. Unemployment is also unusually low in the Washington, D.C., area, owing to our economy's reliance on federal spending, which has not had to impose the punishing austerity of so many state and local governments."[5] Consider this:

8.2 percent

That was the unemployment rate across the nation in that same period. Do you understand why our politicians can't relate to the jobs crisis in America? Things are going just fine where they live and work. There's one place that's creating jobs in America—the federal government.

Now, folks from the Obama administration, just like the Bush administration before that, will tell you that the size of the federal workforce hasn't gone up all that much. It's true that the size of the nonmilitary, nonpostal federal workforce has stayed relatively stable since the 1960s. But that's not the whole story. What has changed is the rising number of contractors who have been hired by the federal government as consultants. In fact it's estimated that, thanks to massive outsourcing over the past twenty years by the Clinton and Bush administrations, there are two government contractors for every worker directly employed by the government.

Federal contracting is the region's great growth industry. A government contractor can even hire contractors for help in getting more government contracts. You could call those guys government-contract contractors.[6] According to the District of Columbia Chamber of Commerce, "Between 2000 and 2010, a period that encompassed two recessions and the events of 9/11, nearly 61,000 jobs were added in the District. By contrast, employment declined in New York, Baltimore and Philadelphia over the same period."

459,016

That is how many federal workers earn more than $100,000 per year. Proportionally that amounts to one in every five federal workers. By comparison, according to the Bureau of Labor Statistics, the median salary in the United States at large was $40,144 per year in 2012. And remember that President Obama isn't paying them these generous salaries. You are.

Government is a booming business—maybe America's only booming business. So much so that people are flocking to Washington, D.C., in droves. In the summer of 2011, and for the first time since the government boom of the 1940s during World War II, Washington, D.C., led the states in year-to-year population growth. The District of Columbia also showed the greatest rate of expansion—2.7 percent—in the nation (relative to state populations).[7]

The construction industry has faced a Great Depression across the nation—due in large part to the incompetent policies of our federal government. The national unemployment rate for construction workers was 11.3 percent in the fall of 2012, significantly higher than the overall unemployment rate. Yet while many parts of this country have crumbling buildings and infrastructure—Detroit, I'm looking at you—D.C. has cranes, cement mixers, jackhammers, and bulldozers on practically every corner.

14 percent

That is how big an increase D.C. has seen in construction jobs *in one year alone* (2011–12). These are the highest levels for the District of Columbia since 1990. Wonder why D.C. politicians don't seem too worried about the housing crisis the rest of us are so concerned about? There isn't one where they live. Quite the contrary, in fact.

The *Washington Post* reports that nine of the top fifteen most affluent counties in the entire United States are now in the D.C. area. This includes one of the toniest suburbs in the nation, McLean, Virginia. If you live in McLean, just a dozen miles from Washington, D.C., here are some of your neighbors:

- Dick Cheney: He bought a lot in McLean, Virginia, in 2000 for $1.35 million, then tore down the house already there and constructed a new one for $1.5 million. As the *Washington Post* reports: "The four-bedroom, nine-bath (including a couple of powders) house includes his and hers bathrooms off the master bedroom on the first floor and his and hers libraries, each with a fireplace, according to a review of the plans. . . . There's a playroom in the basement for the grandkids. A spot above the attached two-car garage has a bedroom, bathroom and bar. The house has the usual elevator that runs from the basement to the second floor."

- Former Speaker of the House Newt Gingrich: He and his wife, Callista, live in a $1.5 million, five-thousand-square-foot home in McLean, complete with five bedrooms and four bathrooms.

With the exception of Dick Cheney, who earned millions as a CEO at Halliburton, the rest made their wealth as a direct result of their time in public service. Of course, you don't have to live in McLean to be rich in Washington. Hillary Clinton, for example, has a $3 million house near Georgetown that has seven and a half bathrooms and a swimming pool. In the first eight years since they left office, the Clintons amassed earnings of more than $100 million. That figure surprised even their friends at the *New York Times*, which called it "an ascent into the uppermost tier of American taxpayers that seemed unimaginable in 2001, when they left the White House with little money and facing millions in legal bills." As the *Times* reported, the bulk of the Clintons' wealth came from speaking fees and their various memoirs, which accounted for almost $92 million. "The former president's vigorous lecture schedule, where his speeches command upwards of $250,000," the *Times* reported, "brought in almost $52 million."

Few people used that old ploy of attacking "the rich" more than Bill and Hillary Clinton as they sought high office. Yet when they left the White House in 2001, what was the first thing the Clintons did? They didn't create a business. They just ran around making speeches, railing against CEOs and Wall Street and rich fat-cat Republicans, and making a bundle. They make the Obamas, two other alleged enemies of "the rich," look like paupers.

$608,611

That's how much President and Mrs. Obama made in 2012, according to their latest tax returns. Lest we feel too bad for them—they aren't even in the same universe as the Clintons—the Obamas did a little better in 2011 ($789,674), 2010 ($1,728,096), and 2009 ($5.5 million). And of course when they leave office, they will likely each make anywhere from $5 to $10 million on their memoirs, plus potentially tens to hundreds of millions in speaking fees or positions on corporate boards. Not bad for a humble community organizer, is it?

All this explains why Gallup's Well-Being Index rates D.C. as the most satisfied large metropolitan area in the United States. Washington residents are said to be more likely to have health insurance than the average American. They're also more optimistic—about the economy and about the future in general.[8]

All in all, Washington is a happy place—except of course if you aren't benefiting from the miniempire government bureaucrats and their supporters have created. In the past decade, as a permanent Washington elite has grown in our nation's capital, they've begun to crowd out and overshadow the large population of Washingtonians, many of them African-American, who have been left out of this new boom. While the haves excel and prosper, the capital's have-nots are in an increasingly deteriorating situation. The poverty rate among Washingtonians who aren't benefiting from this luxury is higher than the national average. The inner-city schools are a shambles. The crime rate remains disturbingly high. As *Time* magazine reports, "White residents enjoy a per capita income nearly three times that of African Americans."[9]

This disparity continues to widen. In northern Virginia, someone even tried to build an American version of Versailles—a twenty-five-thousand-square-foot mansion that was to be called Le Chateau de Lumiere. The northern Virginia palace, which was actually modeled on Versailles, was to have a movie theater, five bedrooms, three two-car garages, an elevator, a pool and pool house, a wine cellar, a billiards room, and a master suite that would occupy an entire wing and would have four rooms and a gallery. Unfortunately for the aspiring Lord of the Manor, the neighbors of this $20 million monstrosity complained and filed a lawsuit to stop it. The neighbors, and their high-priced lawyers, claimed that too many trees would be torn down. The *Washington Post* speculated that the real reason for the neighbors' opposition to the project was the fear that their own property taxes would go up. The plans apparently have been scrapped. For now. But it's only a matter of time before the similarities between Washington and Versailles become overwhelming.

"If the elites in Washington are insulated from the rest of the country, don't grasp what is at stake for everyone else, and have no real incentive to act in those people's interests—then why on earth would we ever look to those elites for our salvation?" asks Robert Tracinski, who has been studying the Washington "bubble." "Why should we give them vast and unprecedented power over the economy and depend on their stimulus money to put bread in our children's mouths?" Tracinski is asking very good questions, questions that are ignored daily by the national media, but working men and women all across America are questioning our elites, our elected officials, as never before.[10] And among the questions that rankle our middle class most is why millions of homes have been foreclosed as their owners were upended by the deep, painful recession of 2008, whose effect is still being felt across much of the country. And why did Washington bail our banks but not homeowners? If there are to be bailouts at all, why institutions and not individuals?

CHAPTER 3

BANKSHOT

I believe that banking institutions are more dangerous to our liberties than standing armies.

—THOMAS JEFFERSON

Few would have argued with Jefferson's sentiment in the depths of the Great Recession. Banks, mostly the biggest banks, and the entire financial system were at risk of collapse in 2008 and 2009. We learned a lot about moral hazard and "too big to fail," and now, as we enter the midterms of 2014, there is a certain frothiness in the air. Banks are pumping out billions of dollars in profits, bank stocks are rising, and all that money spent at the depths of the Great Recession, or "invested" as President Obama said at the time, has paid off handsomely. Many bank stocks have actually tripled in price from their lows of March 2009.

And why should they not be doing well? The economy is certainly not growing as it should, jobs are not being created in sufficient number to provide opportunity for all who want and need to work. An estimated 20 million people remain out of work almost five years after the end of the Great Recession. Small business continues to struggle and big businesses remain steadfastly stingy stewards of their available capital for investment (or if you prefer, simply prudent and wise managers). Businesses large and small are prudent to the point of paranoia, however, when it comes to their payrolls, as they manage their costs and margins. Small and medium businesses work diligently to avoid the adverse impact of Obamacare: limiting the number of employees, relying on part-time employees, even in some cases cutting their payrolls. This is hardly an era marked by adventurous entrepreneurs and effusive innovators trampling one another as they rush to their bank for more capital, ever-bigger loans to fund their rapidly growing businesses.

Big banks and their earnings, whether money center banks or regionals, are doing well in this peculiar economic environment—the hallmarks of which are twenty-five-basis-point returns for commercial bank reserves. The Federal Reserve board, now faced with an economy that seems to require a continuation of stimulus one month and tapering of asset purchases the next, is negotiating one of the most difficult economic periods in our history. Bank earnings are rising despite the threat of ever-greater regulation and the lack of credit demand. Banks are competing, and energetically, when they do find the rare high-quality customer who wants to borrow money rather than deleverage, the customer who wants to invest rather than stockpile his or her capital. The world of banking at times seems upside down, except at the top. Over the course of the last thirty years, commercial bank assets on average have exploded. Their assets are almost five times greater over that period. In part, it's because there's never been so much Fed-driven liquidity in our economy and, in part, it's because there are fewer than half as many commercial banks today as three decades ago.

Banks are getting fewer and bigger, more concentrated, more powerful, and far more difficult to manage and regulate. Take a look at these numbers, which reflect the sea change we've seen in America:

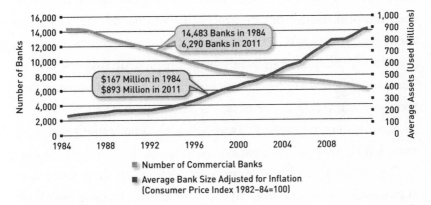

14,483 Banks in 1984
6,290 Banks in 2011

$167 Million in 1984
$893 Million in 2011

Number of Commercial Banks
Average Bank Size Adjusted for Inflation
(Consumer Price Index 1982–84=100)

Source: http://www.stlouisfed.org/publications/re/articles/?id=2283.

And the twelve largest banks in the country make up .2 percent of all banks in America, and control 69 percent of total commercial banking assets.[1] The St. Louis Fed chart makes sense: fewer banks, rising liquidity, bigger average assets. There is no question that by the 1980s we had far too many commercial banks, and by the end of that decade, thanks in part to the S&L crisis, the number of commercial banks had been significantly reduced. Among regional and community banks, competition remains at healthy levels, but not so with the gargantuan institutions at the top of the industry.

The Federal Reserve continues to run stress tests on the nineteen largest banks, and while they pass those stress tests, the tests are administered ostensibly to share the health of the institutions and to disclose the possibility that the Federal Reserve and the federal government will ever have to face the prospect of the moral hazard that brought the U.S. economy to the brink of collapse in 2008. But there is little doubt in my mind that any one of those institutions would be considered too big to fail by the Federal Reserve or the Treasury Department. They draw on the Federal Reserve almost at will, their cost of funds is minuscule, and their margins are all but unlimited. These massive banks represent a potential threat to the economy that is perhaps even greater than pre-2009. A misstep by any one of these truly-too-big-to-fail banks would create upheaval not only in the banking industry, but throughout the entire economy.

But, you say, what about Dodd-Frank? Wasn't that legislation intended to prevent the financial industry from ever again losing management control and to prevent reckless bankers from taking us to the edge of chaos? Well, what about Dodd-Frank? Very simply, Dodd-Frank has done nothing. It's not even implemented. And what about the Volcker Rule? There is no Volcker Rule. And whatever regulations flow from the Dodd-Frank law won't be fully written for at least another year. Yes, bankers have created their own separate reality that at this very moment is well beyond the power of our government to regulate.

Moral hazard is what brought the U.S. economy to the brink of collapse in 2008. The big firms on Wall Street gambled on the housing market, funded loans that homeowners couldn't pay back, and then ran to Uncle Sam to bail them out of their terrible business deals.

In their world, there aren't consequences to failure. There are no risks too risky. If you get big enough, you can't fail. Government won't let you.

This ugly thought is expressed in those four words that should cause American taxpayers agita every time they hear them:

"Too big to fail."

That was the excuse the Bush and Obama administrations used to justify their bailouts of Wall Street. These Wall Street firms became so massive, so integral to the functioning of our overall economy, that we couldn't let them go bankrupt. In President Bush's remarkably memorable phrase, "I've abandoned free market principles in order to save the free market." Mr. Bush had a way with a phrase. As much as Wall Street likes to think of itself as a big ol' free market, there are a few barriers to entry and some decidedly powerful structural competitive advantages in the equities marketplace that render it often something less than a free market. As far as banks themselves, whenever a half dozen institutions command and control 69 percent of an industry, I think it's fair to say that what we have is at best an oligopoly, a group of institutions that is more protected and insulated by government than regulated by it. Of course, regulators and many lawmakers still adhere to "too big to fail" rhetoric, but there's no question that it is the de facto policy of the government of a nation that once prided itself on self-reliance, independence, the rough-and-tumble of truly free markets, and raging, roaring capitalism.

Don't tell anyone, but our free-enterprise capitalism has been replaced in many quarters by something softer, less rigorous, and far less productive. "Too big to fail" is now policy, whether stated or unstated. Crony capitalism has been substituted for full-on free-market competition. And market adherents to such nonsense will have to relearn that "too big to fail" may permit firms to exist to survive calamity, but in the longer term, I believe it is axiomatic that too big is itself failure. And the consequences of not restoring dividing lines between investment banking and commercial banking and carefully regulating our financial industry could well be an economic upheaval too disturbing to contemplate. Republicans needn't adopt left-wing regulatory zeal or antibusiness attitudes and sneers in order to consider the importance of reregulating our banking industry. I would argue that effectively restoring Glass-Steagall, raising equity capital requirements for the largest banks, not merely American banks, but all banks doing business in the United States or with U.S. customers, would ensure that all banks are held to the same standard. And such an agreement among banks should not be difficult to construct and maintain. My comfort in recommending such reregulation is based in history, and the arc of American business experience.

In 1933, the year after the Great Depression began, Congress passed the Banking Act of 1933, which among other things created the Federal Deposit Insurance Corporation (FDIC) and separated commercial and investment banks. The Glass-Steagall provisions of that law prevented commercial banks from using any of their depositors' money to gamble on the stock market, or if you prefer, to underwrite stocks. That wall between commercial banking and investment banking became known as the Glass-Steagall Act and it worked for sixty-five years, through a world war, rampant prosperity, one depression, and quite a few recessions.

Then, in 1999, the stock market was rollicking, stocks doubling and tripling or more in a matter of months. It was the height of the technology and internet bubble, almost everyone owned stock, and it seemed almost every stock was guaranteed to go higher. Life was very, very good, particularly for stock brokerages and Wall Street firms. So good that the commercial banking industry desperately wanted a piece of the action, and a big slice of the profit pie that was getting larger with every passing year. And as he was about to head into the final year of his presidency,

President Bill Clinton signed the so-called Financial Services Modernization Act. With a stroke of President Clinton's pen, Glass-Steagall was no more, sweeping away the lessons of the stock market crash of 1929 and the massive banking failures of the Great Depression.

The Modernization Act was the result of brilliant lobbying and exquisite economic timing. It was all orchestrated by Treasury secretary and Wall Street icon Robert Rubin, and in securing President Bill Clinton's signature on the Gramm-Leach-Bliley Act, Rubin tore down the walls between commercial and investment banking, securities and insurance companies. And the first effect of rolling back Glass-Steagall was to benefit Wall Street's archdealmaker, who had already assembled a massive superstore of investment and commercial banking, and securities and insurance businesses. The dealmaker was Sandy Weill and the firm was CitiGroup. By the way, Bob Rubin left his government post that same year and went to work for Weill. Rubin actually joined CitiGroup just about two weeks before Bill Clinton signed the bill into law. Rubin maintained that his steerage of the legislation had nothing to do with his decision to join Weill at CitiGroup. It took only eight years for Weill, Rubin, Gramm, Leach, Bliley, and their acolytes who voted for the legislation to all be proven disastrously wrong. But so many were so wrong about so much that their names are only infinitesimal footnotes to one of history's biggest economic catastrophes.

The housing market was being driven by the politically attractive idea that every American, no matter his or her financial circumstances, was entitled to own a home. Mortgage origination wasn't a problem. Plenty of money in the economy. No need to worry prospective homeowners with the necessity of having a down payment or, for that matter, the income necessary to pay a mortgage. The interest rates weren't much of a sticking point in any negotiation because everyone relied on what became a painful fiction: that the prices of houses would rise no matter what and do so in perpetuity. Of such stuff, great fortunes are made. And bubbles, too. Government-sponsored enterprises such as Fannie Mae and Freddie Mac offered their own loans or insured others. These originators sold off the debt to other institutions and the market for subprime debt bulged.

All this mortgage debt, so simple in origination, so fraudulent in process, was packaged in complex derivatives and financial instruments known as Collateralized Mortgage Obligations (CMOs). And then a very unfunny thing happened in the housing market. Unfunny, and to many, unthinkable. Housing prices fell. As property value declined, losses spread to investors holding CMOs, and those packaged mortgage bonds were sinking fast. The balance sheets of some of the largest institutions that had bet big on housing and on the assumption that housing prices never fall, or never fall for long, were suddenly holding assets so toxic that some were effectively worthless.

$600,000,000,000,000

That's $600 trillion.[2] It's an absolutely astounding number, an incomprehensible number. In 2007 the *entire world's* GDP was $54 trillion at the onset of the financial crisis. The value of all derivatives was estimated variously at somewhere around $600 trillion. No one knows for sure, because without regulation, without exchanges, the world of derivatives was, and despite all the reforms, still is, an opaque market where no one knows with precision the entire structure or value of the market.

At the first sign that the housing markets were faltering, the mortgage-backed security market was collapsing. By the summer of 2008, a crisis that began in the subprime housing market had spread to other areas of the economy. In September, what had started as a liquidity problem—a lack of cash and credit—became a liquidity crisis, threatening insolvency for Wall Street firms and the country's biggest banks. The commercial paper market was simply paralyzed. The economy was on the verge of failure. Credit and money were disappearing. There were fears in Washington of runs on banks and the onset of a full-blown economic disaster. In fact, the credit markets were frozen and the country had come to a virtual standstill.

As our economy moved into recession, so did most of the world economy. Interest rates spiked, credit became scarce and then unavailable, and markets plummeted. What happens the next time? We can't afford a next time. And the Republicans have an opportunity, as the party of business, entrepreneurship, and free markets, to lead on the issue of what I would call market integrity and secure free enterprise. Republicans need to lead on intelligent and efficient regulation of our markets and to ensure that corporate concentration in any industry is halted before it strangles competitiveness and even the idea of a free market. It is the responsible course for the Republican Party, and it would permit Republicans to speak voluminously and credibly to America's working men and women who deserve far better than the policies of dependency and division of which the Obama administration is now historically emblematic.

The CEOs of J.P. Morgan Chase and Wells Fargo manage vast and unwieldy global businesses, organizations that many believe are so large that they are impossible to effectively manage over time. Anything that big, that complex, with so many people, is bound to make mistakes simply because of the scope of the organization. The only question is how big the mistake will be and when it will occur. The Chase and Wells Fargo CEOs, Jamie Dimon and John Stumpf, are particularly vociferous in their opposition to regulation. It's fine, it's understandable, that two of the smartest bankers in the country believe they require no help from the government to run their businesses. In one sense, they may even be right. They are among the smartest guys in any room, and certainly are so when they go to Washington to lobby politicians for strategic competitive advantage, to roar, kick, and bellow against the emerging guidepost boundaries and shape of Dodd-Frank regulations that are still being written as I write this.

But it is also "right" that the stakes are too high, the risks too great, and the financial and economic consequences so potentially devastating that these institutions cannot be guided by profit motive alone. Nor have they been allowed to do so through most of the past century. The departure of 1999 was created in the midst of an illusion that the United States was the world's only superpower and faced no credible geopolitical or military threat from any power in the world, that the peace dividend that resulted from America's victory over the Soviet Union and Marxist-Leninism would never be spent unwisely, and even if it were, there would be more money where that came from. My God, the federal budget was being balanced, and both Republicans and Democrats had seized on the opportunity, rationalizing welfare, cutting military spending, and reaping enormous tax revenue from an economy that kept growing, driving a period of prosperity that seemed unending. Balanced budgets? Unthinkable only the decade before. America stood atop the world, its only superpower, its greatest economic engine, a surely eternal monument to the greatest constitutional republic in history, and its free-enterprise capitalist economy was the envy of Europe, Russia, and China, and indeed, emerging nations seeking to gain even a portion of our prosperity knew they must emulate our economic and political models. It was an era, the 1990s, of innovation and technology, the popularization and commercialization of the internet, the greatest economic expansion since World War II. The last half of the 1990s was without a doubt a period of hubris maximus.

What a small thing it must have seemed at such a time to almost all in government: the dismissal of the antiquated concerns and restraints of Glass-Steagall as billions of dollars were being made each day on Wall Street and in Silicon Valley, millions of jobs created as never before. But within five months of the Gramm-Leach-Bliley bill's being signed into law, the stock market and the economy were in upheaval, and everything changed in what seemed an instant. With the dawning of a new millennium, we were reminded that fortune only rarely casts a lasting smile upon mere mortals. The first decade of this new millennium made it obvious to almost all that whatever America's destiny, the path to its achievement will be strewn with challenge and conflict, and that all that we as a nation have accomplished and overcome is at risk each and every day. I am not suggesting that CEOs of our largest businesses or the leaders of our government practice the politics of paranoia. We've come perilously close to doing just that at various points since September 11. I'm strongly recommending, however, that we practice both the politics and the economics of prudence, and some modesty. The past decade should demonstrate to all that no matter how bright, clever, innovative and industrious, goodhearted and compassionate a people we may be, we are also in the mainstream of humanity no matter how much we want to believe ourselves to be set apart, and we are not inured to the vicissitudes of history. It all begins, I believe, with reining in all the institutions of government. It begins with limitations on the size of our government at all levels: federal, state, county, local. We must surely find leaders who want to pursue public policy that is far more modest, whether at home or abroad. And we must also insist on some modesty.

I believe it's time for Republicans, even at the risk of losing sizable political contributions, to say, "We will become the party of the national interest, and we will respect and seek out the opinions of business as always, but public policy belongs to the nation." Financial institutions will squeal mightily, but the Republican Party has a unique historical opportunity to do, in big bold bright letters, THE RIGHT THING. Government is not intended to be the handmaiden of bankers, but banks are intended to be institutions of trust in our communities and in our nation.

In the wake of the Great Recession, billions of dollars in settlements and fines have been assessed, levied, and negotiated with commercial banks that failed to follow correct and legal foreclosure practices, violating in many instances regulations and laws, and to be fair, in some instances simply because of the tremendous numbers of properties involved, literally millions. None of which served to help the public's opinion of banks and their standards of conduct.

Neither has the number of banks that have been caught maintaining deposits, laundering money, and providing secretive services and transactions for tyrants, terrorists, and cartels. The failure of the top management of banks, their compliance departments, and certainly government regulators to carefully scrutinize activities and operations also resulted in an international market manipulation scandal that remains under investigation. The LIBOR interest rate scandal may not end the close cooperation and control of the world banking cartel, but it has surely forced changes in the way those banks do business. It's far too early to tell whether it all results in real reform, or just the appearance of such to permit a return to business as usual.

The London Interbank Offered Rate, or LIBOR, has been set by the British Bankers Association (BBA) since 1986, and LIBOR quickly became the most important global short-term benchmark interest rate. And the member banks and firms appear to have rather quickly become a merry band of price-fixers and manipulators, the likes of which the financial world has never before witnessed. Astonishingly, *Wall Street Journal* reporter Carrick Mollenkamp reported that in the depths of the global financial crisis, LIBOR had become unreliable, and there were heightened concerns that banks were masking their then rapidly deteriorating financial condition by manipulating LIBOR. Ironically, the BBA-LIBOR banks worked to report rates lower, which was beneficial to global borrowers of all kinds. As a result of Mollenkamp's clear questions about fraudulent conduct and activity among the BBA panel members, the BBA has moved to increase the number of banks reporting borrowing rates to help calculate LIBOR.

It all turned out to be very true, and with every passing day, it seems more likely to me that central bankers, including the Bank of England and the Federal Reserve, chose not to risk disrupting an already roiled and desperate international financial system, choosing instead to defer any action until times were less turbulent and balance sheets less burdened. Barclay's Bank quickly became the focus of investigators, but at least twenty banks remain under investigation by the United States and Britain, and the scandal is truly international. The government regulatory and law enforcement investigations presage what will likely be years of litigation by particular corporate customers who may have huge claims to litigate. Barclay's was the first bank charged and the first bank to reach a settlement with regulators, while some of the world's biggest banks, including J.P. Morgan Chase, UBS, Citibank, Deutschebank, HSBC, Royal Bank of Scotland, and others, were also involved. The settlements are already in the billions, with civil lawsuits only beginning. And HSBC's problems, as severe as they are, have only worsened.

HSBC's lack of ethical standards extends well beyond the LIBOR scandal. The U.S. government accused the British bank HSBC of transferring funds from Mexican drug cartels through the United States. In December 2012, HSBC admitted this violation of federal law and agreed to pay $1.9 billion as part of a settlement. Although this was the largest penalty ever imposed on a bank, the story somehow escaped notice in the mainstream media.

On its face, justice was served. Yet despite the history-making fine, the settlement ought to concern rather than reassure the American public. Although U.S. authorities sent executives of smaller banks to prison for money laundering, not a single HSBC executive was arrested, despite their monstrous clientele. In full public view, the rule of law was trampled on in the interest of protecting big banking.

Not only was HSBC too big to fail, it was also "too big to indict," despite engaging in illegal activity. And it is more than plausible that HSBC executives escaped indictment *because* the interests they represented were "too big to fail." The government's general regulatory response to the recession and the fiscal crisis of 2008 reflects that not only is that attitude well and alive, it is enlarged. Less than a decade ago, the big banks and credit card companies actually helped write the 2005 bankruptcy law. And both political parties were keen to allow them to do so. Today neither political party is willing to bend or sway quite that much to the will of the financial industry. As I write this, the Federal Energy Regulatory Commission is charging a number of banks with manipulation of the energy markets in California, and the *Wall Street Journal* is reporting that Chase faces fines of up to $1 billion for its alleged role in manipulating the California energy market seven years ago. Chase's reputation has taken severe hits for an institution considered to be the best-run bank in the world.

The concept of the universal bank is, I believe, nearing an end. When Don Regan, the CEO of Merrill Lynch, first contemplated the superstore of finance, he did not envision institutions so large that they created their own capital ecosystem in which regulators, whether federal or state, could not intrude, or if necessary, intervene. We can define the assets of our largest financial institutions, within limits. The reality is we cannot yet define the size of the global derivatives market, or, within precise boundaries, the exposure of our largest institutions to those synthetic and exotic financial instruments, which arguably have created far more risk than they were designed to hedge against. The rough size of that market is not inestimable. Here are some of the estimates:

$700,000,000,000,000

$1,000,000,000,000,000+

That's at least $700 trillion, more than a quadrillion dollars. At that size and scale, 50 percent variances in estimates really don't matter much. Because if the crushing complexity of all those effectively unregulated derivatives were to come crashing down, the world economy would quickly be brought to an abrupt end and an entirely new system of value and wealth would have to be created amid the wreckage. The world economy would quickly shrivel from almost $70 trillion to a fraction of that.

We've emerged from near disaster in the Great Recession of

2008 and 2009 with only the pretense of new and better regulation in our financial markets, and the potential for even greater damage. Neither the president nor Congress, Republicans nor Democrats, have had the guts or principle to construct a regulatory structure for our modern markets, which are conceptual in values, virtual in operation and processing, so complex as to defy full comprehension of even the market actors and participants, but so very real in the potential upheaval that could result from further resistance to regulation. America's markets have for eighty years enjoyed a security premium as we've competed with markets all around the world. I hope that Republicans will lead the way in investing a portion of that premium in the most sophisticated partnership between institutional and market risk management and government regulation of our financial industry and markets. If Republicans don't lead, the result is surely calamity for the nation.

Banking is a major part of the reform we must contemplate. Henry Ford said, "It is well enough that people of the nation do not understand our banking and monetary system, for if they did, I believe there would be a revolution before tomorrow morning." That understanding is setting in, and we have to restore safety and trust to our banking institutions. And banking is far too important to leave to mere bankers.

CHAPTER 4

BLESSED ARE THE CHILDREN

Baby boomers haven't done our children and grandchildren any favors. We will have left them a national debt that
amounts to $17 trillion, unfunded liabilities for all sorts of wel-
fare programs, Social Security, Medicare, that by some measures
amounts to $100 trillion. In short, our generation has burdened
succeeding generations with massive and all but unmanageable;
debt. We've failed to be good parents, positive and disciplined,
too often we've permitted our children to read less, watch TV and
play video games more, immerse themselves in chatrooms, and
put virtual experiences and activities ahead of almost everything
else, including school and family. What we've done to our children as students in many cases is criminal. We've built schools,
provided all the tools of learning, and then said to our young students, "We don't care how you act, how you behave in school, and
if a teacher or administrator tries to discipline you, we'll certainly
put a stop to that."

Imagine a room filled with hundreds of teachers. Some are reading. Some painting. Some are doing yoga. And there isn't a student in the room. And for good reason. This is where teachers who are accused of misconduct, including corporal punishment, sexual harassment, and assault, go. In New York City alone, the school system is spending as much as $65 million a year to keep these teachers on the payroll.[1] What other occupation insists that employees accused of such serious offenses receive what is essentially a paid vacation, rather than unpaid leave or suspension, probation, or prison? In the teacher trade, these big rooms filled with bad teachers are called "rubber rooms." You'll find them in school districts across the country, where thousands of teachers spend their time, taking paid leave after committing offenses against their students. These rubber rooms are waiting rooms. The teachers in them wait sometimes for years for their cases to be heard by school boards and for their appeals—and appeals of appeals—to slowly make their way through the school system. Any rational manager in any rational organization would fire such employees, and they would be appropriately punished in the private sector. But there's very little that's rational about the union-dominated American public education system.

I was raised to believe that public education made all the difference in a child's life. Public education has always been a meritocracy. Hard work, some smarts, and a curious mind would succeed, no matter how much or how little money your parents had, no matter whether you wore designer clothes or blue jeans. And I truly believe, today, that public education remains the great equalizer in American society. It has long been the institution empowering children from all walks of life to fulfill their dreams, their passions, and their visions, where reading, writing, and arithmetic established the foundation to make dreams come true. But sadly the public education system in this country is now failing to prepare enough of our children adequately for an increasingly competitive global economy and marketplace. Perhaps more important, our public education system isn't preparing our students for the responsibilities of citizenship in our constitutional republic. That is deeply disturbing.

Eight years ago, in my book *War on the Middle Class*, I lamented the appalling state of our education system in a chapter called "A Generation of Failure." Little in education has changed in the last eight years, except that matters have worsened. Some of our politicians on occasion give lip service to concerns, but there is little evidence that they truly care about our schools, and that means they do not care enough about our schoolchildren and their preparation for global competition.

How do I dare say this? Haven't we heard for decades from presidents in both political parties offering tear-stained testimonials to America's teachers? Haven't we received pledges year after year from every person who ever sought a seat in Congress about the importance of ensuring "high-quality education" for "the children"? Didn't both Obama and Romney put "improving our schools" at the top of their respective to-do lists after winning the White House? And that's not to mention the countless pictures of politicians in classrooms, sitting with kids or reading them books. While children might make for excellent photo ops or campaign promises, they apparently are not important enough for politicians to ensure they receive a quality education.

How do I say our politicians don't care about education? Because the dismal results speak for themselves. For decades our representatives in Washington have used the same failed tactics to get the same appalling results. You can probably guess what their approach is, since it's the same approach Washington has to everything. Throw money at the problem and hope it goes away.

Consider this number:

$15,171

That's how much the federal government spends of your tax dollars every year on the average pupil in public schools. $15,171 per student. That is almost a 400 percent increase since 1960, when we spent $2,800 per pupil on average. And what exactly have we gotten in return from this generous expenditure of our money? Worse achievement scores than we had in 1960. We could spend days discussing just how badly our public school children are performing. Here's one sobering statistic:

67 percent

That's the percentage of American fourth-graders who can't even read at their grade level.[2] We have increased federal spending on education by 400 percent since 1960, and we have not received any tangible benefits for our investment. Does that sound like progress to you?

If the quality of education in this country could be measured just by how much money we spend, then we'd be on top of the world rankings. If only that were the case. According to tests administered by the National Assessment of Educational Progress, average math and reading scores for seventeen-year-olds have hardly moved since this spending boom really took off in the 1970s.[3] The United States now ranks a dismal fifty-first out of 139 countries in the World Economic Forum's report on math and science education, and twenty-eighth overall in education.[4]

MATH AND SCIENCE EDUCATION, GLOBAL RANKINGS

#1   Singapore

#2   Belgium

#3   Finland

#6   Lebanon

#8   Canada

#10 Barbados

#13 Qatar

#14 Iceland

#31 China

#35 Iran

#41 Bosnia and Herzegovina

#51 United States

How many studies do we need to see telling us that our education system is failing? That our children are scoring lower and lower on achievement tests? How much longer do we want our education system to be worse than Iceland's? Or China's? Or Iran's? That's where we are, ladies and gentlemen. But the bigger point is this: If more than two-thirds of our children are not able to read properly, how can we possibly expect them to graduate from college and attain fulfilling and productive careers? That is, if they even manage to graduate in the first place, as our children have also fallen from first to fourteenth in the world in terms of the share of young adults with a postsecondary degree.[5] To compete and win in this century, especially with the rise of countries like China and India, we are going to have to build a workforce that is highly proficient in math and science. Yet, according to the Organization for Economic Cooperation and

Development (OECD), we are failing to do so; actually, "failing" isn't quite strong enough—we're absolutely tanking. According to the OECD, American students now rank fourteenth in reading proficiency among developed countries, and just twenty-fifth in mathematics—out of thirty countries surveyed. When that test was first administered in 2000, the U.S. ranked fifteenth in reading and nineteenth in math, so we have actually gone backward. When it comes to science, our fifteen-year-olds ranked twenty-fifth.[6] This, by the way, is in spite of the fact that we spent more money per student than any other developed nation in that study (well, okay, except for *Luxembourg*).[7]

This is incredible. It is criminal. And yet no one has the political courage to do a damn thing to fix the problem. We just keep shoveling our tax dollars down a rat hole of failure. What is the famous definition of insanity? Doing the same thing over and over again in the hope of getting a different result.

The level of cluelessness on this issue is overwhelming. All the time you hear politicians patting themselves on the back for another great education success story. Well, the only way this story is a success is if you read it backward.

NO CHILD LEFT UNHARMED

The No Child Left Behind law was supposed to solve many of these proficiency problems. In theory, as a mechanism to ensure schools meet their ambitious goals, states that fail to meet the educational targets it sets are supposed to lose funding. But teachers and students aren't reaching the benchmarks of the legislation. In fact, about half of public schools missed their targets under NCLB over the past school year. That's bad enough. But what was even worse was Washington's response. Did the Obama administration try to apply pressure and push schools to meet their targets the next year? No, that would have made too much sense (not to mention upsetting the all-powerful teachers' unions). Instead, President Obama took the politically expedient way out, issuing waivers to thirty-three states and the District of Columbia to exempt them from the law's requirement that all students be proficient in math and reading by 2014.[8] What an example to set for our children—the federal government is cheating on its own test. Can you think of another industry where failing to meet targets is met with a shrug of the shoulders? Yet where education is concerned, failure is considered acceptable, at the expense of the next generation's future.

Too many politicians in Washington, D.C., think that they can—and should—be telling everyone else what to do, so they implement their pet education policies and slap mandates on local schools, ignoring the fact that public schools receive just 10 percent of their money from the feds. By comparison, schools get 46 percent of their funding from the state, and 44 percent from local sources like property taxes. In a rational world, those who contribute 90 percent of the funds would be making at least 90 percent of the decisions about how schools should be run. But in our country, it seems to be the other way around. How does that make any sense?[9]

The policymakers in Washington, if they are paying any attention at all to our education system, are more interested in telling us what we can't do than what we can do to get out of this mess. We can't criticize our teachers. We can't fire bad ones. We can't give bonuses or promotions to teachers who do well at the expense of others who do poorly. We can't teach values in our schools. We can't even have kids recite the Pledge of Allegiance.

(Although apparently we can force them to recite the Mexican pledge of allegiance!)

We can't give more control to local school boards. We certainly can't empower parents to make decisions for their kids.

And when politicians do pass ambitious laws like No Child Left Behind—and trust me, I have my qualms about No Child Left Behind—they never follow through with the necessary tools that might actually allow them to fulfill their purpose of empowering our schoolchildren (or, at the very least, allow them to not fail so spectacularly). All too often, we see the political class, Democrats and Republicans alike, taking the easy road of issuing exemptions or changing the rules when things don't go as planned. What happened to vision? What happened to political courage in this country?

THE BAD TEACHER PROTECTION RACKET

The dramatic increase in American education spending, and the accompanying cratering of our students' educational outcomes, have coincided with the rise of another significant phenomenon—teachers' unions. Now, I'm always careful to make a distinction between teachers and teachers' unions. I believe most teachers want what's best for our students and our nation and work diligently to help students learn important skills.

Teachers' unions, on the other hand, are a different story entirely. By design, their mission is not really to look out for what's best for children, for teaching, or even for teachers. They are, at their core, a source of political power, utilized primarily to support partisan objectives and candidates. Since the mid-1960s, when teachers' unions first started becoming politically active (initially by forming PACs and supporting local candidates),[10] they have become a dominant force in the Democratic Party.

Meet Randi Weingarten, head of the American Federation of Teachers, who makes $425,000 in salary yearly. One school principal said of Weingarten while she was head of New York City's powerful teachers' union, "Randi Weingarten would defend a dead body in the classroom. That's her job." Or meet Dennis Van Roekel, head of the National Education Association, who makes $362,664 annually.[11] Add in stipends and paid trips to Washington, and both take in close to half a million dollars each year.

That's not the worst of it. According to union expert Mallory Factor, together these two unions collect over $2 billion in fees and dues from their teachers. What do these unions do with the money? Consider some of these numbers:

$100,000—Media Matters

$110,000—Center for American Progress

With these grants from the NEA in 2011, the two George Soros–funded organizations went on the offensive against Fox News and journalists who dared express skepticism about teachers' unions. Unions give to radical activist groups such as Occupy Wall Street. As the head of the New York City teachers' union adoringly described the protesters: "Occupy Wall Street isn't a place—it's an idea, a movement that has brought national and international focus to the danger to our economy that we face because of growing income inequality." Teachers' unions can give to partisan causes, even radical causes, without obtaining the consent of those contributing the dues used to fund them.

And then there's this:

$50,000,000

That's how much the NEA alone spent to elect Democrats in 2008.

And this—perhaps the most stunning number of them all:

$330,000,000

That's how much the NEA and AFT spent together on political and lobbying activity between 2007 and 2011—before Obama's re-election campaign.[12] The numbers for 2012 are not yet available, but one can only surmise that they likely eclipse any previous union spending.

Teachers' unions use their muscle to pick sycophantic candidates for local, state, and federal office—including members of Congress and presidents of the United States. They hold sway with more than a few Republicans, too, even though the vast majority of their campaign cash has typically gone to Democrats. They punish Democrats who even think of suggesting reforms to help improve education by allowing parental choice in education that could steer money away from their fiefdoms. They hate the idea of merit pay to reward good teachers because they know it would mean weeding out the bad ones, who pay union dues, too. Because these teachers' unions are really just organs of the Democratic Party, they are more interested in defeating Republicans than in entertaining free-market approaches to the public schools.

In 2010, Michelle Rhee, the head of the Washington, D.C., school system, sufficiently agitated the teachers' unions that the American Federation of Teachers chose to spend more than a million dollars in order to defeat incumbent mayor Adrian Fenty, her boss, and replace him with a more union-friendly candidate. And just look at what they were able to accomplish in the 2012 elections. In Indiana, the State Teachers Association mobilized local teachers' unions to defeat one of the country's most high-profile education reformers, State Superintendent Tony Bennett. The unions worked aggressively—and successfully—to defeat a California proposition that would have banned automatic payroll deductions for political purposes. In Idaho, they successfully overturned groundbreaking reforms to the teacher-evaluation process and merit pay.

And let's not forget about the biggest prize of all—their support, cash, and campaign efforts were all critical to the re-election of Barack Obama.

Teachers' unions have achieved vast political power for several reasons, one of which is that they have money. Tons of it. The source of much of that money is union dues that are often deducted automatically from the paychecks of teachers, whether they like it or not (and regardless of whether they actually agree with the candidates and causes those dues go to support). According to the Heritage Foundation, as of July 2010, teachers' unions have spent nearly three times as much on campaign ads as all corporations combined.[13] That, my friends, is raw power. And, with a combined membership of more than 4.5 million (which, by the way, represents more unionized staff than any other public or private industry),[14] the American Federation of Teachers and the National Education Association have a loyal army of foot soldiers to deploy in campaigns. If you're a supporter of union causes or political positions, that's a good thing. But if you cross them—and politicians do their best not to—then watch out. Terry Moe, a political scientist at Stanford University, put it this way: "[Teachers unions are] powerful enough that they can go after their enemies. . . . That tends to prevent a lot of policymakers from doing anything." What legislator would want to run for re-election with a phalanx of unionized teachers knocking on doors, buying up ad space, and mobilizing voters against him if he could avoid it? It's no wonder our country's political class has kowtowed to the unions for so long.[15]

But all that power comes at a price. For us as taxpayers, the costs are obvious. Over the last several decades, these unions have used their sway with officials from both parties to win lavish pay and benefits packages that are absolutely unheard of for employees in the private sector. Public school teachers, on average, receive compensation more than 50 percent higher than what they could expect to receive in the private sector, and their guaranteed pension benefits can be worth up to four times as much as the typical 401(k) plan of a private-sector worker (despite their working an average of sixty to seventy fewer days every year).[16] Unionized teachers also make 40 percent more in pay and benefits than nonunion teachers. The costs of maintaining these benefits are prohibitively high, and liabilities associated with teacher pensions in particular threaten to bankrupt state and local governments.

$41,000

That's the average teacher pension in Illinois. In other words, retired teachers there make, on average, almost as much as a working man or woman in Chicago. Teacher pension costs also suck seventy-one cents out of every state education dollar,[17] and a study released by the Democratic governor's office in 2012 projects that, by 2016, the state will spend more on government pensions—for which it already faces about $80 billion in unfunded liabilities—than all the money it spends on education. Pensions already eat up an incredible 12 percent of the state's entire budget.[18]

Moreover, according to Education Sector, nearly 20 percent of our country's public education spending goes toward teacher perks like generous benefit packages and seniority-based pay.

That represents about $77 billion that could otherwise be used for projects or programs that might actually help students in the classroom.

It's hard to begrudge individual teachers who want to defend their pensions—if you had such a sweetheart deal, wouldn't you too?—but at some point it's time to step back and take a look at the overall picture. And that picture is not pretty. If these unions were responsible, if the bosses of teachers' unions were true American patriots who truly cared about this country and its future, then they would acknowledge the immense, unsustainable costs of what they have secured through political arm-twisting. They would offer to work with policymakers to ensure those benefits are viable over the long run. They would concede that some very basic reforms are needed so that our country will not have to keep borrowing money from China, or stealing it from our children and our children's children, in order to fund such outrageous benefits. Of course, union officials do not concede any of this. Instead, they keep demanding more and more, while producing less and less in terms of educational results.

Just look at Chicago.

Fifty-two percent of Chicago's fourth-graders are below basic levels of reading; 32 percent are below basic in math. About 40 percent of Chicago's students drop out, and just 6 percent go on to obtain four-year college degrees.[19]

If ever there were a city in need of major education reform, Chicago would be it. With such sobering statistics as a backdrop (and with Chicago public schools facing an estimated $1 billion deficit),[20] Mayor Rahm Emanuel proposed a relatively modest reform package in 2012 that sought to introduce some actual metrics to the teacher-evaluation system, lengthen the school day, and still provide teachers with a raise (albeit a more modest one than the Chicago Teachers' Union wanted). Before long, the union was on strike, claiming that the proposed teacher-evaluation process put too much emphasis on student test scores. They also wanted a system of raises based on "experience" rather than impact or performance, and they demanded a provision that would force the school system to keep laid-off teachers on the payroll.

They also rejected the mayor's proposed 16 percent pay hike. This despite the fact that they already have the highest average salary of teachers in any major city, making about one and a half times more than the average Chicago worker. In fact, the teachers' average annual salary of $76,000 doesn't even account for their exceptionally generous benefits, such as paying only 3 percent of their health-care costs, or being eligible to retire as early as age fifty and to earn a pension equal to three-fourths of their highest salary at age sixty.[21]

Emanuel promised to dig in his heels and fight for reform, no matter the cost. He certainly put on a good show, but it all turned out to be a lot of hot air. While the national media tried to spin the final, watered-down deal as a win for the mayor, it really didn't do very much to advance education reform in the city.

Just look at the details.

The teacher raises in the contract—which amount to an average of about 17.6 percent over four years when you throw in things like seniority-based pay increases—will add another $295 million to Chicago public schools' already massive deficit. The deal will lengthen the school day from five hours and forty-five minutes to seven hours, and it will expand the school year from 170 days to 180; but all that will do is take Chicago from having one of the shortest school years in the country to falling in line with the national average. And those teacher evaluations? They were previously based on principals' observations; now, in the third year of the contract, 30 percent of evaluations will be based on student performance. Can you imagine? It's going to take a few years, but at least we'll get a small indication of how teachers are actually doing in the classroom. But again, this is not some groundbreaking new concession, as it will just force Chicago to fall in line with existing Illinois state law.[22]

In my view, this was all political theater from the beginning, and the real losers in this deal were the students and their parents. If you think that's outrageous, then consider this; just about one in ten Americans attend private schools, but about 40 percent of the same teachers who signed this deal—you know, the ones supposedly fighting "for the children"—send their kids to private school. They don't even allow their children to go to the same schools where they teach! If your teaching, and that of your fellow teachers, is not acceptable for your own children, why exactly do you deserve a raise? For trying and failing to teach math and reading skills to other people's kids?

So, my question is this: How is any of this helping our children? In what universe would it be possible to work and not expect to be evaluated based on your actual performance? We want our teachers to be well compensated. Who doesn't want that? What we don't want is political extortion. When government officials give taxpayer money to public-employee unions and those unions give the money back to government officials in the form of campaign contributions, that's cronyism at its worst. And, by the way, all this is ultimately funded by you and me. But this is about more than just corruption. The future of our country's ability to effectively educate its young people is at stake.

If we really care about paying our teachers well, and if we want to do so in a way that encourages better educational outcomes, then we need to talk about merit pay. Merit pay is a simple concept; it says that teachers who excel in the classroom should earn more than teachers who perform poorly. I can't think of an industry where that is not the case. Can you? Better lawyers earn more than mediocre ones; salespersons who overperform their sales targets earn bonuses and raises; even the drive-thru attendant at the local fast-food restaurant can expect his pay to be based at least partially on his on-the-job performance. Money is the primary tool by which employers can incentivize their employees to do better and work harder.

Not in the world of teachers' unions. Instead of pay based on performance, teachers are usually paid based on their seniority and, in part, on what certifications and degrees they have acquired. Some of these certifications are meaningful and can enhance a teacher's classroom performance; others are essentially meaningless pieces of paper collected as a way to earn more money under byzantine contract rules. Imagine if this were a private-sector company. Should we pay Gus, the twenty-year company veteran with a master's, more than Susan, a more junior associate without an advanced degree? Of course, as long as they had the same relative on-the-job performance. But if Gus mentally checked out a decade ago, if he punches the clock at 5:00 p.m. every day and loses clients due to inattentiveness, then should he really be making more than employee-of-the-month Susan with her record sales, late nights, and positive attitude? The question, really, is whether Gus should still have a job at all.

This basic logic of incentives and good management does not apply when it comes to America's public schools. Not only can many star teachers not be paid more for their performance, but also bad teachers are difficult—if not impossible—to fire. Teacher tenure laws vary from state to state and from locality to locality, but, in general, many teachers are essentially handed jobs for life once they achieve tenure. In some places, that can happen after just a few years on the job.

Another reason this is all so problematic is that it makes teachers without tenure far more vulnerable to losing their jobs. These are the teachers, by the way, who tend to enter the profession with the greatest idealism and enthusiasm for teaching children. Many of them are younger, are more flexible, and tend to be able to devote after-hours attention to students. These are the teachers who usually earn the lowest salaries and, yet, are often the ones we should actually be paying the most in order to encourage them to stay and continue inspiring our kids. Not only is that not the case, but also these teachers are usually the first to be fired in times of layoffs and budget cuts. Instead of pruning the withering leaves from our schools to make them stronger and more effective (which is theoretically what budget cuts should be doing anyway), teacher tenure rules force the cuts down into the roots, eviscerating the next generation of teachers while leaving the rest of the system unreformed and on a path to further decline. What does that usually mean? More cuts down the line, resulting in even fewer promising teachers—and then the cycle repeats again.

It's maddening.

Since we're on the subject of layoffs, it's worth mentioning that some union contracts make it nearly impossible to stop paying a bad teacher. I alluded to this somewhat when talking about the Chicago strike. But that's really nothing compared to New York City. According to the *Wall Street Journal*, teachers in the Big Apple are "guaranteed pay for life even when their school closes and they are put out of a permanent job." Educators who lose their positions are simply transferred to so-called rubber rooms, where they can theoretically be called up to work as a substitute or perform other tasks. Most of the time, though, they just sit there with nothing to do as they continue to collect salaries that average more than $80,000 a year. Not only is this a stupid policy, but it also costs New York City about $100 million annually.[23] Imagine if that money was used instead to hire good teachers, replace collapsing schools, and help educate the students of New York—about a quarter of whom do not even graduate with the proper preparation for careers or college.[24]

If this were a world of angels, if humans were not motivated by money and the fear of losing their jobs, then maybe—maybe—we could believe that every teacher could work as hard as possible out of the pure joy of teaching our children. But we don't, and they don't. By taking the most effective carrots and sticks out of the hands of principals and school officials, how can we possibly expect our schools to effectively hire, manage, and retain the most effective teaching staffs? We can't.

We've tried to solve this problem the teachers' unions' way. They told us that the answer to all our education problems was spending more money. So we've spent and we've spent. We should give more power to the federal government, they implored. So we gave the feds vast new powers over what had traditionally been a state and local issue. They said that we needed to give in to their demands on gold-plated, taxpayer-funded pension plans and obscene, budget-busting benefit packages. We did that, too. They told us that we should give them all this, but that we should not expect to be able to evaluate unionized teachers based on how they actually perform in the classroom. Check.

And yet, we seem only to keep spiraling downward faster.

Let me make this as clear as possible: Teachers' unions are killing our kids' chances for a better life. More than that, they are destroying our country's ability to compete and win in an increasingly competitive global economy. They are also plunging government budgets deeper and deeper into the red, just as we have begun to witness, in Europe and elsewhere, the terrible consequences of runaway entitlements and unsustainable debt.

If teachers' unions are unhappy about the state of education in America today, they have only themselves to blame. They got everything they wanted. And these are the unfortunate results of bad policies.

LET THE DEVOLUTION BEGIN

It's time to start doing the exact opposite of what the union bosses want. We need to devolve power back as close to parents and students as possible. We need to spend money wisely in ways that can actually help students instead of just spending more to *feel* like we're doing something. We need to institute measures designed to incentivize good teaching, such as merit pay and performance-based evaluations, and we need to lengthen the school day. If we do nothing else, let's at least eliminate some of the more wasteful and downright idiotic policies, like the rubber rooms. And we need to bring teacher salaries and benefits back in line with reality. It's clear that what passes for reality among private-sector workers is worlds apart from what this pampered class of union bosses and cronies has come to expect, all at taxpayer expense. That cannot endure.

Our education system used to be about educating children and preparing them for a successful career. Today, it's morphed into a political tool for greedy adults to advance their own selfish interests and political agenda. It's time for that to change.

Most of the current political class in Washington is either in the pocket of the public-school union establishment, or too timid to challenge it. If our political leaders really want to improve education, if they really want America to compete with China and India and Europe in the twenty-first century, they need to change, too. Or we need to change them. It's time to end the war on children and to wage a war *for* our children. They're counting on us.

CHAPTER 5

A TOUGH ENVIRONMENT

The Earth is warming. Well, parts of it anyway. But what part is climate and what part is climate change? And then, of course, how much of it all is anthropogenic? I'm not satisfied with the answers from the scientists on either side of the argument, nor am I satisfied with the politics and positions of the left or the right, and despite years of debate, I've heard no sensible plan that would create an absolutely benign alternative for either ourselves or for our planet. We hear a lot about so-called green energy. A lot of hopeful talk from politicians about their big plans to bring our nation boundless amounts of energy from clean, "renewable" sources (the sun, the wind, even the oceans) while putting an end to "dirty" coal, oil, and gas.

Celebrities talk about it, too, railing against the oil and coal industries and demanding "green" energy alternatives in our daily lives. Actors have embarked on Facebook campaigns to "unfriend" the coal industry and have supported the Sierra Club in a campaign to go "Beyond Oil." The actor Pierce Brosnan has outfitted his entire home with green energy—including low-flush toilets and other state-of-the-art devices that millionaires like him can well afford. John Travolta, who owns several gas-guzzling private jets (including a four-engine Boeing 707 airliner that consumes two thousand gallons of jet fuel *per hour*), once lectured self-righteously on the need for "alternative methods of fuel"—while riding a motorcycle down the red carpet.[1] A few years back, scads of environmentally conscious pop stars even joined together to put on a Live Earth concert to heighten awareness of green issues (and, in so doing, they left behind a massive carbon footprint equivalent to the emission of about thirty-five thousand tons of greenhouse gases).[2]

Our energy resources matter to ordinary Americans because they directly affect our pocketbooks. The average American household pays more than $1,400 a year in energy costs.[3] And the demand for energy is not slowing. According to the U.S. Energy Department, global energy consumption is expected to rise more than 50 percent by the year 2035.

What this means is that we need to develop a sane, practical energy strategy right now. We can't wait or the costs to the American people will continue to skyrocket. Unfortunately, the most we hear from our leaders is the usual bold talk and empty promises.

Every American president since Richard Nixon has promised to free us from our "dependence on foreign oil" and to devise an independent energy strategy for America. All of them have failed. Some of you may be too young to remember that in the 1970s, Jimmy Carter's brilliant energy strategy was to "strictly conserve" our energy resources and advise Americans to "live thriftily." He turned down the heat in the White House and appeared on television wearing a sweater and sitting in front of a fire. "Some of [my energy] policies," he said in an address to the nation shortly after he was elected, "will require some sacrifice from you."

Maybe it's just me—but I think the most powerful nation in the world can come up with a better strategy than merely putting on extra layers of clothes.

Historically, American ingenuity has driven the discovery and development of new energy technologies. In fact, the United States' two most impressive inventors were essential players in this pursuit. Thomas Edison started the very first coal power station in New York City. Nikola Tesla introduced America's first power grid in Niagara Falls. New inventions created a growing demand for new energy sources. Henry Ford's mass-produced Model-Ts paved the way for exponentially increasing consumption of petroleum, as did the Wright Brothers' aeronautical adventures. It's amazing to think of all the efforts made by individuals working in the private sector that made these groundbreaking developments possible. Government, if you've been paying attention, played a negligible part. Maybe we can give the federal government some credit for its role in nuclear energy, but the last time I checked, our houses weren't nuclear-powered and we didn't drive nuclear-powered vehicles. Actually, the government may have some part in blocking that, too.

Don't get me wrong; saving on energy costs is a great thing. Nobody in his or her right mind would freely opt for a dirtier, more expensive energy source. People have always looked for ways to more effectively harness energy toward useful ends. For example, about 150 years ago less than 5 percent of heat energy expended by an open fire was usable. Then someone came up with a chimney design that upped that number to 15 to 20 percent. Nowadays, heat furnaces can turn up to 97 percent of the energy in natural gas to usable heat.[4] I doubt President Grover Cleveland championed "greener" chimneys in his State of the Union Addresses, much less ran for office on the idea. The market allowed consumers to decide, and look what happened. That's real progress.

Supposedly, green energy has been around for thousands of years (though nobody would have thought about it like that back then). Green energy proponents point to ancient sources to emphasize that we've been using wind, solar, and geothermal energy for a long time—implying that because of that history, those sources are somehow more natural than others. One particularly epic account begins with Odysseus on the Aegean, gloriously transitioning to the "bubbling wakes and billowing sails" of a thousand ships of "commerce and conquest."[5] If only we could return to that golden era of environmentally friendly conquest! Alas, not all that is ancient is clean. Consider if we were still using wood as an energy source—and its 5 percent energy efficiency rate. It's a good thing that we were able to find more efficient fuels—if only for the forest's sake. Of course, the idea that older is more natural is absurd on its face, akin to "Marijuana is just a plant" (so is opium), "Al Qaeda just wants to talk" (have you asked them?), and "animals are people, too." (This one has always confused me. Should animals behave like people or should we behave like animals? Perhaps a compromise?) If we can take one lesson from the fact that wind and solar energy have been around for a long time, it's that they have had a long time to become competitive with coal and oil. And they haven't even come close.

But that hasn't stopped our leaders from promising the moon. Just like every one of his predecessors, President Obama had a grand plan for our energy needs and a lot of promises. On the campaign trail in 2008, he pledged to create "5 million green jobs" within a decade.[6] "I'll invest $150 billion over the next decade in affordable, renewable sources of energy—wind power and solar power, and the next generation of biofuels—an investment that will lead to new industries and 5 million new jobs." He also promised that these jobs would pay well, and that they could not be outsourced.[7]

Millions of jobs, a greener environment, cleaner energy—this all sounds wonderful, doesn't it? That's why politicians love to talk up "green energy" and barely say a word in the defense of the oil, coal, and gas industries when they come under attack. There is just one problem, folks: In the near future at least, green energy is an expensive fantasy, a distant hope at best. The green energy alternatives that the federal government champions do not put a dent in our current energy needs, and they likely won't be a practical solution for decades to come, if ever. Meanwhile the Quixote-like pursuit of this green energy fantasy is destroying jobs in this country. Yes, DESTROYING jobs in the United States. Today.

When we discuss green energy, we ought to get in mind two numbers. The first one is this:

9,200,000

That is how many American jobs the oil and natural gas industry alone is responsible for providing, both directly and indirectly, according to the American Petroleum Institute.[8]

Officials in the Obama administration cite a similarly large number in terms of the green energy jobs they claim to have created. They assert that 3.1 million green energy jobs have been created since Barack Obama took office.[9] That number should have a big, fat asterisk beside it, because there is no federal definition of a so-called green job. That 3.1 million figure includes all sorts of jobs that already exist, such as plumbers who install toilets with "low-volume" flow and even public relations professionals. Bizarrely, the federal government counts lobbying for the oil industry as a green job.[10] As Diana Furchtgott-Roth reports in her book *Regulating to Disaster*, the U.S. Department of Education defines a "green job" as any farmer who sells at least some of his corn to ethanol producers.[11] "Another puzzling class of green workers is the 241,877 employed in public transportation," Furchtgott-Roth writes. "Buses and trains are classified as 'green,' but taxis are not."[12]

Furchtgott-Roth notes that not only is there no federal definition of a green job, but states each have their own varying definitions. The state of New Jersey, for example, acknowledges that a green job is not a newly created job, but one that already exists with the potential to contribute toward improving the environment.[13] The situation is so convoluted that if I started talking about recycling on my television program, I might be considered as having one of these "green jobs" the Obama administration "created," too.

Now consider another number:

4,700

According to the most recent data from the Bureau of Labor Statistics, that is the total number of jobs that actually have been *created* in the United States by generating electricity from wind, solar, biomass, and solar energy. In other words, there are more people working in the executive branch of the Obama administration than there are working in the entire country on "green" energy projects. As a former Obama administration economic advisor admitted while discussing solar plants, "Some of these firms don't employ as many people as you might hope." No kidding.[14]

Don't get me wrong: It is a good thing to look for new sources of energy. Nobody wants America kowtowing to corrupt Middle Eastern dictators for the rest of our lives. But while we look to the future, doesn't it make sense to also recognize today's reality? What the Democrats and their friends aren't saying clearly, and what they may not understand, is how critical our oil, natural gas, and coal industries remain to our economy, and how important they will continue to be for years and years to come. Here is how America's energy consumption breaks down today:

- Oil: 36 percent
- Natural gas: 27 percent
- Coal: 18 percent
- Nuclear: 9 percent
- "Renewable" sources: 9 percent
  - Biomass: 4.3 percent
  - Hydropower: 2.6 percent
  - Wind: 0.9 percent
  - Geothermal: 0.4 percent
  - Solar: 0.1 percent

As you can see, the "renewable" sources the Obama administration just can't stop funding or talking about account for a combined 9 percent of our energy production, not even a tenth of America's energy needs. Solar, geothermal, and wind account for just about 1 percent. Obviously, there's a long way to go before they are ever going to match oil or coal.

Here is why this matters: Millions of American jobs, and nearly all American households, are relying on the continued health and prosperity of our oil, coal, and natural gas companies. And yet the federal government, sometimes with bipartisan support, is working every day to make it harder for them to do business.

The Obama administration says it believes in an "all-of-the-above" energy strategy; in theory, that strategy is supposed to entail developing all our nation's energy resources, renewable and nonrenewable, in pursuit of reducing our dependence on foreign energy. At a Hollywood fundraiser in 2012, President Obama described the Democratic Party's position on energy this way: "I'm big on oil and gas, and developing clean coal technology, but I also believe that if we're ever going to have control of our energy future, then we've got to invest in solar and wind and biofuels, and that it does make sense for us to double our fuel-efficiency standards on cars." On the surface, that all sounds like a good idea—and perhaps it would be, if the president actually backed his rhetoric up with action. Unfortunately, a more accurate term for this president's energy strategy might be "some-of-the-above, and-definitely-not-any-of-the-stuff-that-actually-works."

The Obama administration and its Democratic allies in Congress spent four years demonizing the productive sectors of our energy economy. For example, it's become almost an obsession for the president to call for the repeal of what he calls the "$4 billion in subsidies" enjoyed by American's oil and natural gas industry. "A century of subsidies to the oil companies is long enough," Obama said in 2012.[15] Nancy Pelosi calls them "outdated and costly,"[16] and has frequently advocated their abolition. Yet, as Harry Reid has acknowledged, doing so wouldn't do much to help American families. "We know it's not going to have an effect on gas prices," he said following a failed repeal vote in 2011.[17]

It's fun to attack faceless corporations. Sometimes it is even warranted. The Democrats have been attacking Big Oil for de-

66

66666

cades. But in this case, the charges are totally hypocritical. It is not the government that is subsidizing the oil companies, but the oil companies that are subsidizing the government.

Contrary to the Democrats' assertions, American oil companies do not collect "subsidies" from the federal government. What they receive are the same tax breaks that most other American businesses are entitled to in one form or another. These tax incentives help our businesses grow and compete in the international marketplace.

One of the reasons the president gives for trying to increase taxes on oil companies is that they are profitable. The Democrats have called many times for a "windfall profits tax" on oil companies. President Obama himself once pledged to "make oil companies like Exxon pay a tax on their windfall profits."[18] Here's a thought: When did profit become a bad thing? Why do we want to punish companies that are managed well? Don't we want American companies to be successful and to create more jobs and energy right here in the United States? Some of the ultrawealthy athletes and celebrities who support President Obama make huge profits in the private sector. Katy Perry makes far more in album sales than a CEO of Shell. Sean Penn makes far more from one of his blockbuster movies than the president of Peabody Coal. Why don't the Democrats single out any of these groups as Public Enemy Number One?

The vendetta against oil companies is not only discriminatory—yes, discriminatory—it also flies in the face of all common sense. Here's another statistic to consider:

$1,000,000,000,000

The oil and natural gas industry represents more than $1 trillion of economic activity every year, and it accounts for nearly 8 percent of our country's gross domestic product.[19] As I mentioned, jobs created by the oil industry far surpass those created in the renewable, green energy world. More than that, our traditional energy sector also plays a huge role in enabling our government to fund other federal programs.

ExxonMobil, for example, is the largest oil company in the United States, and it pays an effective average tax rate above 40 percent.[20] When ExxonMobil made $41 billion in profits in 2011, more than $27.3 billion funneled right back to federal, state, and local government budgets. That's just one company, remember. Chevron paid $17 billion in income taxes and ConocoPhillips $10 billion. Combined, the industry returns about $86 million each and every *day* to the federal government in fees, taxes, and royalties[21]—just a fraction of that sector's overall contribution to our economy. Compared to the rest of the twenty-five most profitable companies in the United States, these three companies alone had the highest effective tax rates. In a freakish turn, these companies in effect are funding a federal government that is actively working to undermine them. Yet do we hear any politician—from either party—going to the trouble to point this out? Of course not.

Democrats have steadfastly stood in the way of drilling here at home. They've even been joined by spineless Republicans, who fear the backlash of environmentalists and being pinned with the blame in the event of an environmental disaster like an oil spill. The Institute for Energy Research estimates that there are 1.4 trillion barrels of oil within our own territory, or enough to meet our current oil needs for two hundred years.[22] A significant amount of this oil is in remote locations—sitting offshore, hidden in shale in the West, or locked away in areas of Alaska.[23] It will take creative strategies and solutions to get that energy out of the ground and into our cars, homes, and businesses where we need it—as a first step, Congress needs to get out of the way and allow American ingenuity to drive the development of these critical deposits.

If our leaders won't let us drill here in the U.S., then they also won't let us work with our reliable neighbor to the north, thanks to an insane energy policy that has been hijacked by radical environmentalists who have no interest in allowing our capitalist economy to function.

If you don't know what a prairie chicken is, you're not alone. This obscure species of small bird roams over much of the Great Plains, but they choose much of Nebraska's grassland and windswept sand, known as the Sandhills, as their home. Few animals have ever had such an impact on America's energy future and jobs. Indeed, if it weren't for the prairie chicken, we might today be building a 1,179-mile pipeline, called the Keystone XL, from oil-rich southern Canada to refineries on the Gulf Coast. We might have the additional twenty thousand jobs the pipeline would have created. And we might begin reaping the benefits of $9.6 billion in domestic product the pipeline was estimated to generate.[24]

I understand that politicians like Obama and Pelosi must be getting a lot of pressure from the radical environmentalists who form their political base. That's obvious not just from their systematic campaign against the coal industry, but also in their outrageous decision to block construction of the Keystone XL pipeline stretching across the United States into Canada, a project that a majority of Americans have consistently supported. Not only that, but we've forfeited a sure source of stable, reliable, North American energy from a friendly neighbor. Yet, because of environmentalists championing pet causes like protecting the prairie chicken, the Obama administration has refused to grant permission for the pipeline.

Keystone should have been a bipartisan no-brainer. Instead, the president prioritized currying favor with his liberal base over American jobs and energy independence. Environmentalists claimed the pipeline could have affected an underground aquifer in Nebraska. No one wants to pollute the environment, of course, and we certainly don't want to contaminate our water supply. But Keystone was subjected to what one columnist called "the most exhaustive study of any oil pipeline in U.S. history." What did government studies conclude? That there would not be any significant environmental harm. Twice.[25] Yet still the administration blocked the pipeline anyway and cost our country tens of thousands of American jobs.

The Democrats' all-out war on the coal industry is even more intense. Coal generates 37 percent of our nation's electrical power, the largest source by far when it comes to electricity generation. Coal is also one of the cheapest sources of electricity in this country. You definitely won't hear the administration talking about this, but coal is four times cheaper than natural gas.

Not only is coal America's most abundant energy resource, but it also helps provide our country with hundreds of thousands of jobs. These are real jobs, not phony green ones. We shouldn't be surprised by President Obama's campaign against the coal industry, though; this is exactly what he promised when he ran for president in 2008. "If somebody wants to build a coal-powered plant, they can," then-senator Barack Obama said. "It's just that it will bankrupt them because they're going to be charged a huge sum for all that greenhouse gas that's being emitted."[26]

Earlier in his first term, President Obama urged Democrats in

Congress to pass cap-and-trade legislation that would have devastated the American coal industry and our economy. According to the conservative-leaning think tank the Heritage Foundation, such legislation could have cost as many as 1.9 million jobs, raised electricity prices by 90 percent, and increased families' annual energy bills by $1,500.[27]

When that effort failed, the administration directed the Environmental Protection Agency to impose draconian regulations on coal-fired power plants. The Obama administration has been responsible for substantially blocking and delaying coal production on federal lands, which has dropped to just 272 million tons annually—almost half the 515 million tons per year produced under the George W. Bush administration. Operators are planning to retire a record 57 coal plants in 2012, with another 175 generators scheduled to be shut down over the next five years. The Democrats are destroying—repeat: destroying—the coal industry. And they have nothing to put in its place.

We have enough coal to last for more than two hundred years at current consumption levels; it simply makes no sense to wage a self-destructive war against such a cheap and reliable source of energy that creates so many American jobs—especially if the president really is serious about pursuing an "all-of-the-above" rather than a "some-of-the-above" strategy. Because "oil" and "gas" have become dirty words in Washington, politicians have sharpened the knives to tax them more. In his 2013 budget, Obama raised taxes by $38.5 billion on U.S. energy companies by eliminating existing subsidies. If passed, the scenario plays out in one of two ways: Either the companies are forced to pass on the costs to consumers at gas pumps and on their electricity bills, or they will simply give up and pack up their bags and move to different countries. We've already seen that in the oil and gas services industry.

Halliburton has moved to Switzerland. Transocean and Noble are moving to the United Kingdom.

The Obama administration has made it exceedingly difficult to get licenses to drill for oil and gas on federal lands. It has reduced the number of permits and licenses by 40 percent from the Bush administration. Oil production on federal lands was down by 14 percent in 2012.[28] Gas production was down by 17 percent. At the same time, President Obama has directed his EPA to attack the energy industry with a range of misguided regulations, one of which, the so-called Utility MACT rule aimed at coal-fired power plants, is based on shaky science yet could cost as much as $21 billion in annual compliance costs and lead to more than 180,000 lost jobs every year.[29]

The continuing effort by environmentalists and their allies to degrade, delay, or block development of the energy sources that currently employ millions of Americans, light our homes, and fuel our cars might all be a bit easier to swallow if their "green" investments actually seemed to be paying off. Instead we are investing millions of tax dollars—your tax dollars—in failure.

In 2009, shortly after he took office, President Obama prodded Congress to pass a multibillion-dollar stimulus package that he claimed would get our economy moving again. While it hasn't done much for our economy, the president's American Recovery and Reinvestment Act was successful in securing billions of taxpayer dollars for a wide range of subsidies and government-backed loan guarantees for favored green energy enterprises.

According to the Heritage Foundation, these included:

- $43 million for an energy-storage company called Beacon Power
- $400 million in loan guarantees for Abound Solar

- $500,000 for SpectraWatt
- $118.5 million for EnerDel's subsidiary Ener1

What happened to these companies? Well, for starters, Beacon Power, which received that $43 million from you the taxpayer without your permission, filed for bankruptcy in 2011.[30] Spectra-Watt filed for bankruptcy the same year.[31] Abound Solar, which received that $400 million in federal loan guarantees, laid off about half of its employees and sought bankruptcy protection. So did EnerDel's subsidiary Ener1, which pocketed more than $100 million of your money.

Let's be fair to the Obama administration. Anyone can pick a few losers. That doesn't mean all our money was wasted. Then again . . . it turns out this administration picked more than just a "few" losers. Here are some other companies that were chosen to receive taxpayer dollars for "green" energy programs:

- A123 Systems   ($249 million)
- Raser Technologies   ($33 million)
- Energy Conversion Devices   ($13.3 million)

They're all in trouble too. And here are a few more:

- Mountain Plaza, Inc.   ($424,000)
- Olsen's Crop Service and
  Olsen's Mills Acquisition Company ($10 million)
- Range Fuels   ($80 million)
- Thompson River Power   ($6.5 million)
- Stirling Energy Systems   ($7 million)

And yet some more:

- Azure Dynamics   ($5.4 million)
- LG Chem's subsidiary Compact
  Power   ($151 million)
- Nordic Windpower   ($16 million)
- Satcon   ($3 million)

Every one of those companies is now either bankrupt, heading toward bankruptcy, or laying off workers instead of creating more of the president's vaunted green jobs. And let's not forget about the $3 billion—that's billion with a "b"—in taxpayer-subsidized loans our government thought fit to give to First Solar, the S&P 500's worst-performing stock in 2011. Or the biggest and most corrupt rip-off of all: hundreds of millions to a company that made solar panels, a company called Solyndra.

If you haven't followed the Solyndra scandal, I can't blame you. The mainstream media rarely see fit to mention it. Here's a rundown: In September 2009, the U.S. Department of Energy gave the company, a solar-panel maker, $535 million in loan guarantees. A loan guarantee is, in effect, a check handed to a company without any requirement that the company have a plan to repay it should the company go bankrupt—which, in the case of Solyndra, is exactly what happened. I probably don't have to tell you how ironic it is that an administration rallying against "subsidies" to profitable oil companies has absolutely no problem subsidizing failed environmentalist ventures like this one.

It also helps that one of the company's major backers just happened to be one of President Obama's biggest campaign contributors. George Kaiser raised between $50,000 and $100,000 for Obama in 2008, and visited the White House seventeen times in the years since. He was one of Solyndra's biggest investors through a company called Argonaut Private Equity. Kaiser's associates pressed the White House and Department of Defense officials to buy millions of dollars' worth of solar panels, even though the company was clearly failing.

After injecting taxpayer dollars into the company, the Obama administration praised the company with language they usually save for the leaders of Russia or China, or the dictators in the Middle East. The company represented one of the "true engines of economic growth," Obama boasted. His energy secretary, Steven Chu, also heaped praise upon Solyndra. "It is time to rev up the American innovation machine and reclaim our lead on clean energy. . . . This investment is part of a broad, aggressive effort to spark a new industrial revolution that will put Americans to work, end our dependence on foreign oil and cut carbon pollution."[32] Vice President Joe Biden appeared by satellite to announce the loan grant to Solyndra's employees. Several months later, the president visited the Fremont, California, factory himself, where he said that companies like Solyndra were "leading the way toward a brighter and more prosperous future."[33]

Even then the warning signs about Solyndra were already manifest. The Department of Energy "is trying to deliver the first loan guarantee within 60 days from inauguration (the prior administration could not get it done in four years). This deal is NOT ready for prime time," wrote one Office of Management and Budget official.[34] Before the loan was made, Department of Energy staff knew the company would run out of cash by September 2011. Sure enough, in August of that year, Solyndra filed for bankruptcy. Eleven hundred workers were laid off.

Toward the end of 2011, a federal judge approved a plan allowing the company to exit bankruptcy. The plan would allow the federal government to recoup "just pennies on the dollar on the approximately $528 million it pumped into the company," according to a news report.[35] This means that the bulk of the half-billion dollars our government wasted on Solyndra is likely lost forever.

To this day, the federal government refuses to admit its mistake. Politicians from either party almost never do that. After the ruling, a Department of Energy spokesman told reporters that "from day one, decisions made on loan applications and projects supported by loan guarantees were made on the merits after careful review by experts in the loan program. Our consistent goal has been to manage these critical investments in innovative clean energy technologies in a way that manages the risk to the taxpayers." Talk about utter, indefensible cluelessness.

This is what welfare looks like for the well-connected. It is cronyism in the twenty-first century. Solyndra was unable to get financing from private investors, so they turned to something even better: the U.S. taxpayer. After all, they'd never have to pay back the loan. If Solyndra's dirty little secret never became public, no one would complain.

Since 2009, the federal government has made thirty-eight similar commitments totaling $36 billion to projects like Solyndra. They've gone to French companies to build nuclear power plants ($10 billion). A subsidiary of a Russian steel company ($8.1 billion). The electric car manufacturer Fisker ($529 million). And dozens of other projects, some of which are almost certainly going to end up like Solyndra.

Even when the government is able to create some of these so-called green jobs, they're massively expensive. Just look at Nevada, Senate Majority Leader Harry Reid's home state. He's been pretty successful at pulling those green dollars back home. In fact, Nevada's already received at least $1.3 billion in such funding for geothermal, solar, and wind projects since President Obama took office. So what did all that money create? In terms of jobs, just

288 of them—at a jaw-dropping cost of $4.6 million per job! That hasn't done much to dent Nevada's 11.6 percent unemployment rate, but it has led to the quadrupling of the cost of power in the state.[36]

What may be most disturbing about the pursuit of a fantasy for "green" jobs and renewable energy is that it willfully ignores an energy revolution in America that is actually happening. For a president who claims to want energy independence, he has a funny way of showing it. If politicians were willing to encourage oil and gas production in America, we could become more and more independent from our longtime suppliers in places like Saudi Arabia and Venezuela. Indeed, by the end of this decade, by some estimates, North America could become a net exporter of energy.

Take North Dakota. Help Wanted signs dot the landscape. McDonald's pays fifteen dollars an hour to its workers.[37] With 3 percent, it has the lowest unemployment rate in the nation. Why? Because the Bakken field of oil and natural gas contains an estimated 24 billion barrels of oil, effectively doubling America's oil reserves.[38] With 810,000 barrels produced per day in May 2013, North Dakota now is behind only Texas in crude oil production.[39]

American technological pioneers have developed new ways to get at oil that even ten years ago would have been unimaginable. Horizontal drilling allows rigs to drill through the earth's surface at an angle, miles underneath the ground, allowing access to new deposits. Hydraulic fracturing or "fracking" pumps high-pressure water, sand, and trace amounts of chemicals deep into the earth to dislodge natural gas from rock and sand. New and more unconventional drilling methods are also allowing us to extract energy trapped tightly in rocks like shale. Over the past five years, the development of shale gas—which accounted for just 2 percent of natural gas production in 2000, compared to nearly 40 percent today—has helped drive a massive 25 percent increase in American natural gas production.[40] Moreover, today's natural gas costs a little over $2.50 per thousand cubic feet. That compares to $4.50 in 2010, and a price nearly three times as high in 2008.[41]

A report prepared by IHS estimated that more than 1.7 million jobs are supported by unconventional oil and natural gas development activities, and such jobs can grow to 3 million by 2020.[42] But that's going to happen only if Washington gets out of the way.

Our long-term energy strategy is nonexistent. Our policies are scattershot and make no sense. In the 2012 campaign, most of what we heard was platitudes and empty promises. These are the kinds of things that make Americans so cynical about their government. We see leaders bending to their bases and political paymasters instead of pursuing good policies. We see politicians trying to take both sides of an issue for fear of offending powerful interest groups. All the while, things only seem to get worse in our country. Who is looking out for American jobs and gas prices? Every time we go to fill up at the pump, we're reminded of just how broken our political system has become.

Political leaders owe the American people the truth when it comes to our country's energy needs. There is just no possible way that these green energy sources are going to be able to power our electric grid or the millions of cars we drive for the foreseeable future. The government can dump billions more taxpayer dollars into renewable energy ventures and—assuming they're not wasted outright on more Solyndra boondoggles—it still will not make a difference for decades to come.

That must be why the president continues to pitch more government investment in renewable energy technology, as if renewables were some sort of magic short-term solution, some silver bullet. The problem is, the facts simply do not back up the rhetoric. As is so often the case, when you start looking just a little deeper, when you break things down just a little further, you find that, while renewable energy may be helpful somewhere far down the road, it's nowhere near being in a position to replace fossil fuels or coal in our energy mix. And that's likely to be the case for decades to come, no matter how many government dollars we spend today trying to change that reality.

America's middle class can't afford eight dollars a gallon for gasoline; for that matter, neither can our economy. It will take decades to create true alternative energy in abundance. We fortunately are at the beginning of a renaissance of fossil fuel energy, blessed as well with advanced clean technology that will allow us and millions around the world to responsibly consume that energy. Our fossil fuel wealth is a bridge: a bridge to technology and energy that we have only begun to contemplate and develop. The Republican Party is on the right side of history and the energy resources that will fuel our destiny.

CHAPTER 6

SPACE MYSTERIES AND MISADVENTURES

Americans have been possessed of the imagination and courage to explore new frontiers for more than four hundred years. Americans are by birthright and nature innovative, productive, and among the most ambitious people in the world. Discovering and founding a new world in America, early Europeans who were to become the first Americans braved odds and risked all to found the United States, and by the twentieth century only space remained as the true final frontier. The century began with the discovery of flight. Within two decades aviation was integral to war and in the First World War the world was introduced to Manfred von Richthofen, known as the Red Baron, England's Edward Mannock, and America's Eddie Rickenbacker. The world was overtaken with the romance and adventure of flight, and a new kind of hero was introduced.

Descendants all of Lewis and Clark, still to come were Amelia Earhart, Richard Byrd, Charles Lindbergh, Billy Mitchell, and

Chuck Yeager. These were all Americans who braved the odds, risked all, and explored new territories—the land, the sea, the air. We were on the brink of a new era of discovery in space. What the hell happened?

Like many Americans my age, I grew up dreaming about space and space exploration. And I still do. As children our heroes were cowboys, and growing up we had real-life heroes, the veterans of World War II and Korea. And then the NASA astronauts. It is all but impossible to express the excitement and wonder as we watched the first astronauts of the Mercury program blast off in their Redstone rockets. Alan Shepard became the first American in space, and less than a year later John Glenn became the first American to orbit the Earth. The hardware had changed; Glenn got to ride the Atlas rocket and a bigger, more powerful launch vehicle. Technological advancements were being achieved at a dizzying rate. Mercury astronauts were blending in to the new assemblage of Gemini astronauts. The newspaper and television accounts of our Space Race with the Soviets had moved us into something of a tie despite their early firsts with satellites and then Yuri Gagarin claiming first-man-in-space honors. America's national pride was swelling with each mission success. Then in 1965 Ed White became the first American to exit his space capsule and to walk in space.

It's hard to absorb America's amazing accomplishments in space. In little more than four years from our first spacewalk, Neil Armstrong and Buzz Aldrin were walking on the surface of the moon. Stunning now to remember that glorious, exhilarating pride in all the astronauts and the men and women of NASA and all the contractors who had made it happen. There is no modern-day parallel and there is no way to explain why America has chosen not to return to the moon or to go beyond during the past almost half century. It is as if Christopher Columbus discovered the new world and refused to ever return. The Russians have kept their space dreams alive while we have no vehicle to even reach the International Space Station that we put in orbit more than fifteen years ago. The Chinese are dreaming and dreaming big.

The Chinese declare that they are committed to manned space exploration, and I believe them. At this moment in time we lack the resources, the strategy, and the will to compete with the Russians and the Chinese. We could make up for squandered opportunities and resources and do so quickly. To do so, however, will require new leadership and a new sense of national purpose. I truly wonder whether we have such leaders emerging, whether the American people still have the strength of character and the ambition and the drive and the pure pride to resume our manned exploration of the cosmos.

Few in our government understand any of this. In 2012, our country made history when a groundbreaking, technologically astounding mobile laboratory named Curiosity landed on the surface of Mars. This was the beginning of a two-year mission to decipher the planet's secrets, search for biological clues, and learn more about the elements necessary to support life.

President Obama hailed this achievement, calling it an "unprecedented feat of technology that will stand as a point of national pride far into the future." He called it an achievement that "proves that even the longest of odds are no match for our unique blend of ingenuity and determination."[1] Curiosity, President Obama said, reminds us that "our preeminence—not just in space, but here on Earth—depends on continuing to invest wisely in the innovation, technology, and basic research that has always made our economy the envy of the world."[2]

Meanwhile President Obama, like his predecessors, continued to gut the space programs.

There was no Lyndon Johnson equivalent in the Senate to push for space exploration, and Obama has certainly been no JFK. Curiosity cost NASA more than $2.5 billion and took nearly a decade to design, build, and launch. Its highly sophisticated landing required the flawless firing of seventy-six pyrotechnic devices, never-before-attempted acrobatic maneuvers, and use of the largest supersonic parachute ever deployed in space. The fact that all this went off without a hitch is a glowing testament to American ingenuity. It also demonstrated the vibrancy and innovative capacity of our country's private technology sector.

Indeed, Curiosity would never have made it to Mars without a massive public-private partnership that involved some of our country's best-known and most respected companies. It was Boeing that built Curiosity's nuclear-power generator, Intel that supplied the rover's real-time operating systems, Pioneer Aerospace Corporation that made the spacecraft's parachute for descent landing, General Dynamics that developed the deep-space transponder that allowed for effective communication with NASA, and Aerojet of GenCorp that made the engines that lowered the rover during the final seconds just before landing.

Here's a number worth remembering:

7,000

That's the number of jobs Curiosity helped support.[3]

Yet President Obama has cut NASA's budget almost every year since he took office. And he certainly hasn't shown much love for the Mars program; in the 2013 budget, the administration actually slashed funding from Mars exploration by about 40 percent, cutting it from nearly $600 million to just $360 million. One NASA official who recently resigned put it this way: "The Mars program is one of the crown jewels of NASA. . . . In what irrational, Homer Simpson world would we single it out for disproportionate cuts?"[4]

Obama also proposed a devastating 20 percent cut to the planetary science program. This prompted a sharp rebuke from members of both parties. Congressman Adam Schiff, a Democrat from California, called the proposal a "disaster for leadership in space," and Texas Republican Representative John Culberson said that he grieved for his country and for NASA.[5]

Because of President Obama's actions, NASA has been forced to back out of two joint missions that had been planned in coordination with the European Space Agency; NASA will cease activity related to the ExoMars Trace Gas Orbiter 2016 mission, and it is ending its participation in planning for the Mars 2018 mission concept, which would have included the first direct search for life on the Red Planet since the 1970s. The Europeans are determined to move forward on these projects without us, and they will probably now team up with the Russians, who will reap the benefits while we sit on the sidelines.[6] This whacking away at NASA also threatens to derail our country's efforts to explore other parts of our solar system in the search for life, such as Jupiter's large moon Europa.[7]

I know the argument that Obama and his supporters make. Exploring space is a nice idea. But it's too expensive. This is funny, especially coming from a president who has shown little to no regard for fiscal responsibility during his tenure in office. For several years in a row, President Obama has given us deficits in excess of $1 trillion. He has added trillions to our national debt. And now he's going to gut one of the few government initiatives that actually works and creates jobs? He's going to bring down the ax on a space exploration and NASA budget that, at its peak, cost less than $20 billion a year?[8] The NASA budget for FY 2013 accounted for only about 1.5 percent of total discretionary spending, or just over $17.5 billion. This compares to the $850 billion we spend on the Department of Defense and the $72 billion for the Department of Health and Human Services. We even spend more on the Department of Agriculture than we do on NASA. Just think about that for a moment.[9]

Total FY 2013 Discretionary Spending
Total–$1,264,000,000,000
Department of Health and Human
Services–$72,000,000,000
Department of Housing and Urban
Development–$35,000,000,000
Department of Education–$69,800,000,000
TARP for Mortgage Bailout–$12,000,000,000
NASA–$17,500,000,000

The real reason for the cuts in space is that there is no built-in constituency for them. No one in the president's political base gets much of a cut from the space industry. The Super PACs aren't running ads to support the quest for space. The American people, by and large, don't care much about space either. That's really too bad.

A 2006 report by the Space Foundation found that for every dollar spent on NASA, the economy is boosted by about ten dollars. In fact, the Space Foundation estimated that NASA has annually contributed as much as $180 billion to our economy, with more than half of those benefits coming from goods and services created by companies related to space technology.[10] In fact, another study showed that private industry makes big strides when it works with NASA on research contracts, gaining about $1.5 billion in benefits—mainly through the commercialization of products developed with space technology—from NASA outlays of less than $65 million.[11] That's a huge return on investment. Had the Obama administration had the imagination and had this president truly had the faith in American exceptionalism, he would have included a call for massive new spending on NASA and our space program. Just imagine the stimulus impact on our economy at a time when we desperately needed it. Just imagine that the United States would not have to hitchhike with the Russians, and perhaps soon the Chinese, to get back to the International Space Station. Our nation cries for leadership.

And remember what society gains when we succeed in our efforts to explore space. We learn more about ourselves and about our origins, for one thing. But there is a much more practical side to this as well.

1,400

That's the number of NASA inventions that, since 1976, have led to goods and services that benefit our daily lives, such as CAT scanners, kidney dialysis machines, and the satellite communications that allow for television and GPS navigation.[12]

As he campaigned for office in 2008, candidate Obama called for a "real vision for the next stage of space exploration" and criticized the Bush administration for not committing enough resources for NASA to meet the ambitious goals it had set. "NASA's had to cut back on research, trim their program, which means that after the space shuttle shuts down in 2010, we're going to have to rely on Russian spacecraft to keep us into orbit," he said as he promised to protect jobs threatened by the retirement of the space shuttle. "That's why I'm going to close the gap, ensure that our space program doesn't suffer when the shuttle goes out of service." [13]

Nice words. But has he done anything to follow them up with actions? Did he commit the necessary resources to allow NASA to pursue its back-to-the-moon mission? Absolutely not. In a decision that Neil Armstrong called "devastating," [14] he iced the return-to-the-moon initiative and he canceled the Constellation program, which was aimed at developing the next generation of spacecraft to transport astronauts to worlds beyond. [15] His administration now wants private firms to pick up the slack and fulfill what has traditionally been NASA's role. As *Scientific American* put it: "With the retirement of the space shuttle, the next time NASA astronauts lift off from U.S. soil they will likely do so as paying customers on commercially operated rockets." [16]

And he didn't do much to protect jobs either. Remember that number I mentioned earlier?

7,000

Not only is that how many jobs we can attribute to the Curiosity mission, but it is also the number of workers who lost their jobs as a result of Obama's shortsighted strategy at the Kennedy Space Center alone—and those layoffs triggered another seven thousand job losses in the surrounding community. [17] So that's a total of fourteen thousand people out of work so far because of just two of the president's brain-dead decisions on space. If you've recently spent any time down near the Kennedy Space Center—the Space Coast, it's called—you know the beaches are still great, but it's a depressing place to be. Unemployment is well into the double digits. Restaurants are boarded up. Houses are foreclosed and empty. These are the bitter fruits of President Obama's decision to slash NASA and kill our aspirations to explore deep space.

America is losing the space race. Correction: America already has lost it. Space exploration was once the focal point of our research and development efforts over the course of nearly a half century. Today? We can't even get up to the International Space Station on our own; we have to hitch a ride with the Russians—remember them, those guys we supposedly crushed in the Space Race?—and pay them something like $70 million per astronaut just to get our own men and women up there. We're a nation of hitchhikers now. That is not only an absolute failure. It's a disgrace. Below is a list of nations with space programs. Take a look at the countries toward the bottom of the list. They're building rockets and space vehicles and we're grounding ours.

Fifty years ago marked the beginning of one of the most audacious feats of mankind—the creation of the Saturn V rocket. To send man hurtling toward the moon, NASA engineers knew they needed an engine far more powerful than anything built previously. For the project they enlisted an unlikely mind—Hitler's rocketeer, Wernher von Braun. Von Braun and his team of engineers got to work. They had a challenge. And they set about meeting it. The result was awe-inspiring. The Saturn V was—and a half century later, remains—the most powerful engine ever built. At ignition it could be heard for dozens of miles. The five engines together produced a staggering 7.6 million pounds of thrust at liftoff. The power these engines created was equivalent to eighty-five Hoover Dams or enough energy to light up New York City for seventy-five minutes.[18]

Imagine such an incredible feat of engineering today. It wouldn't happen. With the shortsighted crowd we've got in

LIST OF FIRST ORBITAL LAUNCHES BY COUNTRY

Order	Country[a]	Satellite	Rocket	Location	Date (UTC)
1	Soviet Union[c]	Sputnik 1	Sputnik-PS	Baikonur, Soviet Union (today Kazakhstan)	4 October 1957
2	United States[d]	Explorer 1	Juno I	Cape Canaveral, United States	1 February 1958
3	France[f]	Astérix	Diamant A	Hammaguir, Algeria	26 November 1965
4	Japan	Ōsumi	Lambda-4S	Uchinoura, Japan	11 February 1970
5	China	Dong Fang Hong I	Long March 1	Jiuquan, China	24 April 1970
6	United Kingdom[g]	Prospero	Black Arrow	Woomera, Australia	28 October 1971
—	European Space Agency[h]	CAT-1	Ariane 1	Kourou, French Guiana	24 December 1979
7	India	Rohini D1	SLV	Sriharikota, India	18 July 1980
8	Israel	Ofeq 1	Shavit	Palmachim, Israel	19 September 1988
—	Ukraine[c][i]	Strela-3 (x6, Russian)	Tsyklon-3	Plesetsk, Russia	28 September 1991
—	Russia[c]	Kosmos 2175	Soyuz-U	Plesetsk, Russia	21 January 1992
9	Iran	Omid	Safir-1A	Semnan, Iran	2 February 2009
10	North Korea	Kwangmyŏngsŏng-3 Unit 2	Unha-3	Sohae, North Korea	12 December 2012[j]
—	South Korea[k]	STSAT-2C[7]	Naro-1 (KSLV-1)[8]	Goheung, South Korea[7]	30 January 2013[7]

Washington, it wouldn't even be considered. We have an administration that wants to just wrench the life out of space exploration and the entire scientific community. In fact, if you can believe this, President Obama even told NASA chief Charlie Bolden that one of his most important missions as the head of our country's preeminent space agency should be—are you ready for this?—to engage with Muslim-dominant countries. No, I'm not making this up. "When I became the NASA administrator—or before I became the NASA administrator—he charged me with three things. One was he wanted me to help reinspire children to want to get into science and math, he wanted me to expand our international relationships, and third, and perhaps foremost, he wanted me to find a way to reach out to the Muslim world and engage much more with dominantly Muslim nations to help them feel good about their historic contribution to science . . . and math and engineering," Bolden said.

We're now asking our NASA administrator, a distinguished former astronaut and general, to lead sensitivity sessions instead of actually focusing on, you know, trivial goals like space flight and planetary exploration. This is group and identity politics at its worst, and to say that engagement with Islamic nations should be among NASA's foremost priorities is absolutely silly. It's embarrassing to our nation. It's also devastating to the people at NASA who are losing their jobs.

Let's not just blame Obama and the Democrats for their spacey views on space. During the George W. Bush administration, the decision was made to cancel the space shuttle program. Bush did release a "Vision for Space Exploration" that directed NASA to focus on returning humans to the moon by 2020 and, one day, possibly even sending them to Mars and other "worlds beyond."[19] I'm not sure how NASA was going to pay for this without any money. But the Bushes were never all that good on "the vision thing."

And what big ideas did the Romney campaign have for the future of space exploration? Romney's space plan, as articulated by Congressman Paul Ryan, was to have "a clear space mission, a space program that we know where we are heading in the future, and a space program that is the unequivocal leader on the planet in space travel and space research." His team wanted to focus on developing four priorities: "focusing NASA, partnering internationally, strengthening security, and revitalizing industry."[20]

Those platitudes were Romney's space policy. Sad.

No, President Obama is, in many ways, simply following the well-worn path traveled by many presidents before him, focused on short-term political victories with no vision for the future of our country. Just think about where this country's been in the Space Race—our massive accomplishments in getting to the moon, or the heroes of the Apollo program, or Pathfinder, or the Hubble Telescope—compared to where we are today, and it's clear that a colossal series of blunders have been made by administration after administration when it comes to having a vision for the future of space exploration.

As a country, it's absolutely critical that we spur growth, build wealth, inspire development, and bring ideas to the marketplace. This is especially important given our recent economic challenges, and gutting NASA is not the way to do that. Remember that, as I mentioned earlier, the Curiosity program would not have been possible without the active participation of American business—the same private sector, by the way, that our president regularly degrades and derides, both in his words and in his policies. So how can Obama say with a straight face that investments are important while cutting NASA's spending (and with barely a mention of the role of private-sector businesses in making it all possible)?

NASA's budgets are being cut as Washington consumes itself with building an ever-larger bureaucracy and slicing up and redistributing pieces of a shrinking economic pie to its supporters and cronies. This president talks about hope, but he has failed to inspire any big achievements. He talks about competitiveness, but it's clear that he is more consumed with being a community organizer than an actual visionary. It is an abysmal performance on his part. It's pitiful politics, even worse leadership, and it's no way to get us to where no man or woman has gone before.

Not all is lost, though. Some of the things the government has failed to do—or won't do, or can't do—are starting to be taken over by private industry. Yes, mean, selfish, terrible capitalists are at least helping America keep one hand in the Space Race.

And as usual, American entrepreneurship and private enterprise are achieving at a fraction of the price what massive government bureaucracy could not do. The best example of this is the launch of the Falcon 9 rocket by SpaceX, a private company. Named for the *Millennium Falcon*, this two-stage rocket saw its first successful launch on June 4, 2010, and achieved its second a few months later in early December. This rocket was designed by SpaceX not only to transport satellites into orbit, but also to send its Dragon spacecraft to the International Space Station and other orbiting destinations—with the potential for manned flight.[21]

That a private business accomplished this is an extraordinary achievement, and everyone should be cheering this company on. It's an amazing feat they pulled off, and it's exciting at a time when government is going exactly the wrong way. In fact, private missions could be more efficient than government-run ones by a factor of at least ten.

In 2001 I cowrote a book, *Space: The Next Business Frontier,* that talked about the mining of asteroids and the types of private ventures that we're starting to do now. What we need to do is awaken to the possibilities, and have real leadership that has a vision for our country's future and the contributions that the scientific community makes to our daily lives and our quality of life.[22] Virgin Airlines CEO Richard Branson, for instance, is launching Virgin Galactic as a way to offer commercial space flights as the government folds up its space shuttle operations.[23] That's a great step forward.

The bottom line is this. Private industry is starting to take the initiative to move in and develop new avenues of space travel and exploration. That is great news for our country. But it's also at best only half of the equation. Unlike other areas of public policy, space exploration is not an example of where business can simply take the place of government and provide the same services and results; business can contract with government in a host of areas, whether building and launching satellites for national reconnaissance and surveillance or building advanced weapons and delivery systems and launch vehicles. Business, for its part, can build for private industry launch vehicles and a separate commercial satellite market, as it has. But the important military and national security missions will remain the primary purview of NASA and the U.S. Space Command. We wouldn't want it any other way.

No one is more excited about private space flight than I am, whether it's Richard Branson and Virgin Galactic's private spaceship or Elon Musk and his company SpaceX, which will soon be building a commercial launch facility. I am thrilled to see the realization of the book I coauthored with H. P. Newquist titled *Space: The Next Business Frontier.* We wrote that book thirteen years ago and much of it is coming to fruition. It has taken longer than expected, but space business is happening and succeeding. As my good friend John Higginbotham, who once chaired the venture firm SpaceVest and was one of the earliest believers in the necessity of allowing business to take over much of America's space program, noted, "Government has never been designed as a business, and neither has NASA. They are both fundamentally incapable of running or creating businesses because they are designed by their nature to be procurement oriented."

We need American policymakers to rediscover the vision of the future that once animated our world-beating space policy. That's going to require more government attention and more government investment. That is going to require government officials to work in concert with companies, rather than bashing them or simply standing aside.

When our nation faced one of its greatest challenges—putting a man on the moon—American statesmen from both parties stepped forward and answered the call. They inspired us. They led us. President Kennedy said that the United States should "commit itself to achieving the goal, before this decade is out, of landing a man on the moon and returning him safely to the earth.

"No single space project in this period will be more impressive to mankind, or more important for the long-range exploration of space; and none will be so difficult or expensive to accomplish," he warned. "But in a very real sense, it will not be one man going to the moon—if we make this judgment affirmatively, it will be an entire nation. For all of us must work to put him there."[24]

And so we did, together. We all strived for the goal that President Kennedy established for the nation. The United States succeeded in journeying to the moon. America's is the only flag that adorns the moon's surface. The United States won the Space Race. In so doing, we gained vast amounts of knowledge, and created incredible technology that has enriched both our economy and our lives. We have invested hundreds of billions of dollars in our space program over more than sixty years. But my God, think of the dividends to our nation, our worldwide standing, our own sense of national pride if we were to take up the challenge of manned space exploration and could find leaders capable of restoring our faith in, and yes, commitment to, achieving America's destiny, both on this continent and in all that lies beyond this planet.

CHAPTER 7

FUNDAMENTAL FLAWS
AND FAILINGS

How could there be a question about the necessity to return America to its historical preeminence in space exploration? Our technological advances across a broad spectrum of industries are in large measure a consequence of our national effort to realize our dreams in propelling Americans into space and one day beyond this galaxy. But there are, as we all know, naysayers. And unfortunately President Obama is one of them. President Obama is emblematic of those who declare America can no longer reach for the stars, but at the same time declare we can't afford to fix the most fundamental systems of our nation. He reduced NASA's budget and offers no leadership in returning America to space with heartfelt conviction about what we can achieve and should accomplish. His is a shallow understanding of what a great people are meant to accomplish. He seems to love nothing more than government, and more dependency. It's time for leaders to rescue us from community organizers who refuse to comprehend and acknowledge that our nation has created a higher standard of living for even our impoverished. Local and national leaders somehow think that there is an excuse for the greatest nation on earth to surrender its mantle as the land of opportunity for the title of the world's largest welfare society. Those committed to the latter say America can no longer afford to achieve our dreams, whether at home or in space. These naysayers are the ones who've taken the country deeper into debt, bloated our government without purpose, and wasted trillions without creating wealth or lasting opportunity.

America's political leaders have made maddening choices over the past half century: We have squandered our own wealth on wars of choice, on massive welfare programs that failed to eradicate poverty and indeed seemed to be a requirement to perpetuate chronic structural unemployment, and lost opportunity for millions. Paradoxically, we have created great wealth for most people around the world and, of course, ourselves. But the disparity here at home in income and wealth has grown larger, leading to often bitter political diatribes and exchanges between the left and the right over that gap in income.

But I believe there are greater deficits that require both our attention and our action. And now. The gaps of income and wealth are surely disturbing and we must overcome them. To do so I believe we must recognize them for what they are: They are gaps in education, in lifestyle choices, in environment, in strength of the family, and ultimately in achievement. The acolytes of ever-bigger government have largely succeeded in creating an equation that correlates big-spending welfare programs and the budget deficits that result with what the left likes to refer to as an "income gap," when in fact that gap is far better expressed as a gap in opportunity—the opportunity to work, to go to school, and to have a stable, supportive family. The opportunity gap widens as our budget deficits and national debt grow, leaving an ever-greater burden on succeeding generations and less capital to invest in private-sector businesses that innovate and animate our entire economy.

But government does have a powerful role to fulfill in support of our free-enterprise capitalist economy, and that is that the federal government, and government at all levels, must invest in infrastructure. It is a traditional, essential role for government and one that has sadly and dangerously been neglected to the detriment of our entire economy and society. I don't love the word "infrastructure." I prefer to talk about roads, bridges, highways, railroads, telecommunications networks, and electrical grids. The roads on which our kids travel to school. The highways upon which trucks deliver food, medicine, and consumer products to market. The railroads that carry crude oil and grain and yes, cars and trucks, from one end of the country to the other. The electrical grids that light, warm, and cool our homes. The airports that move people and goods to and from our cities. And our airports are in desperate need of investment and improvements. In the 2013 Skytrax world airport rankings, only one American airport made it to the top thirty. Only three others made it to the top fifty. The *Economist* noted that "it's striking that the infrastructure of the world's lone superpower lags so far behind that of the rest of the world."[1]

Infrastructure is obviously essential to every aspect of our lives, private and public, personal and social. All this is essential for our society and economy. Why, then, have this president and previous presidents allowed some parts of our infrastructure in some regions to begin crumbling and corroding?

Look at this number:

13

That's how many people died in 2007 when the I-35 bridge over the Mississippi River in Minneapolis collapsed. Thirteen people dead, more than one hundred injured, in what was one of the worst bridge collapses in the history of the United States. We don't hear much about that disaster anymore, do we? There are no commemorative anniversaries or specials on CNN.

But back in 2007, that tragic episode received a hell of a lot of news coverage. Politicians across America suddenly schooled themselves on "infrastructure" and fell all over themselves to schedule hearings and draft reports and pass legislation until this nationwide crisis was solved. Back then members of Congress were so concerned about the situation that you almost expected to see Nancy Pelosi and Harry Reid walk out of the Capitol with a shovel and bucket of tar in search of the nearest pothole to fill.

Unfortunately the media's nonstop coverage of the "infrastructure crisis" soon gave way to far more pressing matters. Pray tell, does anyone have the latest update on who Taylor Swift is dating? And similarly, the romance between politicians and our roads and bridges also was short-lived. Their ardor for our infrastructure cooled just about the time the cameras departed Minneapolis.

I know it's fun to blame the politicians for their shortcomings, so let's continue to do so. How much work did the folks in Washington do to solve the bridge crisis after the Minneapolis collapse? I'm sure you can guess the answer. Consider this figure:

1 in 4

That's how many bridges in America are in danger of failing. Today. Actually the number is slightly higher than that. Think about that the next time you're driving to work. How often do we worry about the condition of our roads? Seems like a problem more appropriate for a Third-World country, not the United States of America. Yet according to the American Society of Civil Engineers, the oldest national engineering society in the United States, more than 26 percent of the bridges in this country are deemed "functionally obsolete" or "structurally deficient." I'm not sure exactly what that means, but it doesn't sound too good, does it? In fact, "structurally deficient" was exactly how the I-35 bridge was characterized just before it collapsed and killed those thirteen people.

I know our elected officials are busy people. So many fundraisers, so little time. But surely we can all agree that before engaging in Round 5,000 on abortion, or gay marriage, or flag burning, the most important function of a public servant is to make sure our kids can travel from here to there without their school bus slipping into a massive sinkhole, to make sure their constituents can travel to work and home again without fear that the road beneath their cars will suddenly give way. Surely the least we can ask of politicians is that they do all in their power to avoid putting a new macabre spin on the nursery rhyme "London Bridge Is Falling Down." What can I say? I guess I'm a dreamer.

When it comes to the rest of America's infrastructure, things like roads and waterways, there's bad news and there's really bad news. The most optimistic spin I can come up with about our bridges—other than the hopeful thought that three out of four of the ones you drive on might not collapse while you are riding over them—is that the other components of our infrastructure are in even worse shape.

In 2009 the American Society of Civil Engineers gave America's bridges a grade of C on its periodic report card of the state of our infrastructure assets.[2] This was one of the highest grades they awarded to any of the assets, the only better grade being a C+ for solid waste treatment. I guess a Gentleman's C isn't the worst thing you can get, but it's not really anything to be proud of either. Here are the rest of their grades by category:

Solid waste treatment	C+
Energy grids	D+
Aviation (airports, runways)	D
Dams	D
Transit	D
Drinking water	D–
Hazardous waste	D
Levees	D–
Inland waterways	D–
Public parks and recreation	C–
Roads	D–
Schools	D
Rails	C–

That's not a report card you'd want to bring home to Mom and Dad. Yet that is exactly the report card every member of Congress is presenting to the American taxpayer. Do we really believe that's the best our representatives can do, that Cs and Ds are what we should settle for? Maybe they ought to be expelled. Of course, this terrible situation has profound repercussions for the rest of us.

And when you compare America's infrastructure to that of the rest of the world, our failing effort comes into even sharper relief. In 2008, the United States ranked first in the world according to the World Economic Forum's "Global Competitiveness Index."

In 2012, we dropped down to seventh place. Singapore, South Korea, and almost every single European country were ahead of us. We all rightly express outrage at American corporations that prefer to locate their businesses and assets overseas. But if we look closer, aren't we giving them justification? Fifty years ago Seoul, Korea, was rebuilt by American ingenuity. If we allow our infrastructure to deteriorate much further, America might need to be rebuilt by South Korea.

$130,000,000,000

That was the estimate in 2010 of how much the degradation of America's surface transportation systems cost American businesses and individual households. By 2020, those costs are estimated to rise to $210 billion. By 2040 they could reach $520 billion. The failure to move forward on infrastructure projects also has cost us thousands of jobs, badly needed for the millions still struggling to find employment.[3]

Here's what this means in specific areas. The failure to modernize and overhaul our air traffic control system, for example, likely will lead to increased delays at the airport and potentially unsafe conditions at a time when air travel is on the increase.[4] There are near collisions in the skies above us all the time. It's just that most of the time we are blissfully unaware. The air traffic controller unions have stubbornly resisted any upgrades with satellite and GPS systems because they would rather keep as many of their employees as possible on the payroll instead of relying on safer and more accurate automation. In other words, you can have a GPS system to drive to your aunt Sally's house in your car, but apparently you can't have one in an air traffic control tower to land a 747 from London.

Our inland waterways, which have been an efficient and environmentally friendly way to move goods across the country, are now on the verge of collapse. Thirty of the 257 locks still in use on the nation's inland waterways were built in the 1800s, and approximately half are at least sixty years old, well past their fifty-year life expectancy.[5] When they go, the costs of shipping goods across America will skyrocket, and businesses will pass those costs on to consumers with higher prices.

Our crowded rail lines are in dire need of upgrades and improvements.[6] Approximately one-third of America's major roads are in abysmal conditions, costing drivers nearly $70 million a year in auto repairs.[7] Each year commuters spend 4.2 billion hours idling in traffic because our highways are too small and congested. When you add the car repairs and maintenance needed on account of potholes the size of Volkswagens, the result is a $78 billion drag on our overall economy. Maybe most politicians don't notice because so many of them are used to being driven around.

The number of dams deemed deficient has risen to four thousand, and their average age is fifty-two years.[8] Our nation's levees—the same ones that failed in New Orleans during Hurricane Katrina—also are aging across the country, with repair costs estimated at more than $100 billion.[9]

Our electrical grids are strained as demand for energy continues to rise—that demand has grown by 25 percent since 1990. On the East Coast, we saw how one hurricane could turn off the power to major cities for days. This has not only kept us from using our iPads and iPhones, but put the lives of the sick and elderly at risk. Because of the increase in brownouts and blackouts, more and more Americans have resorted to buying their own generators.

1,250,000

That's how many households in America have generators. That number is spiraling upward, especially after natural disasters like Hurricane Sandy laid bare the truth about the disgraceful state of our power grid. Or remember back to 2003, when if you lived in the Northeast your power was out for two straight days, in what was at the time the second-most-widespread blackout in history. New York City was thrown into a tizzy. Folks almost thought they'd have to start foraging for food again in some postapocalyptic landscape. The most vibrant and powerful city in the world was literally in the dark, humbled by our inability to best Mother Nature.

My wife and I have lived in the same house on a farm in New Jersey for the past thirty years. Over that time we've raised a family and, until the last few years, had never had power outages that lasted more than a day. Our power company is a rural electric cooperative, Sussex Rural Electric Cooperative, and a great organization. But the last couple of years our region has been hit by Hurricane Irene, tropical storms, and even tornados. And after Hurricane Irene I put in a large standby generator for our house and generators for the barns and farm buildings. Just as the weather becomes more unpredictable and occasionally extreme, power generation and the transmission grid are becoming noticeably more unreliable. To one degree or another, we're all becoming hostage to an electrical system that requires far more investment and commitment or we will continue to be hostage to an infrastructure system that is eroding.

As we come to terms with the necessity to invest in, repair, and build out our electrical grid, we are faced with even more demands on our infrastructure dollars. There are nearly 170,000 public drinking-water systems in the United States. The condition of many of them is deemed so poor due to outdated pipes and inadequate storage facilities that it has led to the discharge of an estimated 900 billion gallons of untreated sewage each year.[10]

How much is the federal government investing to resolve this crisis? In practical terms, basically nothing. The United States is today investing about 2 percent of our gross domestic product on infrastructure. That amount is less than half of what the Europeans are spending on their own roads, bridges, and electrical grids and less than a quarter of what the Chinese have spent.[11]

PERCENTAGE OF GDP
SPENT ON INFRASTRUCTURE

United States	2 percent
Canada	4 percent
India	8 percent
Europe	5 percent
China	9 percent

The problem is so severe that some in the Chinese government are now publicly proposing to invest in constructing and repairing American roads and subway systems.[12]

"We hope to achieve cooperation in the area of infrastructure," one senior member of the Communist Party recently told members of the American Chamber of Commerce in China. He said that he was stunned at the high quality of American subways and other infrastructure when he visited twenty years ago but was appalled by how many roads, railways, and ports today were in dire need of renovation. Could anything be more humiliating? Even China, which only a few decades ago was populated by people on bicycles, is now feeling sorry for the pathetic state of our infrastructure.

One reason that the Chinese and the Europeans are investing so much of their own money on maintenance and repair of their roads and bridges is that they realize that improvements to these elements of their infrastructure have a profound effect on their economic productivity. When it's harder for trucks and freight trains to make it across the country, the costs to businesses and our overall GDP increase accordingly. That means you're paying an additional premium for anything you purchase.

$125,000,000,000

According to one estimate, infrastructure problems led to a net loss of $125 billion from America's gross domestic product in 2010.[13] The cost imposed on businesses across the country is expected to reach $430 billion within the next decade, as more and more businesses divert money away from expansion and hiring new employees toward paying for vehicle repairs and associated costs of transportation delays.[14] The total impact of these increased costs will be felt by American consumers. Some contend that the average family will see a drop in their income of almost $900 per year by the end of the decade, all on account of our failing roads, bridges, and railroads.[15]

As I've noted, our politicians are doing almost nothing to create a strategy, an investment plan, and a design for the future of our infrastructure. When our politicians do take up the subject, it's usually more about their own narrow, parochial, political interests than it is about our country's overall benefit.

Nowhere are the twisted incentives and moral compromises that exemplify today's politics more visible than when it comes to the debates over infrastructure. Democrats, and many Republicans, love talking about rebuilding roads, bridges, and highways—as long as these improvements are in their districts. In other words, they support infrastructure investments so long as they can send out a press release grabbing credit in order to boost their re-election bids. Congressional leaders also love to use infrastructure grants to reward those who toe the party line while punishing offenders of Capitol Hill decorum. In other words, if your congressman is not on the right committee or hasn't puckered up to the right chairman, then the chance your road is going to be on anyone's priority list is about as likely as Kim Kardashian winning an Oscar. (And please, let that not happen in my lifetime.)

The other reality is that politicians like shiny new things, so they build new highways and rail lines that they can put their names on. They rarely are willing to undertake the unglamorous work of repairing the infrastructure that already exists, so it decays further with each passing year. We have the incentives backward. Politicians get attention for responding to disasters, not preventing them. You don't get much press attention for fixing something before it is broken.

The last federal "stimulus" package totaled $830 billion. Almost all of that money went to patronage and pork projects and special deals. While $105.3 billion was allocated for comprehensive infrastructure, only $30 billion made it to actual road and highway projects. That sounds like a lot of money, but given the extent of our problems, it is a mere pittance. This is the inevitable result of a political culture that has lost any sense of ethics or morality or public obligation.

The situation is made all the worse by the lack of coverage by today's mainstream media. There are lots of reasons for media lack of interest. The story about our crumbling infrastructure is too complicated for a quick overview in a news report, far too complex for today's soundbite culture. Roads and highways are not by definition sexy. But just as important, even tragic, the number of local reporters working for news departments—the kind of investigative journalists who might be motivated to look at failing roads and bridges in their towns and demand accountability by local and federal leaders—is on the decline. As a result there are very few people available to do that kind of reporting.

How many newspapers are owned by multimedia conglomerates like Gannett and have two or three local editors or reporters working there? Hundreds. Journalists are pains in the neck, not just for us, but for politicians. We need them to be there to report what's going on. And they aren't.

Many of us like to think of the Democrats as being the pork barrel spenders. But they are not alone. The infamous "bridge to nowhere"—the poster child of wasteful Washington spending on infrastructure—was requested by a Republican, the late senator Ted Stevens. Senator Stevens, by the way, felt he owed us no apology for grabbing as much federal money as he could for pet projects in his home state. In fact he actually bragged about it. They all brag about this. Infrastructure has become all about bringing home the bacon, not deploying limited resources strategically for the public welfare. Our politicians look at projects in terms of short-term political gains, not long-term benefits. It's a cliché to call America a short attention-span society, but it is nonetheless true. We have developed a nanosecond attention span. We've made gnats and toddlers look like creatures of concentration.

We have also developed another bad habit: the total lack of common sense. The federal government spends untold millions compensating people for their losses in cases of floods and other natural disasters. I can understand why my taxes are used to help farmers whose crops have been destroyed. There is value to our country in keeping that farm operating and helping its owners recoup their losses. But why should the federal government also subsidize through flood insurance millionaires living on beachfront property? I love beaches as well as anybody but I take issue with paying for some moron who decided to build a shoreside mansion or a fancy development right smack in hurricane alley. There is such a thing as assumption of risk. Or at least there used to be.

What happened to the idea of letting private industry take a crack at things? Why not use our limited resources to partner with or subsidize the private sector? Guess who built the railroads in the first place? Industrialists and entrepreneurs. That turned out pretty well, didn't it? They kept the railroads they owned in tip-top shape. Things got worse as soon as the government moved in.

If you've ever taken Amtrak, you know that "tip-top shape" is about the last phrase you'd use to describe our railroads today. The government-subsidized rail service has squandered millions in taxpayer funding on boondoggles and cost overruns and slush funds. Amtrak's long-serving inspector general was unceremoniously shown the door in 2009 when he proved to be a bit too overzealous in his investigations of waste, fraud, and abuse.[16] Amtrak was hiring outside law firms to obstruct its own internal ombudsman from seeking the truth about a major fraction of $1.3 billion in stimulus funding that had been wasted.

How do things like this happen? "Mr. Amtrak" himself, Joe Biden, proudly tells anyone who listens about the daily 250-mile commute from Wilmington, Delaware, to Washington he made for years on the rail line. He has been Amtrak's biggest booster. His lobbyist son, Hunter Biden, sat on the Amtrak board of governors from 2006 to 2009. The revolving door between Biden's office and Amtrak has swung so many times it'd make you dizzy. Actually, many things that Joe Biden does make me dizzy, but I digress.

The federal government, believe it or not, used to have a brain when it came to America's infrastructure. In the late 1930s President Franklin Delano Roosevelt looked into using the federal government to help build an interstate highway system other than the existing hodgepodge of state-run roads and bridges of varying quality. The president understood that this effort would boost America's competitive edge. The interstate highway system also connected rural and urban areas, with the added bonuses of creating a massive number of jobs during the Great Depression. As part of the Works Progress Administration, a component of the New Deal, FDR's administration oversaw the construction of 78,000 new bridges and viaducts, and improvements on 46,000 more. They paved and constructed 572,000 miles of rural roads and 67,000 miles of city streets.

The first funds for an interstate highway system were appropriated through the Federal-Aid Highway Act of 1956. The act created the Dwight D. Eisenhower National System of Interstate and Defense Highways, also known as the national interstate system. It was billed as the "largest public works program since the Pyramids." It took thirty-five years to complete, but it connected all regions of the country with highways where there had previously been only two-lane back roads. If you've ever driven more than fifty miles from your home, chances are you owe it to the 1956 Federal-Aid Highway Act. Consider these statistics about the project:

Number of miles spanned	47,182
Price tag in today's dollars	$425 billion

In other words, the most ambitious, most successful infrastructure project in human history cost the equivalent of half of the

2009 stimulus championed by the Obama administration. A comparable piddling amount of that stimulus money—$30 billion—went to fixing our nation's roads and bridges. The building of our national interstate system has returned an investment to the taxpayer six times what was invested in the first place.

The truth is our government used to build impressive infrastructure projects—the Hoover Dam, the Lincoln Tunnel. When was the last time we built something so impressive? Instead we are tearing our infrastructure down to protect salmon or a nest of birds. It's insanity. It's pitiful.

President Obama has given lip service to our infrastructure crisis but has done very little. He does seem to understand that we have a problem with infrastructure in the United States. In fact he made mention of the issue at least twice in his acceptance speech at the 2012 Democratic National Convention. The problem is that his solution seems to be what his party has done for years—work with unions to create jobs for themselves rather than focusing on a long-term strategy to improve our situation across the United States. He has had since 2008 to put his plans to work, and has accomplished nothing in all that time. He will not stand up to the special interests in his party and he will not shame Democrats for supporting pork barrel projects.

The Republican position in the last presidential campaign was sadly inadequate. Republican nominee Mitt Romney put together a website listing his priorities and proposed programs should he be elected to the White House. Guess how many references there were to roads, bridges, or infrastructure? Zilch.

Other Republicans have been even more obtuse. Their thinking is that if President Obama is for something it therefore must be by definition sinister. One of the country's leading conservative think tanks, the Heritage Foundation, scoffed at the notion that there was an infrastructure crisis. They put together a whole report on what they characterized as a mythology. Their headline was a classic in self-parody: "Infrastructure 'Crisis' Is About Socialism." Sounds a little bit paranoid, don't you think?

I would hope that each and every Republican candidate in the 2014 midterm elections would take up the issue of infrastructure in every district in every state. Republicans should become the party of the future. And I would hope they would commit to prioritizing one form of nation building. And that, of course, would be to continue to build this nation and to make sure the United States is the leader in the design and construction of all infrastructure. You don't have to go too far back to see just how absurd some of our government priorities are.

Two presidents in a row have chosen to nation-build in Afghanistan and Iraq, where the U.S. government is still rebuilding roads or bridges or improving electrical grids.

$13,000,000,000

That's how much Ambassador Paul Bremer, who was in charge of the Coalition Provisional Authority of Iraq, said the American taxpayer would have to spend improving *Iraq's* electricity grid. And how about this:

$16,000,000,000

That's how much he said it would cost to improve the water system—again, *of Iraq*. Talk about misplaced priorities.

"What is necessary is to achieve an overall strategy and whatever it takes to achieve the strategy, this administration is committed to," President Bush told reporters at the time about these spiraling costs. If only there was the same level of commitment to improving our infrastructure at home.

This free-spending approach is also used to help our neighbor to the south. In 2005, we recently learned, Bush, along with the former leader of Canada, came up with a work plan to increase "a security and prosperity partnership" between the three countries. This was part of the American obsession with the North American Free Trade Agreement, a nutty scheme that made it easier to export American jobs to Mexico. What this proposal turned out to mean was not a surprise: Good ole Uncle Sam agreed to spend untold millions on grants to Mexico, a country that is almost the poster child for lawlessness, official graft, and corruption. The so-called work plan put forward by the Bush administration specifically called for "the establishment of a grant fund for development with U.S. and Canadian resources to finance the development of physical infrastructure in Mexico."[17]

So while American motorists are falling off bridges in Minneapolis, we are building them in Kabul, Baghdad, and Mexico City. I guess that makes perfect sense, if you're senseless.

The other Republican solution is privatization, which admittedly does have some appeal. As I've mentioned, the private sector did a pretty good job with our railroads. But the problem with the mantra of "privatization in all things" is that it is not necessarily an automatic solution, or suitable for all cases.

Take, for example, Indiana governor Mitch Daniels's decision to lease a toll road to private investors. A number of people hailed that as a model for the nation. Other governors began to look at doing the same thing. Yet Governor Daniels just leased something that he didn't pay for. The taxpayers paid for that. The local bondholders paid for that. Are any of them getting that money? Of course not. It's going to go into the state coffers. There should be measures taken to ensure some of that money makes its way back into taxpayer wallets. Still, it was a bold decision, and managed to save the state government $100 million a year from the costs of operating the toll road, in addition to the $3.85 billion Indiana received for the seventy-five-year lease. Leasing the Indiana toll road paved the way for infrastructure improvements in other areas, all possible without requiring tax increases. So while it might not be perfect in all cases, the privatization option remains worthy of consideration as a potential solution where appropriate.

Another Republican "solution" to our infrastructure is simply to sell off parts of our national security infrastructure to foreign governments. I was among the first to break the story in 2006 about the U.S. government's effort to sell as many as twenty-two major U.S. seaports to a company, Dubai Ports World, which was based in the United Arab Emirates. The UAE, by the way, happens to be an Arab monarchy with close economic ties to a number of other countries with which our relations are, shall we say, chilly. Iran, for example.

In December 2005, intelligence officials from the Coast Guard raised concerns that giving a foreign power control over our ports could raise significant security concerns, particularly in an era in which terrorists would love to ship a bomb or dirty nuke into our country undetected. These officials were promptly told to shut up by the Bush administration, which was bound and determined to sell off our ports to these foreign interests in the name of "diplomacy." It later was revealed that the ports that President Bush listed for sale included Portland, Maine; Boston, Massachusetts; Davisville, Rhode Island; New York City; Newark, New Jersey; Philadelphia, Pennsylvania; Camden, New Jersey; Wilmington, Delaware; Baltimore, Maryland; and Virginia locations in Newport News, Norfolk, and Portsmouth. In other words, all these key U.S. ports would be under the control of a corporation that we had no ability to oversee based in an area of the world that was the least hospitable to American interests. This is the sort of dangerous shortsightedness that might have led us to consider selling control over our airports to the Taliban, as long as they had an incorporated business. The controversy ended when Dubai Ports World agreed to sell off the ports to an American company.

If we ever do figure out how to reorient our priorities away from insane ideas like this, then we face an even bigger challenge. We're broke.

$3,600,000,000,000

That was the estimate in 2009 of the amount needed to bring our infrastructure up to a good condition. The number is likely even higher now. Yet our current spending on infrastructure repair is far below that level.[18] We need to spend at least $94 billion every year to repair and maintain our roads, bridges, ports, and so forth, and yet we spend less than $60 billion. We don't have the money to make these repairs even if we did want to spend it. There's nothing left after military spending, education spending, and the massive amounts we spend on entitlement programs, health care, and interest payments on our debt.

Our infrastructure crisis worsens by the day, and the upheaval it portends would certainly be so devastating that America might never regain our prominence as the world's most competitive economy. And both political parties refuse to think, to focus the national consciousness on this critical challenge. But it is the responsibility of President Obama to encourage government at every level to build a partnership with business and academia to create strategies for the rehabilitation of our infrastructure, for the improvement and repair of roads and bridges and highways, our water systems and electrical grids, and to build and extend new infrastructure to ensure the United States has the most advanced infrastructure foundation as America enters the twenty-second century. President Obama's failure to do so has worsened this crisis, but created an immense political opportunity for the Republican Party in the 2014 midterms, and it is an opportunity they should seize immediately, not just for themselves, but in the interest of the nation.

CHAPTER 8

DEMOGRAPHICS AND
DESTINY DISTURBED

Numbers and statistics aren't always boring. Call that "Dobbs's Law of Big Numbers." For example, our world population is just over 7 billion people. Seven billion is one of those big numbers that are basically incomprehensible but do serve to tell us that there are a lot of folks living contemporaneously on our planet. When I look at that number, I tend to ask how in the world will we find enough water for them to drink, food to eat, clothing and shoes, and shelter and housing? But we do. All the more amazing because we've had only thirty years to prepare, because our population has grown by a billion and a half people since 1980. Every day the world is adding people. Every day more than two hundred thousand babies are born. And within fifty years our global population is expected to increase by about 50 percent, reaching 10 billion people. We are on a reproductive rocket to an unquestionably crowded future. In fact the question becomes, why is no one talking out loud about it, the direction we're headed, and the costs and consequences of such rapid population growth?

"Demographics" means simply the measure of our population and its effects. Of all the statistics and formulas in use within the discipline of demographics, the "total fertility rate" is a key measurement, a foundational notion among those who study and calculate the number of children the average woman in any part of the country or world will bear over the course of her lifetime. The number indicates the future growth, stability, or decline of a population over time. Back in 2008, the U.S. Census Bureau calculated America's fertility rate as 2.1.

U.S. Fertility Rate (2008)

2.1

In 2008 the average woman in the United States had 2.1 children in her lifetime. By coincidence, this number also happens to be the "golden number" in demographic calculations. To sustain a population in any country, women on average need to produce 2.1 children. If sustained for two generations, any fertility rate above 2.1 means the population will grow. But if the fertility rate falls below 2.1 the population will decline. And in the four years since the last census, America's total fertility rate has declined to about 1.9 according to the National Center for Health Statistics.

So just for fun, remember this year:

1968

It was in many respects a lousy year. America was at war in Vietnam, it was the year of the Tet Offensive, and it was the year Walter Cronkite told the nation that we faced a stalemate in our war with the Vietcong and the North Vietnamese. Indeed, 1968 was the year of our heaviest casualties in Vietnam, and our combat correspondents and their editors failed to report accurately what in fact was a year of far greater losses for the Vietcong and North Vietnamese, and the result was a propaganda victory for the enemy that turned the war. Martin Luther King and Bobby Kennedy were assassinated, and the entire nation despaired, young and old flailing, trying to understand what had beset our nation.

Nineteen-sixty-eight was the year that one of the most provocative books of the era was published. *The Population Bomb*, by the American biologist Paul Ehrlich, started a revolution across the world that has had dramatic repercussions ever since. "The battle to feed all of humanity is over," the book began, with characteristic melodrama. Ehrlich predicted that "in the 1970's the world will undergo famines—hundreds of millions of people are going to starve to death in spite of any crash programs embarked upon now." In fact, the United States did go through some tough times in the 1970s, but that was thanks to bellbottoms, the Bee Gees, Jimmy Carter, a couple of oil embargoes, double-digit inflation rates, and stagflation—and none of it had anything to do with an exploding world population.

In his book, Ehrlich described a future Earth stripped of its natural resources, with a dwindling food supply, mass starvation, and war across the entire planet. It was not exactly a rosy scenario.

The left loves melodramatic predictions, especially if they mean that big government has to come to the rescue. And Paul Ehrlich instantly became a pop icon. His book sold more than 2 million copies and he found himself on all the major talk shows promoting his doomsday scenario, which was supposedly inevitable unless world governments took drastic action. And that is exactly what many of them did.

The Population Bomb sparked a global movement to combat overpopulation. The U.S. Agency for International Development made birth control a central part of its assistance programs for underdeveloped nations. Disney made a movie based on the book, and translated it into twenty-four different languages. Viewers across the world watched Donald Duck implore parents to reduce the number of kids they planned to have. And the United Nations began to carve out a few million from its obscenely bloated $7 billion budget to celebrate "World Population Day," raising awareness about the perils of overpopulation.

Ehrlich's message is still very much alive today, influencing many of the world's intellectuals and political elite. The Dalai Lama recently opined that overpopulation is "very serious—very, very serious."[1] An environmentalist group called the Population Matters (its motto, "fewer emitters, lower emissions") offers "family-planning credits" to persons who feel guilty about wanting to have children. For $31.70 per year, an individual could fund birth control in sub-Saharan Africa to ensure that carbon-producing kids—labeled "emitters" in that exquisitely Orwellian phrase—would not be born. In other words, for about $30, every child you decided to have could lead to an ended pregnancy for somebody else.

An entire "child-free movement" sprang up in Europe and even here in the United States. If you go to your local Barnes & Noble, you might find books such as:

- *Childfree and Loving It!*
- *Two Is Enough: A Couple's Guide to Living Childless by Choice*
- *Better Never to Have Been: The Harm of Coming into Existence*

That last book begins with this charming dedication: "To my parents, even though they brought me into existence."[2]

Not since Ferdinand Magellan became the first man to sail around the world, once and for all disproving the idea of a flat earth, has such a broadly accepted theory been so roundly and wholly discredited.

Paul Ehrlich's doomsday vision of global overpopulation has not occurred forty years after the printing of his apocalyptic prediction. In fact the planet Earth is a very lucky place for us all to live. We seem to be rescued by the seemingly unlimited resources, water, and oxygen-rich atmosphere that mitigate the consequences of our very human instinct for bad choices, bad policies, and just outright wrongheaded thinking. There's no question that if uninterrupted, we are headed toward global overpopulation. How much water does it take to support 10 billion people? Can we really continue to harvest sufficient crops to feed a hungry world? And what if we're utterly and completely wrong and the low birth rates that we've experienced over the last decade are not an anomaly but a reversal in fertility trends that will lead to depopulation in, first and foremost, the industrial nations and the rapidly emerging economies of China and India.

Thirty years ago Japan was to be the world's next superpower. Toshiba, Toyota, Sony, and Nintendo were fully expected by many economists to overwhelm the United States because of superior technology and work ethic. We were all to be learning Japanese as folks from the other side of the Pacific were buying up the glitziest addresses in Manhattan and Los Angeles. But it turns out that demographics truly are destiny. We watched in amazement as the island nation of Japan built more products; exported more around the globe; amassed massive reserves in foreign currencies, particularly the dollar; and became the second-wealthiest economy in the world. Bedazzled by the gaudy numbers that the Japanese economy was producing, we ignored another set of numbers that would have been a far better indicator of Japan's future. In 1971, total live births in Japan had reached 2 million. Two million babies were born each year in Japan over the next four years. But that five-year period from 1971 to 1975 and 10 million births turned out not to be a trend but rather the peak. Japan's birth rate has been declining significantly ever since, and it continues to fall. At the current trajectory of live births, by 2100 Japan's population will shrink by approximately:

50 percent

The effects of fertility rates of course take time to materialize, but when they do they are often profound in impact. Japan hit the peak of its population of 128.07 million people in 2008. But because its fertility rate has fallen over the past two generations, that population quickly dwindled. Since then, Japan has lost almost one million people from its population. More people in Japan are dying than are being born. At this rate, by the year 2025, Japan's population will decline by another 4 million people. Incredibly, absent dramatic changes in its fertility rate, some projections estimate that by the end of this century Japan's population will be about 57 million, or less than half of its current population. More Japanese consumers are buying adult diapers than are buying baby diapers. Indeed, the health-care costs of a ballooning population of senior citizens will soon test the ability of Japan's strong, vibrant economy to avoid economic collapse.

Obamacare brought great discussion of "death panels" and runaway health-care costs. The debate in Japan has gotten so ugly that in 2013 a Japanese foreign minister urged the elderly to "hurry up and die" without any hint of irony or apology. The remark is all the more extraordinary because of Japan's cultural veneration of the elderly.

There are a number of contributors to and causes of Japan's stalled economy, but certainly not least among them are a population that is aging and a birth rate that has fallen below replacement levels. Just as it is unclear whether this planet can support a population of 10 billion people, it is also unclear whether we have reached an inflection point economically and socially that may result in outright depopulation.

Many of the world's governments have created generous and expensive entitlements that support their elderly, enfeebled, and unemployed. The European Union is at this moment demonstrating that such pervasive support programs are unsustainable. With high levels of unemployment, the working population of most nations simply cannot earn enough or pay enough taxes to sustain the social programs at current levels of funding. And for even the most committed socialists it has become clear that with declining birth rates, smaller workforces, higher levels of unemployment, and aging populations that are bulging the retirement rolls, a crisis is at hand. The Europeans have paid great attention to Japan and its demographic travails. Between 2000 and 2010 Japan's workforce fell by 2.5 percent. This decade, decline continues and the impact will worsen.

As birth rates plummet, particularly in Europe, Asia, and the United States, the elderly obviously make up a larger portion of the population. In fact, Japan's is the world's oldest population. There, people sixty-five or older accounted for almost a quarter of the nation. Italy, another nation caught in deteriorating demographic trends, has the second-oldest population. Just about one in five Italians are sixty-five or older. Sadly, Japan has not only the highest percentage of population sixty-five and older, it also has the lowest percentage of people age fifteen or younger, at 13.6 percent. Japan is caught in a demographic vise that will be catastrophic unless the government acts to counter both trends. I hope you find it as interesting as I do that all these demographic trends are manifesting themselves, but almost solely without comment in our popular national media.

Remember 1968? Well, the great irony of Paul Ehrlich's book *The Population Bomb* is that 1968 was also the year that fertility rates across the world began to decline. Not dramatically, and not in any manner was the decline alarming, or even noticed by most scholars, certainly not by politicians or Paul Ehrlich. Recall that 2.1 is the "golden number" in demographics—the average number of children women need to have in order to reproduce a population. Well, because of the mind-set created among elite orthodoxies in academia, media, and governments worldwide, here are the fertility rates for some of the world's most developed nations:

Russia: 1.61

China: 1.55

Italy: 1.41

Germany: 1.42

Greece: 1.40

Japan: 1.39

Now in the twenty-first century, 97 percent of the world's population lives in countries where fertility rates are falling, but the duration of these declining fertility rates is unclear and uncertain. It is arguable that many of those declining rates will reverse with the return of economic prosperity. It is also entirely possible that with the availability and ubiquity of birth control, we may witness an unparalleled era of declining birth rates that could at some distant point result in a declining world population. There is very little discussion in this country of demographic trends because most political and academic elites consider it politically incorrect to talk about the effects of contraception, what has become a culture of abortion, and the effect on our society and our future.

Looking to other nations and regions, it's somewhat easier to perceive the significant changes that are already taking place.

If European fertility rates remain constant (and that is an exceedingly optimistic hypothetical), Europe's population will decline dramatically by the end of this century, falling from about 740 million people today to under 500 million by the end of this century.[3] Germany, long the economic engine of the European Union, is predicted to lose a net 17 million people by 2060.[4] Italy, the seat of Roman Catholicism, surprisingly has one of the lowest fertility rates in the world. And with its economy's growth slowing to a piddling 1 percent annual growth rate, Italy's aging population is living longer and will require the support of the nation's government-funded health-care system. Italy's aging population will become even greater consumers of health care and may one day bankrupt the nation. The entire Eurozone itself is threatened by the same demographic trend. There simply aren't enough young workers paying into the European welfare systems that disproportionately benefit the elderly—one reason the Eurozone has been in financial crisis for the past four years, far exceeding our own serious fiscal demands. Greece has been only the most extreme example of the dilemma facing Europe's welfare society. American news organizations largely misreported the causation of the Greek upheaval, focusing on unemployment, a failure of both private and public investment, and insupportable welfare programs. The drama that played out was moving and even colorful: demonstrations and riots, Molotov cocktails, parliamentary clashes over whether to enact austerity cuts or risk membership in the European Union and go their own Greek way. The truth was seldom reported in any detail or at any length. The Greek population is declining, it is aging, and compounding the problem of high unemployment is the tremendous burden of Greeks who have retired too early, who are supported by government programs, and who will, at least in terms of the strains they place on the Greek welfare and health-care systems, live far too long.

Russia shares a great deal with Greece, far beyond the billions of dollars that wealthy Russians deposit in its banks. Despite Russia's much larger population, its vast natural resources, and its rapidly modernizing economy, Russia shares with Greece a very similar demographic trajectory and destiny. At the end of the Cold War three decades ago, Russia was home to 150 million souls. Today there are 143 million. And by 2050, one-quarter of its entire population will have vanished. One of the more stunning statistics from present-day Russia is this: For every ten births, there are thirteen abortions. The moral implications of hundreds of thousands of abortions each year aside, a society that places such a low value on life is literally extinguishing itself. Putin may dream of re-establishing the Soviet empire, but Russia's demographic realities will dash such expansionist possibilities.

Even the world's most populous nation is not escaping the power of demographic forces. China's One-Child Policy, put in place thirty-five years ago to limit population growth, was considered rational and responsible by political and academic elites at the time, conforming as it did to the orthodoxy of Ehrlich's *The Population Bomb*. The One-Child Policy ensured that as many as 400 million Chinese children were not born. To ensure that couples do not have more than their allotted one child, the government enforces abortion and sterilization. When women refuse, their houses are torn down and their families are deprived of employment. All this comes out to a fertility rate in China of 1.54. It also results in fewer and fewer working-age men and women having ever fewer children and now imperils China's booming economic growth and continued ascent to becoming a First World nation, which seemed assured only a few years ago.

In time, all this will mean fewer crying babies on flights out of Beijing, and ultimately all-but-vacant residential developments and complexes throughout China, which will ripple out and will mean fewer consumers for American brands from iPhones and Fords to 21st Century Fox movies and Huggies (especially Huggies). A declining population means even a declining demand for birth control pharmaceuticals and, for a time at least, a sales boom for Centrum Silver.

A demographic crisis in Asia and Europe will send shudders through the global economy. We have seen the effect of the European economic crisis on the United States and our stock market. At risk is our robust international trade, and a Europe economically robust enough to support a militarily strong Europe that can be an effective partner in the Western alliance that has persevered through two world wars and the five-decade-long Cold War. America faces external geopolitical and economic challenges unlike any in our history. And to make matters worse, our political leaders, academicians, and national media seem oblivious to the threats that are taking shape but remain still largely in the shadows.

America's demographics are the envy of many of our European allies and friends. We've long been considered exceptional among the industrial nations for many reasons, but certainly in part for our vibrant demographics—our willingness to have kids, and lots of them; our willingness to welcome immigrants, and lots of them. When Ronald Reagan hailed "Morning in America" in 1984, he might as well have been speaking demographically. The population bulge of Baby Boomers were just leaving college and about to enter the workforce to bring American productivity to new heights. Thirty years later, that labor supply is moving into retirement (for many Baby Boomers, that retirement is much earlier and much less plush than imagined because of the 2008 financial collapse). The generational cohort behind the Baby Boomers—Generation X, Generation Y, Millennials—amount to a larger workforce than the Boomers, but they are neither as well educated nor as productive nor as skilled as the generation they follow. Unfortunately, Baby Boomers are carrying with us very large price tags. Because of the Baby Boomers, Americans are retiring at rates never seen before. Never have so many Americans "aged out" with so many government benefits and entitlements: Medicare, Medicaid, Social Security, disability. And despite what you may hear, our entitlement crisis isn't simply caused by the fact that there are fewer workers to support more retirees. To be stated correctly, our problem is that the demographic bulge created by Baby Boomers and the bulge in entitlements and welfare have created an impossible burden for the generations following the Baby Boomers.

The Great Recession of 2008 has only exacerbated the demographic and fiscal crisis that is America's reality. We have fewer workers paying into the entitlement system because there are fewer jobs and the lowest labor-force participation rate since the

Great Depression. For each person who finds a job two other people sign up for food stamps. And the most recent economic reports reveal another disturbing aspect to the altered state of our economy under President Obama. There are more part-time jobs being created than full-time jobs, and those part-time jobs are being created by businesses so they may avoid the additional expense of paying for Obamacare. The left likes to call this "the new normal." It is quite simply an impossible burden for working Americans, an unsustainable array of welfare benefits, tax credits, and entitlements, and it is left to the Republican Party to lead on these most difficult issues and to meet head-on the threats they pose to the future of the world's most successful economy and enduring democratic constitutional republic.

Disturbing signs were revealed in the 2010 Census. Americans have already amazingly begun to dip below the 2.0 birth rate of France. In 1800, the average American woman gave birth to no fewer than seven children.[5] After that, birth rates declined steadily until the end of World War II, when the Baby Boom began.

In 2007, we had a record-high number of births—4,316,233, to be precise, or as precise as such numbers can be. But that peak was followed the next year by the Great Recession. As the real estate market took a dive, credit markets froze, and it all precipitated a stock sell-off that became the most severe and lasting financial crisis since the Great Depression, but also sent birth rates plummeting.[6] If you take a look at the fertility rate of white, college-educated women—a rough proxy for the middle class—the birth rate is 1.6, about the same as that of China or Russia. Take out the effects of particularly Hispanic immigration, and it turns out that America really does look like Europe demographically.

In many American cities and among our urban elites, the fertility rate is European-low. Indeed, there are more households across America with dogs than with children.[7] Pets outnumber children across America by four to one. The fertility rate in New York (1.81) is well below that golden number of 2.1, and the situation in Massachusetts (1.67) is even worse. Only because of states like Utah (2.45), Alaska (2.35), and South Dakota (2.27) will America's population not begin to fall off a cliff. When you break America's fertility rate down into different ethnic groups, it becomes clear why many of our business and political leaders want to throw open our borders. Caucasian women have a fertility rate of 1.8. Hispanics, by contrast, have a fertility rate of 2.73.[8] Between 2000 and 2010, our country increased in population by 27 million people, and more than half of that increase came from Hispanics.[9] That is not meant to be a good or a bad statistic, just a fact. It is arguable whether that increase in Hispanic population includes immigration, both legal and illegal, and not merely a strong birth rate. Under current trends, America's already diverse population will become even more so.

Since 2007, Total U.S. Births Have Declined Sharply
in millions

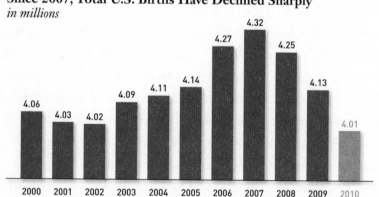

Note: Birth data for 2009 are preliminary, and birth data for 2010 are provisional.
Source: National Center for Health Statistics
PEW Research Center

Within the next decade, many American families won't be producing enough kids to sustain our population. Instead our population will get older, grayer, sicker, and then start to die off. We are on track to follow Japan as massive consumers of adult diapers while migrating to retirement villages in Florida and Arizona. By 2050, America's population is expected to rise to 400 million from 315 million today. But some 20 percent of the population is expected to be above the age of sixty-five (compared to 13 percent today).[10] The median age in America in 1950 was thirty. It was thirty-five in 2000. And our median age is on track to hit forty by the middle of this century.[11] Now, I wouldn't mind turning forty—again—but for an entire country to have a median age of forty will have a powerful and most likely negative impact on our economy, perhaps on our society itself.

I'm sure some are asking, why does any of this really matter? If fewer and fewer people decide to have kids, isn't that a good thing? Less traffic congestion, for one thing, fewer people shopping on Black Friday, lower energy usage, less crowded movie theaters? But fewer young people means fewer people entering the workforce. Fewer people entering the workforce means a smaller number paying taxes that support our economy and also fund Social Security and other entitlement programs for the elderly. In fact, the disproportionate victims of America's population crunch will be the members of our country's middle class, who face slower economic growth, a reduced consumer base to buy goods and services, and a long-term entitlement crisis.[12] Did I mention higher taxes?

Japan, Germany, and Greece have rapidly aging and declining populations, but they are also among the most taxed people in the world. Japan's top individual income tax is 50 percent, and Germany and Greece's rates are at 45 percent. The average tax rate in Germany is 29.8 percent, and in Greece the average tax rate is 25 percent. Taxation necessarily follows demographic contraction, as fewer and fewer workers are producing goods and providing tax revenue for the government and as more and more elderly people require the care of the welfare state. As commentator Mark Steyn has noted, in these societies the traditional family trees we all drew in elementary school are turned upside down: Four grand-parents have two children, who have one grandchild, instead of a widening tree with every generation.

One shrewd observer of demographic impacts, Joel Kotkin, has written: "A society that is increasingly single and childless is likely to be more concerned with serving current needs than addressing the future oriented requirements of children. Since older people vote more than younger ones, and children have no say at all, po-litical power could shift towards non-childbearing people, at least in the short and medium term. We could tilt more into a 'now' society, geared towards consuming or recreating today, as opposed to nurturing and sacrificing for tomorrow."[13] Hence we have the growing power of the AARP—dedicated to the proposition that ever more resources should go to the elderly—which usually wins in contests of resource allocation between the young and old. And the AARP is quite a business, dressed up as a lobbying group. You might remember this largest group for older Americans helped muscle through Obamacare. Why? Perhaps it has something to do with the fact that in one year the group raised as much as 166 million additional dollars from its insurance policies due to the new health-care law, as one congressional report found.[14] Or consider the raw deal for the American people known as Medicare Part D, which AARP and George W. Bush championed in 2003. In 2002, the year before the legislation passed, AARP insurance revenue was $240 million. By 2009, it had tripled to $657 million, thanks in large part to the new entitlement program.

Fewer young people in the workforce also means that America is risking its technological and competitive advantages, and its capacity to invest in our own future. We'll have fewer Mark Zuckerbergs and fewer entrepreneurs who come up with Google and YouTube. There will be fewer people to take on the jobs many of us had as teenagers: flipping burgers, mowing lawns, cleaning pools, and so forth. Young people developing skills, educating themselves, and preparing themselves for ever-higher levels of productivity drive economies. Without them, the future of any nation is bleak indeed. There is a demographic tipping point, and the result will assuredly be one that would threaten a societal homeostasis that we arguably might be incapable of restoring. The questions are: Can our society recover from the demographic trends that are already established, that is, lower birth rates and lower fertility rates? And what public policy should we be pursuing to ensure a high standard of living and high quality of life for American citizens? Those two questions aren't even being asked, at least overtly and directly, by our elected officials. You and I must at the very least insist on the discussion, which will, I hope, lead to policy prescriptions.

What are the reasons for our approaching population contraction, what will be the effects? As to causes, some of them range from the prevalence of birth control to more women in the workplace, who therefore defer and delay having children or forgo them altogether. Increasingly, our culture exalts singles and places a relatively low premium on the family (see, for example, the Obama re-election campaign's cynical but highly effective online campaign called the "Life of Julia" or HBO's hit show *Girls*).

Culture and class do matter. Culture in twenty-first-century America is divided between rich and poor, between the educated and uneducated, and the great arbiter of all things cultural is so bound up in political correctness that too few news organizations will even mention that men and women with higher incomes are far more likely to marry than those who have low incomes. And as Charles Murray makes very clear in his book *Coming Apart*, traditional values of family, marriage, and children, while not unthreatened, are far more secure among those with higher incomes than among the poorly educated, the uneducated, and the poor. A startling 71 percent of poor families have unwed parents.[15] Although just under half of all first babies in America are born out of wedlock, 83 percent of babies whose mothers lack a high-school diploma are born out of wedlock. Five years out from the end of the Great Recession we still find more than 20 million people without jobs or underemployed, birth rates declining, far fewer men than women now graduating from college, and the burdens for women rising as men are finding less work, turning their backs on education, and finding themselves incapable of supporting a traditional family as a result. We have a silent transformation under way, truly an upheaval in our society. Many churches and religious organizations seek to blame homosexuals for the assault on traditional marriage. But as I have already said, that is a distortion of what should be the correct response of people who truly want to preserve marriage and our traditional values. Demographics and economics are powerful stuff, particularly without the countervailing influences of public policies that support values and traditions and exalt the family in our society.

Faith and religion have always been important in our society.

I, for one, believe they are still. Most of us are secular in our politics. But in so being we may have allowed God and religion to be pushed out of the public square and permitted the substitution of political views that are antireligion, anti–traditional values, and I believe we need to have that discussion in this country urgently if we are to succeed in saving the American family. Fewer belong to a church. And there appears to be some demographic difference between those who believe in God and those who don't. One study found that those who believe religion is "very important" had a fertility rate of 2.3 and those with no religious affiliation had a rate of 1.8.[16]

Although the relationship between fertility rates and religious faith is worth discussing, perhaps the most likely explanation for declining fertility is economic.

$169,080

That's how much it costs to raise a single child for American families making less than $59,410 as of 2013. This $169,000 is a daunting number, and one that's likely deterring millions of couples in America's middle class from going forth and multiplying. The costs rise with income level: For families making from $59,410 to $102,870, the cost for raising a single child is $234,900. Families making more than $102,870 face a cost of $389,670. Anyone who has kids can tell you they're wonderful—but they're also expensive. Between education and forgone salaries if mothers decide to stay home, raising kids breaks the bank for a lot of middle-income families. The price of higher education alone has increased by 1,000 percent over the last thirty-five years.

Consider the Smith family, a hypothetical dual-income household in which Mr. and Mrs. Smith each make $40,000 from their full-time jobs. After two years of marriage, Mrs. Smith has a baby and decides to stay home until little Bobby gets to kindergarten, at which point she'll go back to work half-time. Let's see how the math works out:

$40,000 x 5 years staying at home =	
Lost earnings:	**$200,000**
$20,000 x 13 years at half-time =	
Lost earnings:	**$260,000**
Total in forgone wages:	**$460,000**
College tuition & room and board	
$50,000 x 4 years:	**$200,000**
TOTAL COST OF A CHILD =	**$660,000**

And that total does not include the trendy $500 strollers and $1,000 cribs and two-year supply of diapers and organic baby food and the litany of other high-dollar items that many parents feel compelled to shell out for. Even when mothers are able to work full-time, the costs of raising a single child can still add up to $200,000 or $400,000. And those numbers go up for families with two or more children.

These costs make rearing children especially hard on the middle class. And that's why those with an annual household income between $50,000 and $99,000 have the lowest fertility rates of any group of wage earners in the United States: an average of 1.7. Compare that to the 2.04 fertility rate of the poorest Americans, living on less than $20,000 a year.

Middle-class Americans are having fewer kids than members of any other income group, and the high expense of raising children is certainly a large factor in that decision. In our struggling economy, they now have to choose between having kids and paying the mortgage and utility bills. And in more ways than one, it is the middle class that ends up being penalized for an economy with fewer and fewer young people paying into the system. It isn't the middle class receiving federal assistance from food stamps and EBT cards. Instead, they are paying a hefty chunk of change from their weekly paychecks to an expanding welfare state that offers very little, if anything at all, to them. And the federal government will have even less to offer once they pass retirement age and the Social Security and Medicare funds into which they have been paying have been bled dry.

Some world leaders actually are taking this threat seriously, even if their solutions sometimes lead to giggles. Population loss in Russia has Vladimir Putin so worried that in 2008 he instituted a "Day of Family, Love, and Fidelity" to encourage couples to stay home, and, well, enlarge their families. Thousands of curved benches have been installed in Russian parks to encourage couples to get closer together. Signs in Moscow subways encourage childbirth as a patriotic duty.[17]

The German state of North Rhine–Westphalia resorted to an unorthodox solution to its demographic troubles. In order to find workers to care for its growing number of retirees, the local government launched a program to train local prostitutes as nurses to care for the elderly. Without a hint of irony, one official remarked that prostitutes were an especially good fit for the job because they possess "good people skills, aren't easily disgusted, and have zero fear of physical contact."[18]

As silly as some of these ideas sound, compare them to what is being done in the United States. Nothing. Zero. Zippo. When is the last time you heard a politician from either party discussing our demographic crisis? What plan has anybody put forward to study or address this?

Our mainstream media deserve part of the blame for the lack of debate and discussion of demographics. Political correctness scares many in the media away from the topic. Anytime a pundit or academic discusses such issues as the decline of predominantly white populations, he or she is quickly labeled "racist." Can you imagine the response if a politician urged a nationwide campaign for women to have more children? You can see the ads being written now. Candidate So and So is a sexist, a misogynist. Who is he to tell women what to do with their bodies? On and on the insanity grows.

Both parties are AWOL on this issue. We all hear a lot of talk from Washington politicians about their great love for "family values." What they usually are talking about is gay marriage or abortion or drug use or prayer in schools. Left completely out of this conversation is the real threat to the family: its literal decline. The nuclear family—parents and kids—used to be considered the most fundamental building block of our society. Today the United States and much of the developed world are moving into a postfamily era. In East Asia and Europe, for example, as much as 30 percent of the population is choosing to not have kids, even forgoing marriage altogether.[19]

We shouldn't be surprised. When we have a federal government that takes on the responsibilities once assumed by the family and community, the family and community necessarily decline in their critical importance. If Medicare and Social Security will take care of the elderly, children and grandchildren who used to do that become a redundancy—and an expensive redundancy at that. These are the unintended consequences of a government that aspires to provide for all its citizens from cradle to grave.

Yet nobody wants to talk about this. Too controversial. Too messy. Not as sexy as questioning birth certificates or asking to see if a candidate has Swiss bank accounts. Yet if you look at America's most pressing financial problems—our exploding entitlements driving up the national debt to previously unforeseen and unimaginable heights—it can all be traced back to one thing: demographics.

It's not as if we should just throw our hands up and resign ourselves to a European future. There are solutions, and they can be a heck of a lot more effective than prostitute-reeducation programs and installing benches to allow people to canoodle in America's parks. For one, we can fix our Social Security system, which has perversely created a disincentive for having children, because they aren't needed to take care of and support parents when they become elderly. Raising the child tax credit could compensate for this public policy failure. Those who create more taxpayers should be rewarded with lower taxes. Or consider college, which has increased in cost by more than 1,000 percent in real terms since 1980. The higher-education bubble and the idea that every child must go to college or else he or she is doomed to mediocrity must come to an end. National exams or credentials outside college could assure employers of a certain level of competency in a subject instead of having a college diploma. There's also the prohibitive cost of living in urban areas, where most of America's jobs are. If we had a serious effort to rebuild America's infrastructure, which in turn would reduce traffic and allow folks to commute longer and faster, more Americans could move to suburbs, which are conducive to child-rearing, if for no other reason than lower costs.

We need our political leaders to commit to enacting policies to help American families. The eighteen-month family leave that is offered in Europe, while excessive, does make a statement about how valuable children are to society. Now, this should be balanced against productivity and disrupting as little as possible a woman's career trajectory. Other possible solutions exist. While not every business and certainly not every small business can afford day care for employees, on-site day care, which keeps parents in close proximity to their small children, would be one of the healthiest, most supportive, and satisfying steps any employer, or, for that matter, any society, could take. This step would be supportive of the children and reassuring to parents. Altogether, it could create a much healthier alignment of family and work. Truly, I believe women will be dominant in the workforce within the next two decades, and I think the reason for it is shifting patterns. Women are raising fewer children, having children later, achieving higher educational levels, securing more and better jobs in the workplace, and in some areas, such as medicine and law, seem to be beginning to outcompete men. We need to develop policies to support families as both parents work to provide for their children and develop successful and rewarding careers as productive members of society.

When we are concerned about law and order, our politicians immediately begin telling us that "we are a nation of laws." When the issue is illegal immigration, the bromides turn to "we are a nation of immigrants." That's all fine and dandy, but when the family is disintegrating, isn't it time to say we are a nation of families, and align incentives and policies in support of the family, and certainly of children? We can and must do better. The consequences of failing to exalt the family and failing to support the family are profound and long-lasting, and are at the root of many of our greatest ills in America, whether a failing education system, inadequate training for success in our competitive economy, or bad behavior and criminal conduct. We can do better, and most of what is required to repair our society depends on mending our families. That should be something easily agreed upon by both Democrats and Republicans. But first, there must be leadership, and Republicans again are presented with an awesome political opportunity if they will only set aside wedge issues and focus with great energy and purity on the interests of the family, making it a cornerstone of Republican public policy. The result will be a far brighter societal and demographic destiny, one worthy of this great nation.

CHAPTER 9

CHINA'S GOOD FORTUNE

President Obama has not been to this point an aspirational leader of all Americans. He has chosen moments as he pursued the political advantage of group and identity politics. But he has seldom spoken to all Americans at the same time. He even famously deflected the question of American exceptionalism at the 2009 NATO Summit by noting that he believes "in American exceptionalism, just as I expect that the Brits believed in British exceptionalism and the Greeks believed in Greek exceptionalism." It was not the passionate defense of American duty and destiny that one would have expected from the president of the United States. He didn't dismiss that exceptionalism, but he left it rather flat, and ours is not a time for flat. Beset by crises and challenges and threats, recession and war, Americans have always expected of their leaders a passionate and persuasive rallying cry, not a matter-of-fact, monotone reminder of global context. Yes, Mr. President, we know about the Greeks, we know about the Brits. It's about us.

And occasionally as Americans, when confronted with challenge, we need to hear the right words and the right tone and a slap on the back, and Obama's just not good at it. Maybe he's a little too self-absorbed to truly understand us, the folks he's supposed to be working for.

So the problems and the challenges persist, and the questions build. But now the questions center on the leader who has ostensibly failed us. Joblessness. Slow economic growth. Uncertain policies, whether with Russia or China. We don't even hear this talk about India, or our own hemisphere. We're convincingly told he doesn't much like Israel and can't discern for the life of us what his Middle East policy is, what he intends for our future with nations all around the world. We're still a superpower, but this president doesn't act like he's leading one, and he communicates no holistic foreign policy and projects little purpose for his interventions and indifferences. And American anxiety rises because we're told China will overtake the United States as the world's largest economy in 2030 and will be spending 50 percent more on its military by midcentury.

Here is that sobering number:

2030

That's the projected date of the People's Republic of China's ascension to the number-one position as the world's largest economy, according to the National Intelligence Council's Global Trends report. As I write this, that's about a decade and a half away. And while the trend lines seem to assure the Chinese of their economic primacy, at least in total GDP, our position is not so certain. The United States and the European Union, it seems, will contest for the number-two economic spot for the decades to come. India, Russia, Japan, and Brazil will round out the contenders some distance back. The way things are going here in America we might not even have a Republican presidency before then. But as of 2030, according to the experts, China will have the world's largest economy. And how much longer before it has the world's most technologically sophisticated military as well?

Maybe I've been spoiled. I lived in a world where for most of my life the United States of America was the world's top power. We had the strongest, most dynamic economy. We had a military without rivals. We were the country everyone looked to as a role model, as a beacon of hope, a productive, creative, always advancing populace. We were in short what everyone else wanted to be. What everyone dreamed of being. As a boy I thought America would be the greatest nation on earth forever. And it sure seemed that way for a while as we conquered fascism, Nazism, and communism. But we are challenged once again, from within and without.

Yet there is little concern expressed by most American business or political leaders. There's great discussion about trade cooperation, making ours a more productive and competitive economy. Apparently business and political leaders don't want to visualize a world a decade and a half distant, or they simply cannot. Or maybe they think China will be a benign power, whose ambitions will not reach beyond its borders. History has a different view. Just ask the South Koreans, Japanese, Mongolians, Filipinos, Taiwanese, Tibetans, the Dalai Lama, the Falun Gong, or . . . well, you see my point. My God, most Americans can't even agree on whether China is a communist nation. It is, but most Americans think of it as a "special" communist nation. My favorite expression from business leaders who have invested in China is that it is "market-based" communism, which is much the same as saying "totalitarian democracy." But it's seldom that we hear the word "communism" even uttered by our national media, and certainly not by industry leaders doing business in China. It makes things too complicated, perhaps.

When I look at the achievements of the Chinese space program, including the rising number of satellites they are launching into orbit, or at the jet fighter aircraft they are manufacturing, I wonder how long it will be before our political and military leaders choose to publicly acknowledge how similar these Chinese advancements are in design and appearance to our own. The similarities are inescapable, and so is the conclusion that China has carried out the most successful espionage program in history. The Chinese have maintained more than three thousand front companies across the United States, with the specific objective of stealing and acquiring, by whatever means necessary, our most advanced commercial and industrial technology, and of course, our most sophisticated weaponry and military technology. That espionage is carried out daily, with relentless, countless cyberattacks on corporate America, our banking system, including the Federal Reserve, our utilities, national laboratories, our government, even the Pentagon itself. The director of the National Security Agency, General Keith Alexander, has called it the "greatest transfer of wealth in history."[1]

Despite the aggressiveness of the Chinese in their assault on our commercial, industrial, and military technology, our elites in government and business tend to downplay or publicly ignore altogether the pillaging of America's wealth and power. Certainly the Chinese are responsible, and it was only two years ago that the Obama administration had publicly served notice on the Chinese that a cyberattack on the United States could be considered an act of war. The pillaging continues without any response from our leaders, and the Obama warnings have ended. This transfer of wealth is truly our own fault, and one of the greatest failings of this administration and those of Presidents George W. Bush and Bill Clinton.

I know that Hollywood loves to produce movies telling us how terrible capitalism is, and how dangerous those greedy capitalists are. (For that the communist Chinese government applauds you.) But if you think about it, that's really a bunch of baloney. From what I can see, capitalists are the most generous bunch of folks you'll ever encounter. Don't believe me? Well, just ask the Chinese. What they are today, and what they are about to be, is the direct result of policy choices made by our politicians and business leaders.

I don't know how many people out there still watch monster movies. A few decades ago they were all the rage. These enormous creatures like Godzilla and Mothra came out of nowhere to destroy Tokyo over and over again. I'm not sure exactly what that fad was about, but for some reason Hollywood producers loved watching Japanese people run screaming through the streets.

Well, there's a new monster out there that's about to engulf the United States—and Japan, too, for that matter. Except this one didn't come out of nowhere. We created it ourselves.

That's right. China wouldn't be anywhere near the world power it is today without the loving support and generosity of good ole Uncle Sam. Just think what we have done over the course of the past few decades for this previously impoverished, technologically backward, and war-torn nation that is more than four times our size.

1972

That was the year in which unemployment in America was a now-unimaginable 5.6 percent and our federal debt was *only* $427 billion. For you entertainment aficionados, it was the first year that Dick Clark started rockin' down the clock on New Year's Eve. Almost as important, 1972 was also the year that the Nixon administration made its famous opening to the Chinese government.

Up until that moment, the United States had considered the regime of communist dictator Mao Tse-Tung an illegitimate gang of thugs and kooks. This was after all a leader whose more famous sayings included "Political power grows out the barrel of a gun" and "Communism is a hammer which we use to crush the enemy." I'm going to guess that Mao was not a fellow who received good marks for "plays well with others" in grade school.

One might wonder why we'd want to be buddies with this nut in the first place. (Note to the Chinese: I mean that with nothing but the greatest respect.)

But Mao apparently had driven the Soviet Union crazy, too. And by 1972 Nixon and his secretary of state, Henry Kissinger, saw an opportunity to play the Chinese off our main enemy, the Soviets. The Chinese, in turn, shrewdly saw a chance to string us along so they could get as much free stuff from our government as possible.

Jimmy Carter fell for their act completely. Which should come as no surprise given this was the president who even thought the Soviets were his buddies (until they invaded Afghanistan). "[The Chinese] are basically a peaceful country," Carter later reflected, "which gives them another advantage over the United States, when we are much more inclined to go to war." I guess Carter had a point. Unless, that is, you considered the 50 million Chinese some estimates claim were slaughtered by Mao's forces and disastrous policies during the Cultural Revolution and his "Great Leap Forward." Always one you can count on to make matters worse, Carter then oversaw a great American brain drain.

The Chinese were complaining that they lacked technological knowledge. So beginning in the Carter administration we gave them ours—the largest voluntary transfer of knowledge from one nation to another in world history. Student exchanges, science fairs, and government programs were started in China to give them a leg up in their quest for economic development. These misguided and irresponsible policies continued over the next thirty years, all in the name of helping modernize a nation that might someday become our "partner." And in case you haven't noticed, we're still waiting.

A couple of decades ago, China's communist government asked for help in exporting their goods and services to the United States. They wanted "free trade." Which is not the same as "fair trade." But we gave it to them anyway. Over the following decades we sent scores of experts to China—including experts from the World Bank and the Federal Reserve—to teach the Chinese how to compete. Against America. And we gave them this invaluable knowledge for free. Although I suppose the Chinese government might have agreed to pick up the tab for their airline tickets.

Why would our government do such things? It is because we Americans are so arrogant that we actually fooled ourselves into believing we could turn China into a democracy by opening our checkbooks and looking the other way while their communist leaders abuse human rights and act in opposition to American interests in the world. By the way, what the Chinese couldn't get from us freely, they stole. But nobody is supposed to talk about that.

The Reagan and George H. W. Bush administrations went right along with aiding and supporting our "friend" in the East. When, in 1989, a group of brave Chinese students and other dissidents got together to demonstrate against the oppressive communist regime, the United States government in its infinite wisdom stayed silent and did nothing to support those gathering to oppose their brutal government (sounds an awful lot like another president during the Green Revolution in Iran in 2009). We foolishly believed China's assurance that it would treat these demonstrators humanely. Maybe there was a problem with the translation. Because what the Chinese government did was order its army to mow the students down in the infamous crackdown in Tiananmen Square. Those poor students probably believed America was on their side. One wonders what those who survived the massacre thought when American leaders continued their buddy-buddy routine with the Chinese, after only the briefest of pauses.

In 1998, President Bill Clinton even traveled to the scene of the crime, Tiananmen Square, and extended America's declarations of friendship, freedom, and economic vitality to the Chinese government. As Clinton himself said, "There may be those, here and back in America, who wonder whether closer ties and deeper friendship between the U.S. and China are good. Clearly, the answer is yes."[2] He wasn't alone in making such declarations.

His successor, George W. Bush, said the following: "China is on a rising path, and America welcomes the emergence of a strong and peaceful and prosperous China."[3] And not to be outdone, President Obama said America welcomed China's "peaceful rise," which will "help to bring stability and prosperity to the world."[4] I guess naïveté is bipartisan.

Do these leaders have no memory? Or are they simply unable to learn the lessons of history? One need only think back to the Hainan Island incident in 2000, when the Chinese held on to a crashed U.S. military surveillance plane (and its crew) until it had been stripped of all useful information. Or one might consider the millions of cyberattacks that originate in their country against

U.S. government computer systems. Chinese hackers routinely probe and penetrate businesses and classified government systems, stealing sensitive information. They monitor the emails of journalists who cover China to find out who their sources are. With friends like China, who needs enemies?

But it's not only our leaders the Chinese have fooled. They have wowed the Davos jet-setters, the international businessmen and journalists, with their shiny airports, their high-speed rail, their gleaming skyscrapers. Exhibit A is *New York Times* columnist Thomas Friedman, who has nary a complaint about the communist nation. "One-party autocracy certainly has its drawbacks, but when it is led by a reasonably enlightened group of people, as China is today, it can also have great advantages," Friedman gushed in one column. China, after all, can ban plastic bags by diktat without those messy things called elections and legislators here in America. In another paean to the forward-thinking leadership in Beijing titled "Green Leap Forward" (I'm not sure if the nod to 20 million deaths during Mao's collectivization effort of the Great Leap Forward was ironic or not), Friedman lauds China's green energy policies—the ones that are ignored by the hundreds of coal-belching power plants across the country.

I don't know if this impresses Thomas Friedman or not, but along with our technology, America has been giving the Chinese jobs. Our jobs.

I wish I were kidding. Estimates are that due to the Chinese government's currency manipulation alone, Americans have lost jobs to the communist country to the tune of:

2,700,000[5]

In 2000, the United States government conferred on China "Most Favored Nation" status, removing high tariffs on Chinese imports. See what I mean about our capitalists being such nice and generous folks? What that meant of, course, was that American companies could now open up manufacturing facilities in China, hire Chinese workers at irresistibly low wages, and then send products formerly made in America back here to the United States at a much higher profit. In other words, we gave the Chinese jobs while throwing American manufacturing workers into our own unemployment lines.

30 percent

That's the percentage of manufacturing jobs lost since 2001 that have been directly attributed to the decision to give China Most Favored Nation status.[6] Think of all the rhetoric we hear from politicians in America about protecting the blue-collar worker. The factory visits. The trade union hobnobbing. Turns out, one of the greatest enemies to job stability in the workplace is the guy in the White House cutting deals with Beijing, beginning with Richard Nixon and running through to President Barack Obama.

Maybe it would behoove us to take a minute to consider what we actually know about China, which is next to nothing. Other than the fact that we get some nifty remote controls, cell phones, chess sets, and tennis shoes from there. I'll start with one simple statistic.

1/5

Nearly one in five people on this earth is a citizen of the People's Republic of China. And that number would be even larger if China hadn't forced its women to limit their children to one.

1,354,040,000—Current Population of China

300,000,000—Number of One-Child Policy Abortions

1,654,040,000—Population of China w/o One-Child Policy

What this means is that over the past twenty-five years, China has aborted a population literally the size of the entire United States. Had China not begun a policy that required its citizens to have one child or face stiff penalties, it's highly plausible China might well have already surpassed America as the world's economic leader. But it's doing pretty well in any event.

Over the past thirty years, in terms of real growth, China has averaged:

10 percent

Meanwhile, we're struggling to maintain an abysmal 2 percent growth rate. At the beginning of 2013, the U.S. economy actually got *smaller.* To put this in context, beginning in 1933, in the recovery following the Great Depression the U.S. economy still grew by 10 percent.

China also leads all other nations in exports. In fact, the People's Republic is nothing short of a manufacturing dynamo. As of November 2012, China led every other nation in exports to the United States. And they supplied us with much more than T-shirts and bobbleheads. Nearly $200 billion worth of important electrical machinery and power-generation equipment made its way to us in 2011.[7] We are now using Chinese-made and Chinese-powered machines to make products physically here in the United States. These are things that used to depend on American ingenuity alone.

In another sign of their manufacturing prowess, China consumes more electricity than any other nation. A lot more. In fact,

China and the U.S. are the only two nations in the world to use more than a trillion kilowatt-hours per year. And guess by how much China surpasses us in electricity consumption:[8]

China: 4.69 trillion kilowatt-hours
America: 3.741 trillion kilowatt-hours

In 2010 the *China Daily*, China's foremost English-language newspaper, reported an electricity *shortage*.[9] Yes, China can't keep up with the demands of its own booming manufacturing sector. What a problem to have.

I remember the days when America was the leader of the world in innovation and invention. Those days are quickly coming to an end, despite Obama's soaring rhetoric and heartfelt endorsement of such unrealistic concepts as green energy development.

From 2007 to 2011 China saw a 270 percent increase in the number of patents filed.[10] But 2011 was a particularly significant year, because that was the year China surpassed the United States as the world's top patent filer. Analysts expect that by 2015, just two years from now, patents filed in China will exceed those filed by the U.S. by an incredible 25 percent.[11]

By contrast, the United States' biggest inventions are a hand-held cell phone and tablets, most of which are actually produced in China. Our manufacturing has atrophied, and now we are staggered by debt. As I write this, U.S. debt stands at nearly $16.5 trillion. That's about $45,000 per citizen, roughly equal to the average wage in this country.[12] Over the next four years, Obama and his administration plan to add another $5.7 trillion to the debt, raising it to $21 trillion by 2017.

Debt-to-GDP Ratio
US: 101 percent
France: 90.2 percent
Italy: 127 percent
Greece: 159.6 percent

Our debt-to-GDP ratio is historically pathetic. France—the country that recently elected an openly socialist politician to the top office in the nation—has a lower debt-to-GDP ratio than we do.[13] The French, whose last inventions of note were frog legs and the guillotine, are more fiscally responsible than we are.

As our debt increases, so does our obligation to China. The People's Republic has proactively and slyly bought up a good portion of our debt. As of November 2012, China owned $1.28 trillion in U.S. debt.[14] This might all be fine if China truly sought a partnership with the United States, as some deluded American business and political leaders still believe. But China doesn't want partnership. China wants economic hegemony.

Few indicators of their true intentions are as damning as China's currency manipulation—artificially keeping the value of their currency low to ensure that the cost of manufacturing remains low. The Chinese undervalue their own currency—the renminbi—by an estimated 28.5 percent by holding more than $3.2 trillion in foreign currency reserves. This in turn makes it impossible for U.S. manufacturers to compete. Currency manipulation alone has cost our nation more than 2.5 million manufacturing jobs and has added $283 billion to our trade deficit. If China cared about America's economic vitality, why would they so obviously and consistently crush our manufacturing abilities?

A few decades ago, the United States government wasn't so shy about pointing out plain truths, such as China's attempts to cheat. Between May 1992 and July 1994 the U.S. Treasury designated

China a currency manipulator five times. China is, by all counts, a classic case of psychopathic recidivism—a repeat offender. Yet in the nearly twenty years since that time, the Treasury hasn't taken a similar action. Not once. And in the 2012 election, Republican presidential candidate Mitt Romney was attacked for daring to propose labeling China a currency manipulator and addressing this grave problem.

In addition to currency manipulation, China has undertaken predatory trade practices in violation of numerous trade agreements it pledged to abide by. We allowed China to enter the World Trade Organization, ignoring human rights abuses, god-awful conditions at Chinese factories, and the fact that all the nation's major industries from mining and energy to steel and shipping happen to be government-owned.

Chinese leaders vowed to remedy violations of these rules. We nodded our heads in approval. And nothing happened. Manufacturing jobs in America especially have been clobbered by China's protectionist policies. Indeed, the communist government's fingerprints are on more rusted abandoned factories throughout the American Midwest than Barack Obama's are on teleprompters. For all our union pandering, for all the rhetoric and promises, no politician can now claim to have a serious plan to fix our economy unless standing up to China is a major part of it.

Just ask Steve Jobs. When he was alive, the former Apple CEO led the charge to transfer his workforce to China. In 2012 alone Apple employed seven hundred thousand factory workers in China. This is a recurring pattern. American companies invent new technology in the United States, contract with Chinese manufacturing plants, and ship components there to assemble them. Then China exports the technology back to us. It's our own technology we're importing. It's a bizarre, perverse cycle.

U.S. companies are investing billions of dollars in research and development facilities across China. It's only a matter of time before the Chinese realize that "innovation" is just as transferable as manufacturing, especially if we fund it for them and train them.

Our pitiful stance toward Chinese economic aggression combined with our leaders' intent to keep racking up debt has placed us closer to military vulnerability than most of us realize.

Even those Americans showing some concern about China's economic prowess argue that the United States can still hold the Chinese in check with our superior military power. At least we're still the world's big dog when it comes to the armed forces. Well, that may not be true for long either.

The Chinese already have an advantage over America in space, since we've put ourselves out of that business. In fact, China is investing billions of dollars in its manned space program. It has vowed to put a man on the moon in the next decade. Maybe they'll check on our American flag, or just as likely, replace it with a Chinese one. What are we going to do about it if they do? Ask the Russians for help?

In March 2013 Congress failed to avoid sequestration, a procedure that will force an automatic $1 trillion in cuts to the U.S. defense budget along with sizable cuts in other federal departments and major tax hikes. Once the sequestration cuts are fully implemented, the army could shrink to its smallest size since 1940, the navy could become the smallest since 1915, and the air force could become the smallest ever. That's how close we are to turning our twenty-first-century military into one not seen since before Herbert Hoover was president.

Our once-proud military is now teetering on the edge of massive and devastating cuts. Obama and his administration are dead-set on downsizing the military, with or without sequestration.

Under the president's crusade to eliminate nuclear weapons, measures are moving through Capitol Hill that would leave us unprotected and unprepared in a post–Cold War world that remains extremely dangerous and volatile. In a speech at the National Defense University, Obama proclaimed, "We're moving closer to the future that we seek, a future where these weapons never threaten our children again, a future where we know the security and peace of a world without nuclear weapons." A nice thought—one that China probably loves. And has no intention of taking seriously.

While China is undoubtedly more than happy to watch the United States take off its armor, the Chinese are doing the opposite. Quickly. In the span of one year, from 2011 to 2012, the Chinese government upped military spending:

11.2 percent

That translates to a rise in spending of 670.2 yuan, or about $106 billion. These are official numbers. Some, however, such as the RAND Corporation, a think tank that studies defense issues, suggest that China is publishing lower numbers than the actual reality.[15] In 2012 the *Wall Street Journal* reported that the Pentagon had noted rising numbers of Chinese naval vessels, including a greater proportion of modern ships, which can take on anyone, especially in the South China Sea, the site of one-third of global commercial shipping. Therefore the one nation that controls those shipping lanes has an incredible influence on world trade. Since World War II, the United States and a coalition of nations have worked to keep these sea lanes open and generally free from one nation's dominance. That's hard to do with an American military atrophying and also committed to nation-building projects all over the Middle East.

In order to exert influence over that vast an area, however, China needs superior air power. And, to date, that is exactly what China is working to develop. Aircraft carriers are the linchpin of this plan. In mid-2012, China launched its very first carrier into the waters of the South Pacific. With this capability, People's Liberation Army aircraft have the capability to conduct missions in any part of the region. And they have plans to complete two more carriers by 2015. By contrast, the U.S. has only one carrier in the region, as does Japan.

China is less than two years away from arming its submarine fleet with nuclear weapons. Submarines give a nation the capability to house nukes anywhere, even just off the U.S. coastline. During the Cold War, the USSR sent attack and nuclear submarines into American waters with abandon. But even as recently as 2012 Russian subs have appeared along our coastlines. In August of that year, a similar sub spent a month in the Gulf of Mexico.[16] The day before the 2012 election, a Russian submarine was found cruising two hundred miles from the Eastern Seaboard.

Now China is investing in them, putting every nation in the South China Sea on notice for an ever-present Chinese nuclear presence. During the Cold War, U.S. superiority in submarine warfare played a large role in deterring the Soviet Union. Will the Chinese similarly be able to exert such a strong deterrent effect on the United States and our partners in the region?

Arming its submarines is only a part of a larger Chinese nuclear weapons initiative. There are three major ways to deliver a nuclear warhead: by sub, by plane, and by ballistic missile. This unholy trio has been achieved only by a few nations, and China is eager to join them. This is, however, no arms race, since only one nation is actually competing. Unlike the original four nuclear nations—the United States, Russia, the U.K., and France—China is actively expanding its nuclear forces. And no one is saying a word about it, let alone doing something to counter the threat.

The People's Liberation Army isn't merely gaining more nuclear weapons. It is also working to ensure that its arsenal is thoroughly modern. In addition to nuclear-warhead-equipped submarines, China recently developed a mobile nuclear weapons platform that can strike American cities. Seattle already is well within their range. Why the nuclear buildup? What are the Chinese afraid of? Or what are they planning? We have no clue.

To make matter worse, we don't even know where all China's missiles are located. We have evidence from our intelligence sources that the missiles are loaded onto rail lines disguised as passenger trains, making the system mobile and harder to hit in a retaliatory strike. If the Soviet Union had acted this way, most of the American government would be panicked. With the Chinese, there's barely a shrug. The way our government acts, you'd think the Chinese were our allies. But that's certainly not the case.

Recently the militaries of China and the United States conducted a joint exercise. This was supposed to be a demonstration of the supposed cooperation and goodwill between our armed forces. Predictably, many media outlets blindly portrayed it that way. But on the last day of the joint exercise, China decided to test the capability of its nuclear missiles, using the United States as their imagined adversary. In their scenario, Chinese nuclear missiles were deployed that were capable of hitting U.S. cities.[17] Are these the actions of a friend?

By any conventional measure, the United States military still dwarfs China in terms of numbers of ships, aircraft, and the like. But China is working to compensate for that in various ways. Since our power in Asia depends on our aircraft carrier force—

specifically the Seventh Fleet—China is developing technology to undermine it. The communist nation is developing antiship cruise missiles, or "carrier killers." Their intention is hardly a secret. The missiles are designed to crash through the atmosphere and into the deck of a U.S. aircraft carrier, disabling the flight deck and not incidentally killing our sailors. A single successful strike could sink a ship with five thousand Americans aboard, making Pearl Harbor look like amateur hour.

The second, and perhaps even more insidious, of China's offensive tactics centers on an area of warfare we still have not completely grasped—the cyberworld. Most people haven't heard about spear-phishing, but it has a deadly effect, and the Chinese are very good at it. A technician targets a specific group or individual through email in order to gain access to the entire computer system to which he is connected. Our cybersecurity industry is not yet proficient enough to fend off this threat. Anup Ghosh, CEO and founder of the cybersecurity company Invincea, warns, "The White House, every Fortune 1,000 and Global 2,000 organization—medium-sized businesses, small businesses, consumers—ALL are at risk from spear-phishing attacks."[18]

In October 2012, the White House issued a report that demonstrated the dangers ahead. It revealed that a hacker had made his way into their computer system. That's right—what should be one of the most secure places on earth was penetrated. The intruders reportedly gained access to a system used by the United States military for its nuclear commands. The hackers were identified—wait for it—as Chinese. The accompanying White House statement was chilling. "These types of attacks are not infrequent," an official warned.[19] How are we going to devise a way to counter these cyberattacks? We'll probably have to use programs produced in China.

We have done this to ourselves, folks. We have lost the economic ingenuity that once made us the envy of the world. We have lost our lead in innovation and technological advances. We have stood idly by while American companies—does any company even call itself American anymore?—move to China, hire Chinese workers, and then ship their goods back to us here at home. The Chinese in turn do little to make it easy for us to sell our goods to their customers. What are we doing? Why are we selling out our own economy to help a nation that sees us as a competitor, even an enemy, but certainly not a friend?

Our leaders entertain the idea of shredding our own military while China builds up its armed forces. Before too long, if we stay on our current trajectory, the Chinese will claim dominance over the Asia-Pacific region and anywhere else they so desire. All this while we speak naïvely about a "peaceful rise" and bury our heads in the sand.

I don't think the Chinese people are innately more industrious or enterprising than Americans. I think the problem is that Americans have forgotten how to be industrious and enterprising. Our government has beguiled many of our citizens with a culture of entitlement and handouts. We have regulatory and tax policies that punish companies and cripple job growth. We have a manufacturing strategy that is either nonexistent or a complete failure. We have national leaders from both parties who have convinced themselves that China is a partner, a friend, or who simply care more about selling products to China's billion-plus population than they do about the damaging effect our policies have right here in America.

This will not change without leadership that recognizes the challenges ahead of us and commits to winning our economic contest with the Chinese. This will not change without engaged, productive citizens who insist on holding their elected representatives accountable for vision, for governance, and for success. There is no reason in the world that the United States of America—the nation that invented the telephone, the personal computer, penicillin, the fax machine, Coca-Cola, the Saturn V rocket, the nuclear submarine, McDonald's, and the artificial heart—should drift into a second tier of world powers. We are too exceptional a country, too smart and ambitious a people, to passively allow ourselves to surrender our destiny. To anyone. Ever.

CHAPTER 10

THE SHARIA SPRING WE SPRUNG

So I have known Islam on three continents before coming to the region where it was first revealed. That experience guides my conviction that partnership between America and Islam must be based on what Islam is, not what it isn't. And I consider it part of my responsibility as president of the United States to fight against negative stereotypes of Islam wherever they appear.

—BARACK OBAMA, JUNE 4, 2009, CAIRO, EGYPT

The president's words, spoken early in his first term, serve as something of a guide to the personal religious and political perspective that sets him apart from previous presidents. To add to his duties as president the role of protector of Islam is breathtakingly egotistical, and created lots of questions early in his administration about his commitment to the role of commander in chief. It would be difficult to imagine President Franklin D. Roosevelt worrying over the spiritual and religious heritage and belief system of all Europe while commanding our army, navy, and air force in war. Or President Harry Truman taking on the role of cultural and spiritual interpreter and explaining the Japanese traditions of Shinto and its importance to their culture. Obama's 2009 Cairo speech at points seemed intended to join him with Islam and fiercely set him apart from other Western leaders who had been led to believe that Presidents Bush and now Obama sought victory in the war against terrorism, not a curiously constructed defense of a religion that is neither his nor, for that matter, America's or Europe's. The bloody experience of radical Islamists and Muslim extremists is, however, a shared and tragic experience.

It was as if this president sought to compensate for his lack of foreign-policy knowledge and acumen by assuming a pose of moral superiority over the very people he was elected to serve and projecting that perception to the world. I don't recall this president ever declaring with conviction and passion that he would fight radical Islamists to the death—that he would battle against radical Islamist terrorism—but he does declare that he will pick up the unidentified standard and fight heroically against amorphous and vague "negative stereotypes" of Islam wherever they appear. He doesn't identify who is guilty of such stereotypes, who is communicating them to whom or where. The stereotypes he projects and against which he feels compelled to war seemingly live only in his mind, part of the inventory of straw men, false choices, and convenient contrivances he so readily employs in his speeches and public utterances. He seems at times to relish criticizing Americans, his fellow citizens, and apologizing for them, and interestingly, never to them. The Cairo speech was truly a sorry one, unbecoming of the president and outright embarrassing to our nation and to our allies. The left loved it.

If there is anything that signifies the drift, the weakness, the ti-

midity, and the lack of foresight of President Obama, it is his foreign policy. The United States has long confused foreign policy
with foreign aid, handouts with deft diplomacy. Administrations
of both political parties over the years have used foreign aid,
and hundreds of billions of taxpayer dollars, to prop up corrupt
regimes, destabilize ones we don't like, and maintain at least neu-
trality where we judge the United States can afford neither opposition nor an enemy. History is filled with plenty of examples, but
the Egyptian experience has been sadly the result of the Obama
administration's poor understanding of Egypt, its politics, its society, Islamists, and the Muslim Brotherhood. Most important, the
Obama administration has not demonstrated an ability to fashion
a foreign policy for the Middle East, for Egypt, that is consonant
with our values and advances our interests in the region and
around the world.

In January 2011, thousands gathered in the heart of Cairo.
By all outward appearances, those who assembled didn't appear
menacing. Many were dressed in Western clothes. Bearded and
dark-robed Islamists were nowhere in sight. The media reported
that these were crowds generated through Facebook and Twit-
ter, and, in fact, a Western-educated Egyptian Google executive
emerged as a spokesman for what would become a revolutionary
moment, that had nearly all the trappings and usual elements of a
revolutionary movement: students, women, the Islamist faithful,
academics, secularists, Salafists, minorities, merchants.

These disparate revolutionaries told Western reporters that
they wanted to depose the thirty-year dictator of Egypt, Hosni
Mubarak, long an ally of the United States, to whom we'd
given billions for decades, and who had also upheld a landmark
peace treaty with Israel. In his stead, they told the media, a democracy would emerge. They insisted they didn't want Sharia law,

or rule by Islamic clerics. They wanted free elections, a new constitution, and an independent judiciary. *Time* magazine reflected the conventional wisdom that these were twenty-first-century Thomas Jeffersons unleashed through the power of the internet, dubbing the upheaval "the Facebook revolution."

But because Mubarak had been such a steadfast ally of the United States, the Obama administration, to no one's surprise, did not have a clue what to do. For nearly a week, the president and his people watched in amazement the pictures being streamed live across satellite TV. Statements from the White House podium vacillated. They started with fulsome words of praise for Mubarak, then shifted to tepid support, then shifted again to a statement that he had to go.

From the White House, President Obama praised the revolutionaries. "The people of Egypt can find the answers, and do so peacefully, constructively, and in the spirit of unity that has defined these last few weeks; for Egyptians have made it clear that nothing less than genuine democracy will carry the day." He then waxed eloquent about "the wheel of history," which "turned at a blinding pace as the Egyptian people demanded their universal rights."

On February 11, Mubarak resigned. In his place, an interim government led by the Egyptian military promised free and fair elections soon to follow. American experts fell over themselves on cable news with visions of a new, vibrant Egyptian democracy dancing in their heads.

At the beginning of the revolution, the major groups involved in the protests against Mubarak included civil society forces, young people, women, and minorities such as the Coptic Christians. The Muslim Brotherhood, suppressed under the Mubarak government for its subversive activities, at first took a backseat to the other factions involved in the protests. The Brotherhood initially claimed it was not looking to take a leading role in the revolution, and this was ultimately a strategic decision. When Western citizens looked at media coverage of the revolution, they saw average citizens struggling for freedom, rather than a fundamentalist group seeking to seize power from a leader who, while authoritarian, was generally helpful to the United States in its efforts against terrorist threats and an important ally in the region. Had the world seen footage of Islamist slogans and Brotherhood members leading the protests, there would probably not have been a great outpouring of support, and Mubarak might still be in power today. However, citizens around the world, especially Americans, identified with the ordinary people they saw protesting for their rights in Egypt, and this support enabled the American government to pressure Mubarak to step down and throw its support behind the protesters.

But any casual observer of the Middle East could have told you that the best-organized opposition to Mubarak's government was the Muslim Brotherhood—a group of ruthless ideologues who would look to America's Constitution only if they needed kindling. Historically, the Brotherhood has often been an influence on violent organizations, despite its pledge of nonviolence. Sayyid Qutb, a prominent early figure within the Muslim Brotherhood, has provided intellectual foundations for modern-day jihadi and terrorist organizations, including Al Qaeda. His work was influential on the development of *takfiri* ideology as well as the idea that so-called illegitimate Muslim rulers need to be overthrown. Adherents to *takfiri* ideology believe that Muslims who do not follow a sufficiently fundamentalist form of Islam can be declared apostates, and are therefore legitimate targets for attacks and killing. The vast majority of the Muslim world believes that only properly qualified religious scholars have the authority to make such a decision.

Although the Brotherhood has shrewdly attempted to work within existing political institutions, it is important to be aware of its ideological and historical ties to overtly violent movements and individuals. The renunciation of violence can be seen as a tactic to better position the group for political influence in a country, perhaps opening a path to the goal of an Islamist government. The group has a long history of offering to work within a political system, as it once promised in the initial years of Anwar Sadat's rule, only to shift to violent tactics once it received an opening. The group has vowed war with Israel. It has sought second-class status for Christian and Jewish minorities and has sought to impose Sharia or Islamic law on all Egyptians, including the country's five-plus million Coptic Christians.

The Muslim Brotherhood's radical ties should have been another serious concern for the Obama administration. The Muslim Brotherhood has well-established ties to Hamas. Hamas was itself initially established as a Palestinian branch of the Muslim Brotherhood. Although President Mohamed Morsi used these ties to negotiate a truce between Israel and Hamas after the 2012 outburst of violence in Gaza, there is certainly cause for concern. One unexpected outcome of the rocket attacks and subsequent truce was to increase Hamas's legitimacy in Gaza and in the region, particularly after then-president Morsi met with leaders of Hamas. The Sinai, sharing a border with Hamas-controlled Gaza, remains a cause for major security concerns, as armed Islamic factions dominate in the area. Although the militants in this largely Bedouin region of Egypt were suppressed under Mubarak's rule, they have seized the opportunity presented by the security vacuum resulting from the revolution to take control of the region once again.

But that's not what the Obama administration wanted to believe. President Obama's director of national intelligence, James Clapper, said the group was "largely secular." Experts went on to tell us that the Muslim Brotherhood was a minority and marginal faction on the Egyptian political scene, not a threat to take power. However, the administration vastly underestimated the superior organization of the Brotherhood, particularly when compared to the various disorganized factions that made up the larger part of Egypt's revolutionaries.

As the revolution in Egypt moved forward, the Brotherhood took larger and larger steps to the political forefront. First, the Brotherhood won a majority of the seats in Parliament in the November 2011 elections, even using the disputed tactic of running candidates for seats reserved for independents. Despite its initial claims that it would not run a candidate in the presidential elections, the Brotherhood finally entered Mohamed Morsi in the race. After Morsi, running on the ticket of the Muslim Brotherhood's Freedom and Justice Party, took control in the presidential election of June 2012, running on promises of social justice and political inclusion, the result was instead large strides toward consolidated control by the Brotherhood and a push toward an Islamist government. The Brotherhood benefited from its widespread network of support throughout the Middle East, and sympathetic coverage from Qatar-based Al Jazeera. The Brotherhood used its majority in Parliament to push through a Sharia-based constitution widely criticized for its insufficient protection of the rights of citizens, especially women and minorities. The Brotherhood also sought to undermine the power of the military, which has well-established ties to the U.S. through foreign aid. Morsi used executive power to undermine the power of the judiciary. Disturbingly, he also said he would push the United States to release "The Blind Sheik" Omar Abdel-Rahman, the Egyptian cleric and mastermind of the first World Trade Center bombing.

Both the Obama and George W. Bush administrations saw promoting democracy as central to their foreign policy, and this can be a worthy goal if tempered by sound judgment and careful application. "The change in the conversation about the Middle East, where people now routinely talk about democratization, is something that I'm very grateful for and I think we had a role in that," said George W. Bush's secretary of state, Condoleezza Rice. Rice, of course, had engineered the ambitious, if hasty, plan to push for democracy in the Gaza Strip that was ultimately abandoned after Hamas handily won elections.

In Egypt, the transition to democracy had struggles of its own. President Morsi ran into popular protest beginning in 2007 over his attempts to consolidate power and run roughshod over opposition groups and politicians, as well as his government's failure to take substantial steps to address Egypt's struggling economy. Unrest developed in response to his attempts to consolidate power, as well as continued high unemployment and a weak economy. Morsi became so out of touch with ordinary Egyptians that he appointed Adel el-Khayat, a member of the radical Gamaa Islamiyya, as governor of Luxor. Gamaa Islamiyya is the group responsible for the 1997 massacre of fifty-eight tourists in Luxor, as well as a violent campaign against the government. The people of Luxor protested; they realized the damage this could do to the vital tourism industry, even if Morsi was more concerned with consolidating Islamist support. The protests were significant enough that el-Khayat was forced to resign. As discontent grew, the Obama administration did not take significant steps to pressure Morsi to include the opposition in governing the country.

Ultimately the Obama administration underestimated the Egyptian people's desire for real democratic change, and their desire to have leaders focus on improving the economy and enacting policies that improve ordinary people's lives, rather than engaging in power struggles and promoting religious fundamentalism. That fact was proven on June 30, 2013, the anniversary of President Morsi's assuming the presidency, when popular protests larger than those that ousted Mubarak convinced the Egyptian military, led by Defense Minister General Abdel Fattah el-Sisi, to step in and remove President Morsi from power three days later. Popular anger was also focused on President Obama and Ambassador Anne Patterson, who were both seen as siding with the Muslim Brotherhood due to the Obama administration's failure to pressure Morsi to step aside. In the Egyptians' eyes, why would the man who called for Mubarak to step down in the wake of large protests refuse to call for Morsi to step down in the face of even larger protests?

Notably, Defense Minister el-Sisi called for the Egyptian people's support against terrorists and extremist groups. These are the same goals shared by the United States. While the U.S. government should exert pressure on the Egyptian military to ensure that proportional force is used in response to violent protest, and to ensure the rights of peaceful protest, the opportunity to build a relationship with a government that could be a partner in the war on terror should not be wasted. Extremist forces threaten stability in the Sinai, and the Muslim Brotherhood has called for continued unrest. It is in the United States' interest to work toward building a relationship with the interim government led by Adly Mansour, working to ensure that appropriate steps are taken to work as quickly as circumstances permit toward writing a new constitution and holding elections, as well as working toward rebuilding Egypt's embattled economy. However, now is not the time to give a cold shoulder to a country, long an ally in the region, and squander the opportunity to see a country that could potentially be both democratic and an ally of the United States.

In failing to recognize that the Egyptian people truly wanted leaders who would work on behalf of their interests and the good of the nation, the Obama administration committed a major foreign policy error from which this country will be working to recover for some time. It is clear that a serious rethinking of our Egyptian foreign policy is in order.

SPRINGTIME FOR MUBARAK, GADDAFI, AND ASSAD

After the Arab Spring began, first with the overthrow of President Zine El Abidine Ben Ali in Tunisia, then with the overthrow of Mubarak in Egypt, popular protests soon spread around the Middle East, affecting nearly the entire region. In February 2011, Libyan president Muammar Gaddafi was suddenly facing elements of opposition and then an outright uprising after he used overwhelming force to crush what began as largely peaceful protests. Given Gaddafi's long history of supporting terrorism and opposing American interests, it was no surprise that President Obama quickly announced that the Libyan dictator had to go. Much of the world shared a sense of outrage over the cruel treatment of Libyan protesters, and the United Nations Security Council even supported a resolution for installing a no-fly zone in the country to protect civilians.

NATO ultimately decided to intervene on behalf of the Libyan opposition forces. NATO forces, led by the United States, France, and the United Kingdom, installed the no-fly zone and bombed Gaddafi's forces, but even with this assistance, the conflict dragged on until October 2011. The rebel groups suffered from problems of disorganization, and it took months for Gaddafi to be killed and his forces defeated. President Obama struggled to clearly define the stakes involved, and the importance of helping the Libyan opposition. Public opinion therefore was not heavily behind the campaign, and Obama faced domestic criticism over his decision not to obtain a declaration of war from Congress.

Although there was an opportunity to help the Libyans, led initially by the National Transition Council, move toward establishing a new constitution, elections, and ultimately a new democracy in the region, problems quickly began to surface. The Libyan conflict exposed the significant danger that radical Islamist extremists and terrorist groups could take advantage of power and security vacuums in countries struggling to regroup after the overthrow of their authoritarian rulers. In Libya, this was exactly what happened. Disparate militias and rebel groups fought against Gaddafi in the civil war. However, it soon became clear that some of these groups were composed of fundamentalists, and even terrorists in some cases. The weapons provided by supporters of the revolution inevitably ended up in terrorist hands. Even after the conflict had ended and the rebels declared victory, the militias still refused to disband as of summer 2013, nearly two years after the end of fighting. Some of these militias were sympathetic to or even affiliated with Al Qaeda. The weak transitional government in Libya was in desperate need of assistance to disband and disarm militias, and to help integrate their members into police and army forces where possible.

The Obama administration spent more than a billion dollars

to intervene in the Libyan civil war. The payoff should have been at least a transitional government working to provide security to its people, and taking substantive steps toward establishing a democratic, representative government. Instead, the American people were shocked by the brutal September 11, 2012, attack on the U.S. consulate in Benghazi, where our ambassador, a State Department employee, and security personnel were killed. The rebel capital had become a hotbed of Islamic extremism, which is why our diplomatic buildings had been bombed twice before the coordinated September attack. By 2013, the situation on the ground remained precarious. Public frustration and anger with Islamists grew by 2013, and following the assassination of revolutionary leader and human rights lawyer Abdelsalam al-Mismari, protesters stormed the headquarters of political offices, targeting Islamist parties in particular. This shows rising distrust for fundamentalism, extremist militias, and a climate of fear reigning in Libya, where violence has remained all too common. The administration needs to ensure that the Libyan government can consolidate its control over its territory, disband the militias, and provide security for its citizens. In addition, porous Libyan borders make it all too easy for extremist fighters and weapons to migrate through North Africa, threatening to fuel violence in Mali, Algeria, and the entire North African region. It is imperative that the United States take action to prevent radical groups and terrorists from gaining a foothold in the region.

Now the United States is faced with a decision to intervene in the Syrian civil war, a brutal conflict that has been going on since 2011, and has already claimed more than one hundred thousand lives. But intervention in this conflict would be far more complicated than even the NATO intervention in Libya. Syria's leader, Bashar al-Assad, is much more firmly entrenched than

Gaddafi ever was, and is firmly backed by Iran and its Lebanese proxy militia, Hezbollah. Despite the fact that the vast majority of the Arab and Western world supports the opposition, Russia has steadfastly remained in Assad's corner, and still intends to follow through with weapons shipments to the embattled dictator. Although President Assad leads an oppressive regime, is aligned with our enemies in Iran, and has supported terrorist groups such as Hamas and Hezbollah over the course of his rule, not to mention his suspected involvement in the 2005 assassination of former Lebanese prime minister Rafik Hariri, there will be significant obstacles to a successful intervention. As of the summer of 2013, President Obama had announced his decision to send arms to the Syrian rebels, but Congress had stalled the actual delivery of the weapons.

As the United States government weighs the costs and benefits of escalating its aid to the Syrian rebels, such as sending weapons and military trainers, or establishing a no-fly zone, it must take into account the disturbing rise of extremist groups such as Jabhat al-Nusra. Although the regime of Bashar al-Assad has certainly been no friend of the United States, given its firm alliance with Iran and its willingness to allow insurgents into Iraq during the United States operation there, not to mention its long-standing role as a state sponsor of terrorism, arming rebels could be a losing proposition if those weapons fall into the hands of terrorists equally (or more) opposed to the United States. Jabhat al-Nusra has already declared its allegiance to Al Qaeda. It is vital to develop sources and relationships within the various opposition factions in order to better assess their motivation and goals for a post-Assad Syria. The second step would be to assist and strengthen those militias that are more moderate and eschew terrorism and fundamentalism. Currently Jabhat al-Nusra and other

Salafist or militant groups enjoy fund-raising advantages over the more moderate factions that could place the radicals at an advantage in a struggle for power if the rebels do force Assad to step down. Any decision to escalate support to the rebels must ensure that aid does not fall into the hands of terrorists who could use those weapons against the United States.

The rebels remain disorganized, and suffer from a severe lack of unity and cohesion. The government in exile, known as the Syrian National Coalition, has had numerous leadership challenges, as Saudi Arabia and Qatar struggle to promote their favored leaders. But the Syrian National Coalition has little if any influence over events on the battlefield, and has no command over the countless militias and rebel groups fighting Assad's forces. The Free Syrian Army, which at least in theory is leading the opposition, has recently lost significant numbers of its fighters to the extremist Jabhat al-Nusra. Other relatively moderate groups have faced similar problems. Fighters can be lured by power, weapons, and momentum for a given militia as much as they can be motivated by ideology, so aiding more moderate forces could help those groups rebuild strength and forces. In addition, the possibility of radical, Al Qaeda–aligned forces gaining control over Syria's chemical weapons opens up a serious national security threat to the United States, given Al Qaeda's determination to attack the United States and the West.

The conflict also threatens to inflame sectarian divisions and conflicts across the entire Middle East. The rising role of Hezbollah in the Syrian civil war is indicative of the growing sectarian implications of the conflict. The opposition forces are primarily Sunni, fighting against Bashar al-Assad's government, dominated by Alawites (a sect of Shi'a Islam). Hezbollah, itself a Shiite group, is fighting to defend the Assad regime. The rising power of extremist Sunni forces serves to fuel anti-Shi'a prejudice, not just in Syria, but also in neighboring countries and around the region. Neighboring Lebanon, which itself has a long history of sectarian conflict, has already seen spillover violence, including attacks by Syrian rebels on Hezbollah strongholds. Tensions with Israel have risen, as Israel has attacked weapons shipments bound for Hezbollah, and Assad has threatened to strike back. The violence in the region is spreading, and containing it will be vital to preserve security in the region.

Unfortunately, it seems that from Egypt to Libya to Syria, the Obama administration has not given sufficient thought to what could or should replace the authoritarian rulers and dictators whom we were seeking to remove from power. In recent congressional testimony, Defense Secretary Leon Panetta said, "We've unleashed a lot of forces here." That is certainly true, and it appears that the administration has not prepared adequately for how to manage and respond to these forces and the potential threats they pose to the United States and our interests. Despite our obvious miscalculations, Panetta added, "We can direct those countries in a better direction." But in order to help move the outcome of events in a direction favorable to the interests of the United States, it is necessary to first develop an understanding of the governments, societies, and histories involved in order to formulate specific, effective foreign policies.

THE FACE OF THE ENEMY

I've taken both the George W. Bush and Obama administrations to task for their blindness to the threats posed by radical Islam. They refuse to even use the word "Islam" in connection with any act of terrorism. "The global war on terror" is what Bush called it. The name is inadequate, as it merely refers to a tactic but fails to mention the actual enemy using it. If our leaders can't even identify our enemy, how can we possibly expect to win the war? And if we're paralyzed by concerns about offending the enemy, how can we possibly hope to defeat it?

In 2008 a memo was circulated in the Bush administration offering guidance on how to talk about Islam. "Never use the terms 'jihadist' or 'mujahideen' in conversation to describe the terrorists," the memo stated. "Calling our enemies 'jihadis' and their movement a global 'jihad' unintentionally legitimizes their actions."[1] This was not an *Onion* parody. This was a government memo. In other words, if you don't mention the enemy or its intentions, then they won't exist. It was the government equivalent of avoiding making eye contact with a bully in the futile hope that he'll just go away.

President Obama takes the Bush tendency to create convenient fictions about Islam to a whole new level. Instead of "global war on terror"—which at least gave us the idea that we were fighting against something—we now have "overseas contingency operations." They label the terrorist massacre by Nidal Hasan at Fort Hood as "workplace violence," as if it was just some employee angry about the size of his paycheck. Obama chose to ignore the contact Hasan had with radical Al Qaeda cleric Anwar al-Awlaki, a man later killed in a drone strike for his role in the terrorist group. The Obama administration no longer calls Guantanamo detainees "enemy combatants."

If President Obama wants to ensure that America wins this war, he needs to display the fortitude to identify our enemies for who they are: radical jihadist terrorists. We cannot allow ourselves to become shackled by political correctness and fears of offending

Muslims. Our nation has a long and proud history of religious freedom and religious tolerance. These values are an important part of the culture that shaped our politics, laws, Constitution, and society. Anyone who believes in the foolish idea that America is at war with all Muslims need only look at our communities, where people of all faiths live in harmony. Our leaders need to find the courage to identify our enemies correctly in order to ensure our citizens understand the nature of the conflict and the ideologies behind it. Only when our leaders and our citizens have an accurate understanding of the threat we face can we develop successful strategies and policies to win the war.

THE AMERICAN WAY NO MORE

It would be one thing if we could ensure that the fallout from the Sharia Spring stayed in the Middle East. But if we pay close enough attention, we're now finding out that it's changing our fundamental principles such as freedom of religion and freedom of speech here at home. It's entering our courts, where judges are taking Sharia into consideration, instead of our Constitution and own legal precedents. It's even changing the way our country thinks about warfare. Out of the desire to not offend, the U.S. military is changing its doctrine to be more politically correct.

Sometimes suffocatingly, absurdly so.

Remember the pastor down in Florida? The one who created a worldwide media sensation by announcing he would burn a copy of the Quran? This preacher, with a congregation that numbered at most thirty to forty people, was seeking media attention far more than salvation. And he got far more than he bargained for. I'm against burning books of any kind, but it is a right protected in our Constitution—the right to offend, to enrage, and to say what we please as long as it does not endanger the lives of our neighbors is purely American. If we didn't have the right to offend, I'd have a lot less to say. But over the last decade, some of our leaders have seen it quite differently.

President Obama called on the pastor to call off the Quran burning, saying it could be a "recruitment bonanza" for Al Qaeda. From thousands of miles away, leading our forces in Afghanistan, General David Petraeus, of all people, decided to weigh in and called the wayward minister's burning of the Quran "hateful" and "intolerant," thereby elevating both the preacher and the stunt to global magnitude. General Petraeus was of course exactly right; the act was hateful and intolerant. But he was wrong to bring the authority of his position of national prominence and rank to bear on what should have been just a piddling passing moment in the public circus. Senate Majority Leader Harry Reid vowed to investigate the matter and contemplated congressional hearings. Senator Lindsey Graham astoundingly said, "I wish we could find a way to hold people accountable. Free speech is a great idea, but we're in a war." This was from the mouth of someone widely considered to be John McCain's choice for attorney general if he won election in 2008. Thank the Lord for small favors.

The Obama administration at times appears committed to an unctuous policy of religious and cultural sensibility that leads to farcical exhortations from the president or his administration, whether over the burning of Qurans by a backwater preacher or blaming a third-rate video titled *Innocence of Muslims* for the Benghazi attacks and the murders of four Americans. Despite knowledge to the contrary, the Obama White House persisted in broadcasting the fiction that a silly YouTube video so angered Muslims that they were storming the gates of U.S. facilities in the

region, and that the date of September 11 was simply coinciden-
tal to those acts. The American embassy in Cairo issued a statement: "The embassy of the United States in Cairo condemns the
continuing efforts by misguided individuals to hurt the religious
feelings of Muslims." President Obama denounced the film at the
United Nations General Assembly. "The future must not belong
to those who slander the prophet of Islam," he said. Hillary Clinton's State Department then bought airtime on Pakistani TV for
commercials that showed Obama and Clinton apologizing for the
video. How much did that cost taxpayers?

$70,000

How have we gone so wrong? How have we thrown the immuta-
bility of free speech under the bus in an effort to appease religious
fanatics who rage and riot and kill at the slightest pretext? Instead
of condemning the provocateurs and fringe lunatics, how about
we condemn those who actually commit crimes? If anything
is "Islamophobic"—a word that gets tossed around with great
abandon—it is the idea that a video or a cartoon of Muhammad
will inflame a billion Muslims around the world.

In 2006, Somali cabdrivers in Minneapolis, Minnesota, refused
to pick up passengers who were suspected of carrying alcohol with
them. In my home state of New Jersey, a newly married Muslim
couple began having domestic disputes. The husband routinely
abused his wife physically and sexually assaulted her. In 2010,
the wife asked for a restraining order. Despite the indisputable
evidence that her husband had beaten and assaulted her, the New
Jersey court refused to grant the restraining order. The court
cited the husband's belief that it was his religious right to have
nonconsensual sex with his wife and held that that belief pre-
cluded any criminal intent. He therefore could not be punished,

the court ruled. Fortunately, the decision was later overturned and rationality prevailed.

MILITARILY GOOD ORDER, POLITICALLY CORRECT

Terry Pasker was a few months from retiring from the military. As soon as he was out, he planned to start a family with his wife. He was on his third tour to Afghanistan in July 2011, when an Afghan intelligence officer—a supposed ally—gunned down the Iowa National Guardsman. "The U.S. military considered the area so safe that soldiers didn't wear body armor, so as not to offend the friendly locals," the *Des Moines Register* wrote in an article about Sergeant Pasker's death.[2]

The fear of offending others has percolated through American culture into our military institutions, and even into the ways we fight wars. This development is unfortunate, as the United States military should have a very straightforward mission—defeat the enemy. There should be no ambiguity about what to do with the enemy. Capture or kill them. Now we're told that our brave soldiers and Marines shouldn't wear body armor to protect themselves, lest it be considered offensive. In 2012, more than sixty U.S. soldiers were killed by their supposed allies in the Afghan military. While it is important to build strong and trusting relationships between our soldiers and Afghan communities in order to build support for our troops and our mission to help the Afghan people build a strong and secure nation, we must never forget that our first and primary responsibility is to aid and protect our own men and women in uniform. While cultural sensitivity is necessary, it seems that concept has often been confused with political correctness. A recent draft of one army handbook on how to avoid confrontations with Afghan soldiers was instructive in this regard.

Etiquette Violations Best Avoided by [coalition forces]
Taboo conversation topics include:
- Anything related to Islam
- Mention of any other religion and/or spirituality
- Debating the war
- Making derogatory comments about the Taliban
- Advocating women's rights and equality
- Directing any criticism toward Afghans
- Mentioning homosexuality and homosexual conduct
- Bottom line: Try to avoid highly charged and emotional issues.[3]

We are supposed to be allied with the Afghans, fighting the same enemy. Why should insulting the Taliban, our common enemy, be deemed offensive? In a way, it's totally logical that we've arrived at this sad point. This is what happens when we have a government and two political parties that are willing to cave at the slightest allegation of religious discrimination, and all too eager to bow to the demands of political correctness.

THE ISLAMIST LOBBY

Like almost any identity group in Washington, D.C., the Islamists have their own lobbying group. Consider the Council on American-Islamic Relations, or CAIR. Its mission couldn't appear to be more benign: "to enhance understanding of Islam, encourage dialogue, protect civil liberties, empower American

Muslims, and build coalitions that promote justice and mutual un-derstanding." That sounds like a wonderful, worthy mission, but upon closer examination, it would be easy to conclude that one of CAIR's principal purposes is to blunt criticism and that they often try to delegitimize critics who raise questions about the influence and strategy of radical Islam and the encroachment of Sharia law into Western society, including our own. CAIR seems to have a difficult challenge in maintaining balance between fairly repre-senting Islam and often becoming entangled in what appears to be defenses of Islamists, even radical Islamists.

CAIR has been linked to Hamas and organizations that funnel hundreds of thousands of dollars to the terrorist organization in no fewer than three separate federal court filings.[4] Its leadership has on occasion sounded like wild-eyed Truthers, maintaining that 9/11 could not have been perpetrated by Al Qaeda terrorists, despite all evidence to the contrary. "Who really benefits from such a horrible tragedy that is blamed on Muslims and Arabs?" the leader of the New York CAIR chapter asked. "Why would the Bush administration allow 9/11 to happen?" asked another.

CAIR has on occasion used its tax-free, nonprofit status to raise money and launch aggressive lawsuits against individuals and news organizations, claiming religious discrimination. "The Mus-lim community realizes that it has to respond to these allegations and to these attacks, otherwise, the people who are promoting these defamatory remarks will win in the court of public opinion," said a CAIR spokesman in 2005. They've gone after the *Washington Times*, *National Post*, and *National Review*. *National Review* won its case, but only after spending $650,000 on legal fees. CAIR appears to have become considerably less aggressive in the wake of the *National Review* case, but I believe the effect may be more pernicious: It may well be that CAIR has succeeded in creating the chilling effect it sought in the national media.

A TIME FOR CHOOSING

Most Americans agree that Ronald Reagan was one of our greatest presidents. And for most Republicans, Reagan is nothing less than a hero. Except for those Republicans so intent on engaging the United States in the Middle East. Republicans and Democrats should closely follow Reagan's foreign policy choices and doctrine.

In 1983, terrorists bombed the U.S. Marine barracks in Beirut, Lebanon, killing 241 Americans. At the time this was the worst terrorist attack on Americans in our country's history. In response, Ronald Reagan rattled a lot of sabers. But here's what he didn't do: send hundreds of thousands of Americans into that country and get into a long, drawn-out war in Lebanon against the terrorist group and Syria—a war that would have exhausted our resources, killed potentially thousands of Americans, and distracted us completely from winning the Cold War and leading a U.S. economic recovery.

Some prominent Republicans, among them Senator McCain and Senator Graham, are calling for intervention in Syria and for the establishment of no-fly zones. I firmly believe that the United States should not engage in conflicts in the Middle East, or anywhere in the world for that matter, unless they have a direct bearing on the interests of the United States. Ronald Reagan managed to keep the United States out of senseless, protracted, and inconclusive conflicts for eight years. Even as the Obama administration further weakens our military with budget cuts of over a half-trillion dollars over the next decade and the elimination of twelve combat brigades, our leaders are putting this country into an exposed strategic position, constantly increasing the missions that we call upon our military to fulfill, while reducing the number of service members available to fulfill those missions. I sincerely hope our leaders will begin to emulate Reagan's constraint, his understanding of America's unlimited potential, and his understanding of the limits of power, even as he forged our American forces into the preeminent global military power. We must, in my opinion, never surrender that preeminence.

OUT OF ONE, MANY

The American Indian movement. The fat acceptance movement. The fathers' rights movement. Feminists. Gay Pride. La Raza. The NAACP. American Irish Historical Society. These are just a handful of the hundreds upon hundreds of organizations based on heritage, race, and nationality in this country. Each of these groups is defined by its separateness. One is either a member of each group or not. The groups organize by the national, racial, or ethnic identity of their members and their differentiation from the rest of society. Group and identity politics are the order of the day in political candidacy and campaign strategy. A nation whose founding values speak to equality and classlessness, equal rights and opportunity, has become a nation in which our founding values have been assailed by multiculturalism rather than holding to the truly American ideal of E Pluribus Unum.

E Pluribus Unum

The Latin phrase for "out of many, one" is the essence of our more than two-hundred-year history. Ours was a nation of immigrants building new lives, a nation of laws that bound Americans to one another, an independent, self-reliant people who limited their new government and asserted individual liberty as no other government had before it. "E Pluribus Unum" expressed the forging of one nation from thirteen colonies, the emergence of all who made up those colonies into one people to be known simply as "Americans" with the formation of the union.

In 1782, with the American experiment in its infancy, a man named J. Hector St. John de Crèvecoeur wrote a series of articles titled "Letters from an American Farmer." Much of Europe was curious about the new country, the only democracy on the face of the earth, a constitutional republic that most thought would be short-lived.

"What then is the American, this new man?" Crèvecoeur asked himself in his letters. An American, he wrote, is one who leaves behind "all of his ancient prejudices and manners, receives new ones from the new mode of life he has embraced, the government he obeys, and the new rank he holds. . . . Here individuals of all nations are *melted* into a new race of men, whose labors and posterity will one day cause great changes in the world." This, it is believed, was the origin of the phrase "melting pot," a notion later attributed to Ralph Waldo Emerson just before the beginning of the American Civil War.

Americans once proudly proclaimed our nation to be the great melting pot of the world, but we seldom even hear the expression, let alone the bold assertion that we remain so. Where once American immigrants turned their backs on their national, cultural, or racial origin and heritage, we have permitted ourselves to be defined by our government, our political parties, and special interest groups, by our differences, by our "otherness": class, race, gender, age, ethnicity, and yes, national origin. America is no longer perceived by many of its citizens and those who would be citizens as a great melting pot, but rather as a multicultural Mecca that insists upon a static adherence to old cultural and social customs, a refusal to let go of national identities that are no longer a part of life in America.

Multiculturalism is on its face anathema to the very ideals of this nation, most specifically a nation of immigrants becoming first and foremost Americans, people celebrating what binds them, their commonalities, their shared purpose. But the multiculturalists, usually with an ideological purpose, celebrate differences of origin, race, and even values. Multiculturalism is a pejorative term because it conflicts so strongly with the American experience and ideals. Our universities and corporate America could not ultimately rationalize multiculturalism and soon turned to the now well-worn term "diversity." The word is so often used and misused that it has become a confusing expression that is more of a totem than a descriptor.

"Diversity" is too often a dog whistle in government and corporate America for racial quotas and gender preferences. University admissions departments often talk about the diversity of students on campus, but what do they mean? Usually they are referring to skin color. In some instances they use the term diversity more broadly to include national origin, and occasionally they will include a variety of economic and regional backgrounds and experiences, but only rarely. In America today, diversity has become the opposite of its original intended meaning, particularly in government and business. Diversity, which was once supposed to be a description of an open assembly of Americans, whether in a university or in a corporation, has become the new code word for exclusion. It is a peculiar word. And isn't it odd the times at which the politically correct who have institutionalized the word neglect to insist upon across-the-board policies? Why is it important to diversify the employees of a restaurant but not of an NFL football team? Why is it important for a university to be diverse in racial and ethnic origin but not in economic circumstances, religious belief or nonbelief, or, certainly, in diversity of thought among both professors and students? Why no insistence on diversity and balance of liberal and conservative thought, independent thought and philosophy? Odd, don't you think?

And how to enforce diversity? Right now, for reasons not clearly understood, far more women are going to college than men. In part, this happens because men have failed to meet their basic obligation to study in high school, with too many dropping out and too few preparing for the highly competitive admissions process. Men are becoming educational wusses. They don't want to read, they don't want to study, they don't want to work hard. But that is not a healthy trend for men, the American family, or the country. Naturally, our politicians are ignoring the issue as best they can.

Think about the political campaigns and all their commercials that will infest our airwaves this election year. It's an orgy of vapidity, "otherness," and oh yes, plenty of nastiness. Those ads are designed and carefully targeted by high-priced political consultants to appeal to us as members of different groups, to distract and divert us, and, of course, to pander to the groups with which we identify based on our differences. Right now legions of experts are in dank basements, plying their dark trade to prepare campaigns designed to seek out voters who will vote for their candidates despite their often woeful inadequacies, checkered pasts, and highly questionable capacity and character to lead the nation. Don't misunderstand me; there are some highly capable and effective representatives in both Congress and the Senate. But they are not an overwhelming majority.

The Obama campaign organization of 2012 will be in the field for this midterm election. They will be spending untold millions targeting women in suburban areas of swing states. Their ads offered women the preposterous notion that their right to abortion and access to contraceptive devices were under siege by the Republican Party. Not only was this utter nonsense, it was an insult to women across America. Think about what the Obama consultants believed. Women weren't supposed to care about the economy or job creation or strong national security. Those, presumably, are issues better left for males to worry about. Instead women were expected to focus on abortion and what Mitt Romney did or didn't say about Planned Parenthood. (Typically, he said all kinds of things about Planned Parenthood, and not much of it made a lick of sense.)

The subliminal message of that ad campaign was equally offensive, or should have been, because of the people they didn't want to reach. The Obama campaign seemed to be saying to people like me that they didn't care about my vote. Or that as a white male, I had no right to an opinion on abortion or access to contraception for my daughters. That's a women's issue alone.

There are political ads especially designed to rile up minority groups on a case-by-case basis. Spanish radio stations talk about "Latino issues." Television programs with predominantly black audiences talk about affirmative action or threats to the black community. There are gay ad campaigns, and Asian campaigns, and Muslim campaigns. This is the way our political elites have divided the country in election cycle after election cycle. We are all special interests now, divided by race, or gender, or religion, or sexual orientation. That's not *E Pluribus Unum*. That's "look out for me and those who look or act like me." It inverts the idea of "community"—the idea that all Americans have a social bond in some way—and defines it as an agglomeration of different interest groups that have much more differentiating them than they have in common.

47 percent

You might remember during the 2012 campaign how much grief Mitt Romney received when at a private fundraiser he decried the so-called 47 percent of Americans whom he didn't "have to worry about" to win the 2012 presidential election. Let's be blunt. What Romney said, whatever his explanation, was stupid, plain and simple. No American president should be talking that way, in public or in private, about groups of his fellow citizens. A president more than anyone should be about representing all the people, not 53 percent of them. Or, in Mitt Romney's case, 47 percent, as the vote turned out to be.

But what was most interesting about Mr. Romney's comment was the total hypocrisy of his critics. Liberal columnist David Corn, who broke the story for some magazine almost nobody ever heard of called *Mother Jones*, attacked Governor Romney for "denigrating nearly half the electorate as 'victims' who do not take 'personal responsibility and care for their lives.' " Former Bush speechwriter David Frum attacked Romney's comments as "angry" and "divisive." The Obama campaign, predictably, took similar advantage of the remarks, also painting Romney as a divisive figure.

Pray tell, how is what Romney said, as foolish and inelegant as it was, any different from what every other public figure in America believes? They divide people by race, class, and gender all the time—into even smaller percentages than 47 percent—all in the guise of empowering different groups against the rest of America.

Now, I understand that freedom of association is protected in our Constitution, I think—but these divisive interest groups of today are abusing the privilege. It is time we took a closer look and realized that these groups by definition pit one section of our country against another, working against the unity of American society.

1909

Consider that year for a moment. That's a long time ago—more than a century. It was the year that Senator Barry Goldwater was born and the year that the United States Army purchased its first military airplane from the Wright Brothers. That was also the year when the National Association for the Advancement of Colored People was established.

Let me ask a question that few people dare ask these days, lest they be branded a racist or a member of the Klan: Is there a reason we need the NAACP anymore? I'm serious. When this organization was started, American society was dramatically different for African-Americans from what it is today. We don't even use the term "colored people" anymore. So the organization's very name hasn't kept up with the times.

Of course, no one would be so stupid as to state that our racial problems in America are cured. They likely never will be. But surely we can acknowledge that the legal institutions of racism— the poll tax, segregation laws—have been removed, thanks in large part to the courageous efforts of civil rights activists and the NAACP's founders. Today we have a black president who has been elected to two terms of office, for goodness' sake. What is the purpose of a group that is still based on the interests of one race against everyone else? Or does the NAACP think we need to keep an eye on Obama, too? Does the NAACP serve any purpose now, other than as an excuse for the Democratic Party to boo Republicans who deign to show up at their events, or to run commercials attacking GOP candidates? Are they really helping African-Americans become empowered and part of the overall society or are they dividing black Americans from the rest of the country by cultivating a victim mentality—an "us versus them" system? I'm just asking questions here.

But consider that groups like the NAACP by definition have to make their members feel aggrieved or shortchanged. Their existence depends on cultivating a belief that society hasn't gone far enough—in perpetuity. Otherwise what do we need them for? Can you ever imagine the NAACP's leaders closing its doors and saying, "Racism is solved now; job well done"? It will never happen.

Similarly, why is there still a National Organization for Women? The original mantra of NOW was "to take action to bring women into full participation in the mainstream of American society now, exercising all privileges and responsibilities thereof in truly equal partnership with men." Women have the right to vote. They serve in public office. They are CEOs and professors and lawyers. Women are now allowed to serve in combat. Diane Sawyer is an evening news anchor. *The View* is one of the most popular talk shows in America. Hillary Clinton was almost the Democratic nominee for president—and she's a front-runner for 2016. Are women—52 percent of the American population—still an oppressed minority?

Have we not reached a point in our nation's evolution when there is no disagreement that all Americans deserve equal economic opportunity? We want every American to advance in our society, do we not? Then why do we so amiably tolerate those who would use physical, ethnic, racial, cultural, and gender characteristics and distinctions to perpetuate differences in our society as more prominent and more deserving of our consciousness than our commonality and our shared space in this time, all united in the values and ideals of this great nation.

So why do we have a National Organization for Women, other than to create another organization whose most effective activities seem to be opining for and working on behalf of the Democratic Party. That's primarily what they have been doing for decades. These great advocates for women barely raised a peep when a Democratic president of the United States was turning the Oval Office into the Oral Office, taking advantage of women barely out of their teens and allegedly groping any number of others. If a Republican president had behaved in a similar fashion, he or she would have been vilified by almost every Democratic officeholder and liberal group or organization to the point of public personal destruction.

But you've got to give NOW credit for adapting to the times, for as women have become the majority in our society, the National Organization for Women no longer stands just for, well, women. They've expanded NOW's mission and are now marketing NOW's membership to include every group grievance there is. This is the organization's new mission: "NOW is one of the few multi-issue progressive organizations in the United States. NOW stands against all oppression, recognizing that racism, sexism, and homophobia are interrelated, that other forms of oppression such as classism and ableism work together with these three to keep power and privilege concentrated in the hands of a few." It appears that NOW has become so ambitious in its broad grievance charter that the only group NOW is no longer representing is women.

Indeed, with so many different interest groups represented, it's reasonable to ask, "Who isn't included in NOW?" The answer is simple: able-bodied white, straight men. They of course remain the enemy. It's "us versus them" America. Not out of many, one.

Some on the left have been brave enough to point this out. In *Time* magazine in the fall of 2012, columnist Joe Klein offered the following observation:

> The Democrats have a serious problem. It is a problem that stems from the party's greatest strength: its long-term support for inclusion and equal rights for all, its support of racial integration and equal rights for women and homosexuals and its humane stand on immigration reform. Those heroic positions, which I celebrate, cost the Democrats more than a few elections in the past. And they caused an understandable, if misguided, overreaction within the party—a drift toward identity politics, toward special pleading. Inclusion became exclusive. The Democratic National Committee officially recognizes 14 caucuses or "communities," most having to do with race, gender, sexual orientation or ethnicity.
>
> Many of these groups had a purpose in the beginning. African Americans had the ultimate historic complaint. The lesbian, gay, bisexual and transgender caucus (LGBT, if you're scoring at home) worked effectively and won the Democrats' support for a full roster of human rights, including marriage. The women's caucus represented perhaps the most successful civil rights movement of our lifetime. Women are moving beyond equality now toward dominance as more of them graduate from college than men—and fewer of them drop out of high school—and take their

places atop major companies, government agencies and, someday soon, the presidency.

We've become a nation of interest groups and organizations. America is no longer about the individual; instead we have entered the era of the special interest group. They share a lust for ideology and politics, and an aversion to paying taxes. Almost all are nonprofit 501(c)(3)s. So what is the point of NOW, or for that matter, the U.S. Chamber of Commerce? People think of their local chambers of commerce as helping the little guy maneuver through complex government regulations and other red tape. Maybe that's true. But everyone in Washington knows that the U.S. Chamber is an organization totally devoted to the interests of big business, major corporations that can afford to deal with federal regulations, interests that are far removed from those of small business owners and entrepreneurs across America. Why do we still need a group that just makes the system easier for those at the top and more difficult for the businessmen still trying to make it to the top?

Goldman Sachs
Texaco
Chevron

These are among the biggest donors to the U.S. Chamber of Commerce. Hardly a group of local business guys looking out for the average American Joe. The Chamber has supported a slew of proposals that would help major international conglomerates, like Chevron, but would do little other than wipe out small businesses across America. They supported, for example, so-called free-trade agreements like NAFTA that shipped American jobs and factories to Mexico. The U.S. Chamber supported an early version of Hillary Clinton's nationalized health-care plan, which ultimately migrated into Obamacare, which is destroying small business owners across the country. The U.S. Chamber is a major supporter of amnesty for illegal immigrants, which will overwhelm and bankrupt small communities dealing with the enormous costs of the influx. The Chamber's slogan is "Fighting for your business." Really? Often they mean if your business is big enough, if your business is in Mexico, or more urgently, if it's in China. Not a lot of Chamber symposia on job creation, repatriation of capital, or employee empowerment. And that's too bad.

One of the real problems with special interest groups like these is that thousands, if not millions, of ordinary Americans actually believe the groups are doing work essential to our economy and society—they think these groups really are fighting for them, representing them, and work complementarily with local and state governments in many cases. But in some cases, they are either undermining them or using the nonprofit structure to further unseen or hidden agendas. Many if, not most, 501(c)(3)s are civic and charity organizations, but the abuses are numerous and often substantial, and for the most part unexamined. Nonprofits have proliferated explosively in American society, now numbering more than a million and a half organizations. It seems almost everyone has a special interest and a special purpose for their nonprofit. Perhaps no individual or nonprofit has run into more controversy than Al Sharpton and his National Action Network.

$250,000

That's how much PepsiCo paid Al Sharpton between 1998 and 2007. He received this money as the company's "diversity consultant." Reverend Sharpton had organized a minority boycott of

Pepsi because he claimed that the company's ads didn't include enough African-Americans. As soon as Pepsi forked over money to him, however, his concerns were apparently ameliorated and the company's advertising markedly improved, at least in the Reverend's good opinion.

Sharpton's social engagement and diversity consultation have taken on a predictable shape, the process is all too familiar, and the outcome seems always to be the same. Sharpton and Reverend Jesse Jackson have for decades raised the consciousness of corporate chieftains and managed to win considerable financial support from public coffers with which to further the social consciousness of even more corporate chieftains. Sharpton educated Pepsi, Jackson educated Coca-Cola. Their tactics may have become tiresome over the years, but the reality is that both Jackson and Sharpton have done some considerable good. It is also unquestionable that they have done themselves some good.

The controversy that follows Sharpton and Jackson has become an issue of balance, a debate over how much of their activities is good for them, how much is good for the companies and individuals they target, and how much is good for society. For example, in 2000, Reverend Jackson put together a busload of Coca-Cola employees claiming that the company was racist. Jesse loves a fight, and he took to the airwaves, and he loves to talk, and he's pretty good at both. Jesse's language can be tough and it can be lyrical. "Either the buses will roll or justice will roll as water down a river stream," Jackson vowed. The media, of course, loved it.

Coke didn't. Coke did its best to deny the allegations, but Fortune 500 companies are usually not nimble enough, or courageous enough, to engage Jackson or Sharpton, and they're also not often pure enough to win. Coca-Cola ultimately decided to settle the lawsuit, despite all the company's previous denials of the racial charges. Prior to the settlement, Coca-Cola already sponsored Jackson's various organizations such as the Rainbow Coalition and PUSH. Reverend Jackson claimed that his organization even bought shares in Coca-Cola. Jackson succeeded in one of the most efficient, and apparently profound, conversions of any corporation in history from racist to enlightened. His group later signed agreements with other companies Jackson was threatening, including Burger King and 7 Up.

Let's be clear about what all this is. These are shakedowns, and no one has ever explained why this kind of political and economic coercion isn't used by every kind of special interest group in the country. When Al Sharpton, Jesse Jackson, and others go into action, they are as likely as not to have their way and further fund the Rainbow Coalition and the National Action Network. Sharpton and Jackson are the Chrysler and GM, the Exxon Mobil and Chevron, of the grievance-victimization media complex.

The *New York Post*—one of the few large newspapers in America that have ever covered these shakedown operations in any detail—demonstrated how Sharpton worked General Motors. From 2000 to 2006, Sharpton's organization asked for contributions from the company. Each time these requests were refused.

By the end of 2006, according to the newspaper, "Sharpton threatened to call a boycott of the carmaker over the closing of an African-American-owned GM dealership in the Bronx, and he picketed outside GM headquarters on Fifth Avenue." In response, GM forked over a $5,000 donation. And then another the following year. The scheme had been successful for years with other companies:

- "In November 2003, Sharpton picketed DaimlerChrysler's Chicago car show and threatened a boycott over alleged racial bias in car loans. 'This is institutional racism,' he bellowed. In May 2004, Chrysler began supporting NAN's conferences, which include panels on corporate responsibility and civil rights and a black-tie awards dinner to honor Martin Luther King Jr. Last year, Sharpton gave Chrysler an award for corporate excellence."

- "In 2003, Sharpton targeted American Honda for not hiring enough African-Americans in management. 'We support those that support us,' wrote Sharpton and the Rev. Horace Sheffield III, president of NAN's Michigan chapter, in a letter to American Honda. Two months after American Honda execs met with Sharpton, the carmaker began to sponsor NAN's events—and continues to pay 'a modest amount' each year, a spokesman said."

- Anheuser-Busch reportedly gave his group, National Action Network, "between $100,000 and $499,000" in one year alone. Other companies on bended knee to Sharpton were Colgate-Palmolive, Pfizer, Macy's, Wal-Mart, FedEx, Continental Airlines, Johnson & Johnson, and Chase Manhattan.

And their operations, such as PUSH and the National Action Network, are seemingly unaccountable to anyone, including the government, or as we learned in the IRS Tea Party–targeting scandals, perhaps especially the government. All nonprofits belong to a cycle of favor, that is, the election cycle, because many of these organizations are decidedly political and ideological in nature, and they benefit from the patronage and protection of whichever party happens to be in power in Washington.

Then there is the group "La Raza," which literally means "The Race." As in one race versus the rest. This too is an organization that encourages race-based grievances against the rest of America. In the fall of 2012, the controversial group made headlines when it attacked the Disney Corporation for an upcoming movie featuring a Hispanic character who did not look Hispanic enough. Whatever that is supposed to mean. La Raza purports to represent all Hispanics in America, but is now a radicalized organization that seems to be interested in perpetuating its own existence and winning sufficient federal government funding and grants to do so. For years, its principal lobbying efforts have been to win amnesty for illegal immigrants and to maintain an open border with Mexico.

La Raza's radicalized and hostile attitude is part of La Raza's extreme campaign. La Raza is behind a new curriculum, called Raza Studies. According to the magazine *National Review*, for example, "The Tucson Unified School District (TUSD) has, in fact, welcomed Raza Studies in its classrooms for about a decade." Overcoming a significant amount of resistance, the author of the *National Review* piece managed to uncover the curriculum of this program, which, as he described it, "included texts with titles such as *Occupied America and The Pedagogy of Oppression*." A Tucson teacher told the magazine that the focus of Raza Studies was "that Mexican-Americans were and continue to be victims of a racist American society driven by the interests of middle- and upper-class whites." Radical, divisive, and wrong. The federal government is spending taxpayer money to fund left-wing ideology and racial agendas.

A late entry to the grievance-victimization media complex is the Council on American-Islamic Relations, whose mission at times appears to be to accuse America of hating Muslims because we insist on defending ourselves against radical Islamist terrorism. The council has itself been accused of having ties to terrorism, including allegations of helping finance Hamas. The effect of the council's attempts at intimidation, particularly of the media, has been to position CAIR as a source of reflexive accusations of religious intolerance and racism against America and Americans. Consider what happened aboard a US Airways flight back in 2006. On November 20, 2006, a member of the crew of US Airways Flight 300, en route to Phoenix, received this frightening note from a passenger:

Passengers and some of the flight staff reported that they observed other behavior they deemed suspicious. These passengers, all of them Muslim imams, reportedly refused to sit in their assigned seats. Passengers thought they fanned out to different sections of the plane. At least one of the imams apparently asked for a seat belt extension—which is an elongated strap that might be used for other purposes. Some on the flight crew apparently were under the impression that some of the imams had no baggage and were flying on one-way tickets—which TSA always considers to be suspect circumstances that trigger further inquiry. Because of similar vigilance on the part of passengers on another flight, the shoe bomber Richard Reid was caught before he could blow up an American Airlines plane in 2001.

The imams were taken from the plane for questioning, and you would think the rational reaction would be to thank US Airways authorities for their vigilance and precautions. But no. The imams were furious. They appealed to CAIR, and CAIR filed a complaint against the airline on the imams' behalf, claiming religious discrimination.

A US Airways spokesperson said, "We've done what we typically do in a situation where there is a removal or some kind of customer service at issue.... We talked with crew members and passengers and those on the ground.... We found out the facts are substantially the same, and the imams were detained because of the concerns crew members had based on the behavior they observed, and from reports by the customers.... We're looking at it as a security issue and as a customer-service issue and where we might need to do outreach." Subsequent investigations, including one conducted by the Department of Homeland Security, found no evidence to support charges of discrimination.

What could possibly be CAIR's motive in supporting legal action against the airline other than to discourage passengers or airline crews from acting expeditiously when confronted with suspicious activity in the future? Did CAIR's action make Americans more or less safe? Did they help the cause of Muslim-Americans or make them seem more separate or more detached from the rest of America?

As if we didn't have enough separate groups and organizations, there are others busy working to create new ones, more novel

classifications to differentiate ourselves from each other. The
Democrats, for example, have fallen in love with a group called
"Native Hawaiians." So much so that they have doggedly pursued legislation with the seemingly innocuous name "The Native
Hawaiian Federal Recognition Act." This may sound like a nice
idea. Why not allow some native group to get a little love from
the United States Congress? Well, it turns out this legislation
amounts to something more than creating the Hawaiian equivalent of Black History Month.

The proposed law, introduced by former senator Daniel K.
Akaka, a Democrat from Hawaii, would create a Native Hawaiian government that would be allowed to negotiate with state
and federal governments. Supporters of the bill, including some
big-name Republicans desperate to ingratiate themselves with a
minority group—*any* minority group—claim that what they propose for Native Hawaiians is the same thing that already exists for
Native American groups. The difference, however, is a big one.
Native Americans have existed for centuries in distinct political
entities known as reservations. The Native Hawaiians have no
such organization. They live in cities all across America. Creating
a separate Native Hawaiian government would mean that Hawaiians wherever they live suddenly would be exempt from state and
federal laws. There is absolutely no historical precedent for this
and the ramifications are enormous.

As former senator Jon Kyl, a Republican from Arizona, wrote
in opposition to the legislation, "On a practical level, it is difficult
to imagine how such a government would interact with the rest of
Hawaii's people. Tribal Indians on a reservation generally are immune from state laws—from the taxes and regulations that apply
to other residents of the state. But unlike reservation Indians, Na-

tive Hawaiians do not live in one area of the state that is set aside for Indians. They live in the same cities and neighborhoods, and on the same streets, as other Hawaiians do.

"Would the citizens of the new Native Hawaiian government—like reservation Indians—be immune from state laws, regulations, and taxes? Would a Native Hawaiian-owned business—like a reservation Indian business—be exempt from the taxes that its non-Native competitors must pay? If Congress were to create a separate tribal government for Native Hawaiians, it would be imposing just such a system on the people of Hawaii. Persons of different races, who live together in the same society, would be subject to different legal codes. This would not produce racial reconciliation in Hawaii. Instead, it is a recipe for permanent racial conflict."

If Native Hawaiians get their own government, how long will it be before Sharpton and Jackson are demanding a separate government for African-Americans? Or one for Hispanics, Irish-Americans, or Indian-Americans? When does it stop, and my God, how did we ever let it begin? Multiculturalism with the force and power of government. Multiculturalism unassailable because of what is now a deep-rooted political correctness that sucks up all reason and passion for truth and free speech.

The political correctness that would ossify the spirit of this great land has led a pliant national media to question only the hearts and motives of those who would secure our borders, insist on sovereign control of our immigration system, and reserve to our government the right to decide who shall become a citizen of this great country of ours. The national media for the most part have already absolved those who have entered our country illegally, have found there to be no national impairment to granting citizenship en masse to all who are here illegally, no questions permitted about whether a nation that has the highest high-school dropout rate in the world really needs another 20 to 30 million mostly unskilled, uneducated people in its economy. Also, in the course of a decade, it has become impolite, if not subversive, to believe that English should be America's official language. Consider, if you will, this number:

8

That is the number of countries in the world that do not have an official language. To put that another way, 185 out of 193 nations in the world have at least one official language. In fifty-one of those countries English is the official language. English is the language of global aviation, it is the language of global commerce, and, of course, it is our language: in government, in law, culture, and heritage. But if you dare so much as suggest that English be the official language of America you will be called without hesitation and from all directions a racist or xenophobe, or both. In large measure because the national media have decided that because we have permitted all those illegal immigrants into our country, the number of Hispanic-Americans has risen to such a level that one might as well speak Spanish. Not only are we now convincingly multicultural in the minds of the national media and the left-wing ideologues, but we are next I suppose to be multilingual. As a matter of fact, the signage of some big-box stores such as Lowes is now bilingual. There's been no vote, of course, either permitting or encouraging bilingual signage in stores or publications, but big business is insisting on a future of its design. And that future is ironically much the same as that envisioned by our political left wing in this country. The media, the left, and big business maintain that insisting on English as the official language is insulting to Hispanics, to Latinos, which couldn't be further from the truth. Here's another number for your consideration:

96 percent

That's how many foreign-born Latinos say that teaching English to immigrants is "very important."[1] Similarly large majorities of Hispanics believe that learning and speaking English is the key to succeeding in America and being part of the culture of the United States. And of course they are right. Those advocating English as the official language are trying only to help all our citizens find a common frame of reference amid our diversity. Ninety-two percent of Americans speak English. It makes perfect sense that English—not Spanish, not Swahili or French—be the official language of the country to build a sense of community. In human relationships, what's more important than the ability to communicate with one another? English is the obvious way to do that, to bring people together, to build a sense of community, to be one nation. From many, one. Not from one, many.

The left in this country is responsible for much of the nonsense: opposing English as our official language, multiculturalism, which is a not very sophisticated political effort to attack the foundation of a country that is despised by many on the left. If the politics of division, as practiced by the left and this president, succeed, America will not. If so-called community organizers and leaders persuade enough African-Americans to believe themselves aggrieved, a separate class of citizens, victimized still by American society, they are likely to also believe that they need big government, big handouts, and as a persistent dependent class, they will want Democrats, particularly the left, to ensure that their needs are met by ever more generous, ever bigger government. And the left uses the same tactics with women, gays, Hispanics, and on and on down the list.

Democrats and the left without question bear the greatest responsibility for the politics of division, of group and identity politics, in our American life, but it is not the American way. I am utterly confident that we will reverse these corrosive, negative trends in our society, and it will largely be up to the Republican Party as to when that occurs. Republicans in 2014 must understand that if they are to reverse multiculturalism as a viable alternative to our melting pot heritage, then Republicans must include all races, all ethnicities, and the Republican "big tent" must become a reality now. "We" and "us" are the appropriate references when we talk about race, poverty, education, jobs, and prosperity. To do so, Republicans will have to acknowledge that corporate multinationals and the wealthy establishment will not be the beacons of our national future, nor will they be the final voice on important public policy direction. Quite simply, Republicans must be the party of Teddy Roosevelt, Dwight Eisenhower, and Ronald Reagan. That is an exciting prospect. For all of us.

NOTES

1. CONSEQUENTIAL ELECTIONS 2014

1. All campaign finance numbers from http://elections.nytimes.com /2012/campaign-finance.
2. http://www.gallup.com/poll/154838/Pro-Choice-Americans-Record -Low.aspx.

2. DIMINISHING, DISTANT DREAMS

1. http://www.huffingtonpost.com/2011/05/24/members-of-congress-get -a_n_866387.html.
2. http://www.nytimes.com/financialtimes/business/FT1075982783472 .html?ex=1393131600&en=84995e065fb67b58&ei=5007&partner=US ERLAND&_r=0.
3. http://www.time.com/time/magazine/article/0,9171,2115062,00.html #ixzz2KEU24w70.
4. http://www.washingtonpost.com/business/capitalbusiness/dc-regions -unemployment-rate-fell-to-55-percent-in-feb/2012/04/10/gIQAJNT V8S_story.html.
5. http://nymag.com/daily/intelligencer/2012/08/why-washington-accepts -mass-unemployment.html.
6. http://www.time.com/time/magazine/article/0,9171,2115062,00.html #ixzz2KEkYFnRk.
7. http://www.dcchamber.org/external/wcpages/wcmedia/documents /DCCCAnnualReport2012.pdf.
8. http://www.time.com/time/magazine/article/0,9171,2115062,00.html #ixzz2KETkPUNB.

NOTES

9. http://www.time.com/time/magazine/article/0,9171,2115062,00.html #ixzz2KEnwTnr0.

10. http://www.realclearpolitics.com/articles/2012/08/16/the_washington _dc_bubble_115129.html.

3. BANKSHOT

1. http://thinkprogress.org/economy/2013/01/28/1502421/chart-largest -bank-assets/.

2. Given the complex modeling of CDS, it's a difficult number to pinpoint, but $60 trillion is as close as anyone has come. For more details see Kevin Dowd's article in the 2009 *Cato Journal*: http://www.cato .org/sites/cato.org/files/serials/files/cato-journal/2009/1/cj29n1-12.pdf.

4. BLESSED ARE THE CHILDREN

1. Mallory Factor, *Shadowbosses*, p. 125.

2. "Statistics About Education in America," StudentsFirst.

3. "Statistics About Education in America," StudentsFirst.

4. "Roadmap for Growth," Business Roundtable, http://www3.weforum .org/docs/WEF_GCR_Report_2011-12.pdf.

5. "Roadmap for Growth," Business Roundtable.

6. "Statistics About Education in America," StudentsFirst.

7. "Chalk Talk: U.S. Increases Spending on Education, But Is It Helping?" *Lou Dobbs Tonight*, 8/21/12.

8. "Chalk Talk: U.S. Increases Spending on Education, But Is It Helping?" *Lou Dobbs Tonight*, 8/21/12.

9. "Chalk Talk: U.S. Increases Spending on Education, But Is It Helping?" *Lou Dobbs Tonight*, 8/21/12.

10. http://www.eric.ed.gov/ERICWebPortal/search/detailmini.jsp?_nfpb =true&_&ERICExtSearch_SearchValue_0=ED299659&ERICExtSearch _SearchType_0=no&accno=ED299659.

11. http://www.foxnews.com/us/2012/07/14/teacher-union-bigs-rake-in -dough-despite-budget-cuts-across-education-sector/.

12. http://online.wsj.com/article/SB100014240527023036440045775 2084 1038165770.html.

13. "Political Power," Teachers Unions Exposed.

14. http://usatoday30.usatoday.com/news/education/story/2012-06-28/Teacher-unions-education/55993750/1.

15. http://usnews.nbcnews.com/_news/2012/11/08/15025083-teachers-unions-show-renewed-strength-in-wake-of-elections?lite.

16. http://www.usnews.com/debate-club/are-teachers-overpaid/average-public-school-teacher-is-paid-too-much.

17. "Chalk Talk: Collusion Behind End to Chicago Teacher Strike?" *Lou Dobbs Tonight*, 9/19/12.

18. http://www.foxbusiness.com/economy/2012/08/06/illinois-to-spend-more-on-pensions-than-on-education/.

19. "Chalk Talk: Teachers' Unions Hurting the Educational System?" *Lou Dobbs Tonight*, 9/11/12.

20. "Chalk Talk: Collusion Behind End to Chicago Teacher Strike?" *Lou Dobbs Tonight*, 9/19/12.

21. "Chalk Talk: Public Teachers' Impact on Illinois Taxpayers' Wallets," *Lou Dobbs Tonight*, 9/10/12.

22. "Chalk Talk: Collusion Behind End to Chicago Teacher Strike?" *Lou Dobbs Tonight*, 9/19/12.

23. http://www.freerepublic.com/focus/news/2582614/posts.

24. http://www.nbcnewyork.com/news/local/Statistics-115590474.html.

5. A TOUGH ENVIRONMENT

1. "With five private jets, Travolta still lectures on global warming," *London Evening Standard*, 3/30/07.

2. Gregg Easterbrook, "Before we get to the NFC preview, some cupcakes," ESPN.com, 10/1/07.

3. Dennis Cauchon, "Electric Bills By State," *USA Today*, 12/13/11.

4. Smil, Vaclav. *Energy Transitions: History, Requirements, Prospects*. Santa Barbara, CA: Praeger, 2010. Print.

5. Righter, Robert W. *Windfall: Wind Energy in America Today*. Norman: University of Oklahoma, 2011. Print. Pp. 5–6.

6. Andy Sullivan, "Analysis: Obama's 'green jobs' have been slow to sprout," Reuters, 4/13/12.

NOTES

7. "Barack Obama's Acceptance Speech," *New York Times*, 8/28/08.

8. "Oil and Natural Gas Power America's Economy," American Petroleum Institute.

9. "EMPLOYMENT IN GREEN GOODS AND SERVICES-2010," Bureau of Labor Statistics, 3/22/12.

10. "HEARING: ADDRESSING CONCERNS ABOUT THE INTEGRITY OF THE U.S. DEPARTMENT OF LABOR'S JOBS REPORTING," House Committee on Oversight and Government Reform, 6/6/12.

11. Furchtgott-Roth, Diana. *Regulating to Disaster: How Green Jobs Policies are Damaging America's Economy*. New York: Encounter Books, 2012. Print. P. 46.

12. *Regulating to Disaster*, p. 48.

13. *Regulating to Disaster*, p. 52.

14. Daniel Halper, "Former White House Economist Admits 'Clean Energy' Firms Don't Create Many Jobs," WeeklyStandard.com, 4/5/12.

15. "Remarks by the President on Energy," WhiteHouse.gov, 2/23/12.

16. "Pelosi to Boehner: Schedule Vote Next Week to End Taxpayer Subsidies to Big Oil After You Said They Should Pay 'Fair Share,'" DemocraticLeader.gov, 4/26/11.

17. Darren Goode, "Senate rejects repeal of oil incentives," POLITICO, 5/17/11.

18. "Obama says he would impose oil windfall profits tax," Reuters, 6/9/08.

19. "API President and CEO Jack Gerard's remarks at the USEA's 6th Annual State of the Energy Conference," American Petroleum Institute, 1/13/10.

20. Christopher Helman, "When It Comes To Paying Taxes, Big Oil Takes The Biggest Hit," Forbes.com, 4/16/12.

21. "Taxes," American Petroleum Institute.

22. "The NRDC's Oil Ignorance," Institute for Energy Research, 1/17/12.

23. "North American Energy Inventory," *Energy for America*, 12/11.

24. Diana Furchtgott-Roth, "Obama's Keystone slow-walking hurts jobs creation," *Washington Times*, 12/8/11.

NOTES

25. Charles Krauthammer, "The great pipeline sellout," *Washington Post*, 11/17/11.

26. Daniel Halper, "Obama Warned that His Policies Would Bankrupt Coal Power Plant Owners," WeeklyStandard.com, 5/11/12.

27. William W. Beach, Karen Campbell, Ph.D., David W. Kreutzer, Ph.D., and Ben Lieberman, "The Economic Impact of Waxman-Markey," Heritage Foundation, 5/13/09.

28. http://video.foxbusiness.com/v/1908399881001.

29. Robert Murphy, "Wind Jobs Apparently More Valuable Than Coal Jobs," Institute for Energy Research, 10/2/12.

30. Tom Hals and Roberta Rampton, "Beacon Power bankrupt; had U.S. backing like Solyndra," Reuters, 10/31/11.

31. Andrew Herndon and Michael Bathon, "Intel, Goldman Sachs–Backed SpectraWatt Files for Bankruptcy," *Bloomberg*, 8/23/11.

32. http://dailycaller.com/2012/10/17/obama-backed-bankrupt-solyndra-sues-chinese-solar-companies/#ixzz2AAqP7AYd.

33. John Harris and James Hohmann, "10 quotes that haunt President Obama," POLITICO, 10/2/12.

34. *Regulating to Disaster*, p. 107.

35. Greenwire, "SOLYNDRA: In blow to feds, judge approves company's post-bankruptcy plan" (Tuesday, October 23, 2012).

36. "Nevada Receives $1.3B for 288 Green Energy Jobs," *Lou Dobbs Tonight*, 8/8/12.

37. http://money.msn.com/investing/unemployed-go-to-north-dakota-cnbc.aspx?page=0.

38. http://online.wsj.com/article/SB10001424052970204226204576602524023932438.html.

39. R2D 188.

40. "America's New Energy Future," *IHS*, 10/12.

41. http://online.wsj.com/article/SB10001424052702303343404577514622469426012.html.

42. "America's New Energy Future," *IHS*, 10/12.

6. SPACE MYSTERIES AND MISADVENTURES

1. "Statement by the President on Curiosity Landing on Mars," White House.gov, 8/6/12.
2. "Statement by the President on Curiosity Landing on Mars," White House.gov, 8/6/12.
3. "Chalk Talk: The Cost of a Mission to Mars Too High?" *Lou Dobbs Tonight*, 8/6/12.
4. "Obama Administration Proposes Big Cuts to NASA's Mars Programs," *Scientific American*, 2/13/12.
5. "Congress grills NASA chief Bolden over budget cuts," MSNBC.com, 3/21/12.
6. "Obama Administration Proposes Big Cuts to NASA's Mars Programs," *Scientific American*, 2/13/12.
7. "Europe Turns to Russia as NASA Cuts Loom," *Wall Street Journal*, 2/2/12.
8. "Chalk Talk: The Cost of a Mission to Mars Too High?" *Lou Dobbs Tonight*, 8/6/12.
9. "How Much Does NASA Cost," About.com's U.S. Economy Guide, 4/22/12.
10. "How Much Does NASA Cost," About.com's U.S. Economy Guide, 4/22/12.
11. "How Much Does NASA Cost," About.com's U.S. Economy Guide, 4/22/12.
12. "How Much Does NASA Cost," About.com's U.S. Economy Guide, 4/22/12.
13. "60 Minutes highlights Obama's broken promise on space program, jobs," Miami Herald Blog, 4/2/12.
14. "First moonwalker blasts Obama's space plan," NBCNews.com, 4/13/10.
15. "First moonwalker blasts Obama's space plan," NBCNews.com, 4/13/10.
16. "Obama Administration Proposes Big Cuts to NASA's Mars Programs," *Scientific American*, 2/13/12.
17. "High joblessness in the home of U.S. space flight," *60 Minutes*, 4/1/12.

18. http://www.popularmechanics.com/technology/engineering/1280801.

19. "The Future of NASA: Space Policy Issues Facing Congress," Congressional Research Service, 1/14/10.

20. "Gingrich criticizes Romney-Ryan space plan," NBCNews.com, 9/23/12.

21. http://spaceflightnow.com/falcon9/004/falcon9.html.

22. "Administration Gutting NASA," Fox Business, 5/22/12.

23. "Gingrich criticizes Romney-Ryan space plan," NBCNews.com, 9/23/12.

24. "Special Message to the Congress on Urgent National Needs," John F. Kennedy Library, 5/25/61.

7. FUNDAMENTAL FLAWS AND FAILINGS

1. http://www.economist.com/blogs/gulliver/2013/04/airport-rankings.

2. "Report Card for America's Infrastructure," American Society of Civil Engineers, 2009.

3. "Failure to Act: The Economic Impact of Current Investment Trends in Surface Transportation," American Society of Civil Engineers, 2011.

4. "Report Card for America's Infrastructure," American Society of Civil Engineers, 2009.

5. "Report Card for America's Infrastructure," American Society of Civil Engineers, 2009.

6. "Report Card for America's Infrastructure," American Society of Civil Engineers, 2009.

7. "Report Card for America's Infrastructure," American Society of Civil Engineers, 2009.

8. "Report Card for America's Infrastructure," American Society of Civil Engineers, 2009.

9. "Report Card for America's Infrastructure," American Society of Civil Engineers, 2009.

10. "Failure to Act: The Economic Impact of Current Investment Trends in Water and Wastewater Treatment Infrastructure," American Society of Civil Engineers, 2011.

11. "Metropolitan Transportation Infrastructure Survey," U.S. Conference of Mayors, 2011.

12. Joe McDonald, "China Wants to Invest in U.S. Infrastructure," Associated Press, 12/2/11.

13. "Failure to Act: The Economic Impact of Current Investment Trends in Surface Transportation," American Society of Civil Engineers, 2011.

14. "Failure to Act: The Economic Impact of Current Investment Trends in Surface Transportation," American Society of Civil Engineers, 2011.

15. "Failure to Act: The Economic Impact of Current Investment Trends in Water and Wastewater Treatment Infrastructure," American Society of Civil Engineers, 2011.

16. http://michellemalkin.com/2011/02/09/culture-of-corruption-whos-policing-amtrak-joe-bidens-53-billion-rail-boondoggles/.

17. "Transcript," *Lou Dobbs Tonight*, 6/21/07.

18. "Report Card for America's Infrastructure," American Society of Civil Engineers, 2009.

8. DEMOGRAPHICS AND DESTINY DISTURBED

1. http://www.boston.com/bostonglobe/editorial_opinion/oped/articles/2008/06/18/the_coming_population_bust/.

2. Quoted in *What to Expect*, p. 23.

3. United Nations, Department of Economic and Social Affairs, Population Decision, *World Population Prospects: The 2010 Revision*, 2011.

4. http://www.spiegel.de/international/germany/volunteers-help-save-germany-s-shrinking-towns-a-880352.html.

5. http://online.wsj.com/article/SB10001424127887323375204578270053387770718.html.

6. http://www.pewsocialtrends.org/2011/10/12/in-a-down-economy-fewer-births/.

7. http://usatoday30.usatoday.com/news/nation/census/2011-06-03-fewer-children-census-suburbs_n.htm?csp=hf.

8. *What to Expect*, p. 6.

9. *What to Expect*, p. 12.

10. http://www.smithsonianmag.com/specialsections/40th-anniversary/The-Changing-Demographics-of-America.html.

11. *What to Expect*, p. 69.

12. http://www.newgeography.com/content/003133-the-rise-post-familialism-humanitys-future.

13. http://www.newgeography.com/content/003133-the-rise-post-familialism-humanitys-future.

14. http://washingtonexaminer.com/article/143004.

15. http://www.economist.com/news/united-states/21569433-americas-marriage-rate-falling-and-its-out-wedlock-birth-rate-soaring-fraying.

16. Sarah Hayford and Philip Morgan, "Religiosity and Fertility in the United States: The Role of Fertility Intentions," *Social Forces* 86, no. 3 (2008): 1,163–1,188.

17. http://www.nytimes.com/2008/07/09/world/europe/09russia.html.

18. Quoted in *What to Expect*, p. 67.

19. http://www.newgeography.com/content/003133-the-rise-post-familialism-humanitys-future.

9. CHINA'S GOOD FORTUNE

1. http://www.defense.gov/news/newsarticle.aspx?id=67713.

2. http://www.youtube.com/watch?v=BkpOutDufXQ.

3. February 22, 2002—President Bush Speaks at Tsinghua University, Beijing, People's Republic of China. http://beijing.usembassy-china.org.cn/uploads/images/KOjXhn4S9Ke2fLD-JqMBjg/President_Bush_Speaks_at_Tsinghua_University_.pdf.

4. http://articles.latimes.com/2012/feb/14/news/la-pn-obama-welcomes-xi-jinping-20120214.

5. http://www.usnews.com/news/articles/2012/08/24/report-america-lost-27-million-jobs-to-china-in-10-years.

6. http://www.usatoday.com/story/opinion/2013/01/20/obama-inauguration-china/1843059/.

7. https://www.uschina.org/statistics/tradetable.html.

8. https://www.cia.gov/library/publications/the-world-factbook/rankorder/2042rank.html.

9. http://www.chinadaily.com.cn/china/2010-08/16/content_11155397.htm.

10. http://ipstatsdb.wipo.org/ipstats/searchresultsTable.

11. https://www.uschina.org/statistics/tradetable.html.

12. http://www.ssa.gov/oact/cola/AWI.html.

13. "Chalk Talk: Is US Headed Down Europe's Economic Path?" *Lou Dobbs Tonight*, 5/7/12.

14. http://www.treasury.gov/resource-center/data-chart-center/tic/Documents/mfh.txt.

15. http://www.rand.org/content/dam/rand/pubs/monographs/2005/RAND_MG260-1.pdf.

16. http://freebeacon.com/silent-running/.

17. "Missile Mania," *Washington Free Beacon*, 12/4/12.

18. "Washington Confirms Chinese Hack Attack on White House Computer," FOXNews.com, 10/1/12.

19. Ibid.

10. THE SHARIA SPRING WE SPRUNG

1. http://www.washingtontimes.com/blog/watercooler/2012/sep/24/picket-muslim-advocacy-groups-influence-heavily-us/.

2. http://militarytimes.com/valor/army-sgt-1st-class-terryl-l-pasker/6567860.

3. http://online.wsj.com/article/SB10001424127887324024004578171561230647852.html.

4. http://www.investigativeproject.org/documents/misc/122.pdf.

11. OUT OF ONE, MANY

1. http://pewhispanic.org/files/reports/25.pdf.

ACKNOWLEDGMENTS

President Obama likes to remind us that elections do have consequences. So do the public policy choices of the winners of those elections, and so does the leadership tone of the chief executive. Mr. Obama's choices and manner have divided Americans, alienated millions who've lost their jobs, their businesses, their savings, their homes, and their faith in America's leadership, whether Democrat or Republican. This year's midterm elections give us a long-awaited opportunity to at the very least begin to mitigate and perhaps overcome the consequences of the elections of 2008 and 2012.

The Republican Party must create a vision and new direction for the country in order to persuade Americans that they can restore belief in our nation's future, and that they will face up to the powerful forces that have diminished our confidence, our faith in our government and our society. The GOP party leaders and strategists have long believed they could simply do the bidding of the Business Roundtable, the Chamber of Commerce, and big-money donors, and if they failed, they at least had lined their pockets and could simply await the next election. That is one reason that Republicans have not been enormously successful in winning elections. If Republicans are to win this year, they must articulate as never before how their policies and values will improve the lives and prospects of working men and women, describe in straightforward language how Republican policies will benefit our middle class and assure the American dream for millions who've lost hope over these past six years. To those ends, I've set down here a few thoughts that I hope you will consider, and if you agree, then urge upon Republican leaders all around the country. I still believe it is entirely within our power as citizens to direct the course of this great nation. Hopefully, you will find this book helpful in doing so.

There are many folks I want to thank for assistance in the writing of this book: first, thanks to my editor at Threshold, Mitchell Ivers, for his support, encouragement, and forbearance throughout; my agent, Wayne Kabak, for his subtle nudges from time to time and good counsel. Thanks to my daughter, Heather, who did amazing research and contributed so much. Thanks to the Javelin team, Keith Urbahn and Matt Latimer, to my colleagues at the Salem Radio Network, and to all my colleagues at the Fox Business Network and Fox News Channel. Thanks to the FBN brass Kevin Magee and Brian Jones, and my appreciation to the terrific folks I get to work with closely on our daily broadcast: Brad Hirst, Tom Holmes, Lilah Sabalones, Abby Penn, Bob Regan, Leanne Miller, Mike Demarest, Brooke Clemency, and Rose Bagley. Thanks to our extraordinary leader Roger Ailes, who returned me to the arena, and who inspires us all. Thanks to my wonderful family for their love and support, and especially my wife, Debi, who keeps us all in line, and still makes me laugh after all these many years.

INDEX

A123 Systems, 103
AARP (American Association for Retired Persons), 164–65
ABC News, 44
Abdel-Rahman, Omar "The Blind Sheik," 204
abortion, 32–33, 157, 158, 159, 170, 185, 225
Abound Solar, 10, 102, 103
Aerojet of GenCorp, 114
Afghanistan, 143, 180, 216–17
African Americans, 17, 50, 51, 225, 242. *See also specific person or organization*
Agency for International Development, U.S. (USAID), 152
Agriculture Department, U.S., 116
air traffic controllers, 133
airports, 129, 132, 133
Akaka, Daniel K., 239
al-Awlaki, Anwar, 212
Al Jazeera, 203
al-Mismari, Abdelsalam, 208
Al Qaeda, 201, 207, 209, 210, 212, 214, 218
Aldrin, Buzz, 112
Alexander, Keith, 178
Alexandria, Virginia: stimulus grants and contracts awarded to, 45
Alston & Bird, 41
American Airlines, 238
American Chemistry Council, 42
American Crossroads, 21
American dream/values
    and American way, 5–6
    and axis of upheaval, 6, 11–12
    changing attitudes about, 5–6
    culture and, 166
    E Pluribus Unum and, 221, 222–43
    education and, 70–71
    family as central to, 166, 170

government influence on, 10
and group/identity politics, 221
middle class and, 35
multiculturalism and, 221, 223, 240
Republican Party as party of, 26–28, 31
social contract and, 5–6
subversion of, 4
American exceptionalism, 117, 175–76, 195
American Federation of Teachers (AFT), 77, 78, 79
American Future Fund, 21
American Honda, 235
American Petroleum Institute, 93
American Recovery and Reinvestment Act, 102
American Society of Civil Engineers, 131–32
Americans: definition of, 222
Americans with Disabilities Act, 37
Americans for Job Security, 21
Americans for Prosperity, 21
Amtrak, 140
Anheuser-Busch, 235
Apollo space program, 122
Apple, 188
Argonaut Private Equity, 104
Armstrong, Neil, 112, 118
Assad, Bashar al-, 208–11
automobile industry, 7
Axelrod, David, 17
Ayotte, Kelly, 20
Azure Dynamics, 104

Baby Boomers, 160
bailouts, 18, 27, 52, 56, 116
Bakken field (North Dakota), 107
Bank of England, 65
Banking Act (1933), 58

bankruptcy law (2005), 66
banks
  axis of upheaval and, 11
  bailout of, 27, 52, 56
  Bush (George W.) administration and, 57
  commercial, 54–55, 57–59, 64
  decline in number of, 55
  division between investment and commercial, 57–59
  earnings of, 54
  expectations for, 64
  failure of, 59, 64
  financial crisis of 2008 and, 53, 60–61, 67–68
  free market and, 57, 61
  Great Depression and, 59
  importance of reform of, 68
  legal actions against, 64, 65–67
  mortgages and, 59–61
  Obama administration and, 53, 57, 68
  as oligopoly, 57
  politics and, 63
  post-2008, 54, 64
  regional/community, 55
  regulation of, 7, 54, 56, 57–58, 62, 63, 64, 66, 67–68
  scandals involving, 64–66
  stimulus for, 54
  stress tests for, 55–56
  as threat to U.S. economy, 56
  "too big to fail," 53, 56–58, 66
  universal, 67
  See also specific bank
Barclay's Bank, 65–66
Bayh, Evan, 41
Beacon Power, 10, 102, 103
Beirut, Lebanon: bombing of Marine barracks in, 219
Benghazi attack (September 11, 2012), 11, 208, 214–15
Bernanke, Ben, 38
Biden, Hunter, 140
Biden, Joe, 105, 140
biofuels, 93, 96
biomass, 94–95
bipartisanship, 6–8
birth control, 152, 157, 159
birth rate, 154, 155, 156, 161, 162–63, 165, 166
Blumenthal, Richard, 44
Boehner, John, 38

Boeing, 114
Bolden, Charlie, 121
Boyd, James W., 38–39
Branson, Richard, 124
Brazil, 13, 176
Bremer, Paul, 143
"bridge to nowhere," 139
bridges, 130–32, 141, 143, 146
British Bankers Association (BBA), 65
Brosnan, Pierce, 90
budget, U.S.
  balanced, 62
  See also deficits, budget
Buffett, Warren, 9
Bureau of Labor Statistics, U.S., 47, 94
Burger King, 234
Bush, George H. W., 181
Bush (George W.) administration
  approval rating for, 19
  banks and, 57
  China and, 179, 182
  and dividing the electorate, 30
  energy issues and, 101, 102
  financial crisis of 2008 and, 37
  foreign policy and, 204
  infrastructure projects of, 143–44, 145
  and insider trading by congressmen, 37
  and Islam, 211–12
  Medicare and, 164
  Middle East and, 204
  and outsourcing of jobs, 47
  prescription drug plan of, 41–42
  September 11 and, 218
  and size of federal workforce, 46
  space program and, 117, 121–22
  terrorism and, 198
business/corporations
  axis of upheaval and, 11
  Chamber of Commerce and, 231–32
  China and, 177, 178, 179, 183, 184, 188–89, 194, 232
  elections of 2012 and, 16
  and English as official language, 241–42
  failure of leadership of, 8–10
  health care plans and, 232
  influence of, 7
  infrastructure and, 132–33, 137
  Obama administration and, 9, 29
  and on-site day care, 172

INDEX

overseas relocation of American, 37,
101–2, 132–33, 231–32
post-2008, 54
regulation of, 18
Republican views about, 18–19, 23,
26, 28
Republicans as party of big, 23
subsidies/welfare for, 7, 27, 28
taxes of, 23, 27, 97, 98, 194
and U.S. as divided nation, 243
Business Roundtable, 8–9
Byrd, Richard, 111

CAIR (Council on American-Islamic
Relations), 217–19, 236–38
Cairo, Egypt: Obama speech in, 197–98
Canada, 73, 99, 136, 143, 144
cap-and-trade legislation, 101
capitalism, 57, 179
Carson, Benjamin, 20
Carter, Jimmy, 90–91, 151, 180–81
celebrities: environmental issues and, 90
Census Bureau, U.S., 150
Center for American Progress, 77
Center for Responsive Politics, 44
Chait, Jonathan, 46
Chamber of Commerce, District of
Columbia, 47
Chamber of Commerce, U.S., 8–9, 41,
136, 231–32
Chase Manhattan Bank, 235
chemical industry: Dooley as lobbyist
for, 42
Cheney, Dick, 1, 48–49
Chevron, 98, 231, 234
Chicago, Illinois: schools in, 81–83, 85
"child-free movement," 152–53
children
cost of raising, 167–69
national debt as legacy for, 69
parents as failing, 69
traditional American values and, 166
China
abortion in, 185
ambitions of, 177
Apple workforce in, 188
Bush (George H. W.) administration
and, 181
Bush (George W.) administration and,
179, 182
Carter administration and, 180–81
Clinton administration and, 179, 182

as communist nation, 177–78, 179
currency manipulation by, 187–88
demographics in, 153, 156, 158–59,
184–85
economy of, 176, 181
education in, 73, 88
elections of 2012 and, 188
energy in, 183, 185–86
espionage/cyberworld program of,
178–79, 182–83, 193
infrastructure in, 136
innovation and invention in, 186, 189
jobs and, 183–84, 188, 194
manufacturing in, 185–86, 187, 188,
189
media and, 183
military of, 12–13, 176, 177, 178, 190,
191, 192–93, 194
modernization of, 181
Most Favored Nation status for,
183–84
Nixon administration and, 180, 184
nuclear weapons and, 191–92
Obama administration and, 176, 178,
182, 184, 186
One-Child Policy in, 158–59, 184–85
politicians views about, 179
population of, 153, 184–85
Reagan administration and, 181
Russia/Soviet Union and, 180
space program and, 113, 117, 178, 189
technology and, 181, 188–89
and Tiananmen Square, 181–82
trade and, 177, 181, 185, 187, 188, 190,
194
U.S. business/corporations and, 177,
178, 179, 183, 184, 188–89, 194, 232
and U.S. as economic superpower, 12,
62–63, 176–77
U.S. generosity and support for,
179–84
U.S. lack of concern/knowledge about
dominance of, 177, 178, 184–85,
187, 192, 194–95
U.S. military and, 12–13, 178, 189,
192–93
and U.S. national debt, 187
as world's largest economy, 176–77
Chrysler, 234–35
Chu, Steven, 105
Citibank/CitiGroup, 59, 66
citizenship, 71, 240–41

Civil Rights Act, 37
Clapper, James, 203
class issues: demographics and, 166
Clinton, Bill
  affluence of, 49–50
  women and, 229
Clinton (Bill) administration
  and bank regulation, 59
  China and, 179, 182
  and outsourcing of federal jobs, 47
  welfare reform and, 27–28
Clinton, Hillary, 49, 50, 215, 228, 232
CNN, 130
coal/coal industry, 89, 95, 96, 99,
  100–101, 102, 109, 183
Coalition Provisional Authority, 143
Coca-Cola, 233–34
Cold War
  U.S. winning of, 2
  See also Russia/Soviet Union
Colgate-Palmolive, 235
collateralized mortgage obligations
  (CMOs), 60
communism: and China as communist
  nation, 177–78, 179
"community": and U.S. as divided nation,
  226
Congress, U.S.
  approval rating for, 36, 43
  bank regulation and, 68
  and deferring of action on national
    issues, 31
  elections of 2012 and, 16, 17
  Libya and, 207
  Native Hawaiian legislation and,
    239–40
  as part-time occupation, 39
  sequestration and, 189
  Syrian civil war and, 209
  workweek of, 36
  See also House of Representatives,
    U.S.; Senate, U.S.; specific person
congressmen
  as exempt from laws, 37
  financial disclosure forms of, 39
  insider trading of, 37–39
  and lobbying as post-public service
    career, 39–43
  net worth of, 44–45
  pensions/retirement plans for, 36
  raises for, 37
  re-election rates for, 43

salaries and perks of, 36, 37
staff of, 36, 43
See also specific person
ConocoPhillips, 98
conservative organizations: IRS targeting
  of, 11, 235
Constellation space program, 118
construction industry, 48
consultants, government, 47
Continental Airlines, 235
contraception, 15, 225
contractors, government, 47
Corn, David, 226
corporations. See business/corporations
Council on American-Islamic Relations
  (CAIR), 217–19, 236–38
Crèvecoeur, J. Hector St. John de, 222
Cronkite, Walter, 150
cronyism, 6–8, 57, 83, 106, 123
Crossroads GPS, 21
Cruz, Ted, 20
Culberson, John, 115
culture: demographics and, 165–66
Curiosity (mobile laboratory), 113, 114,
  118, 122
currency manipulation: by China,
  187–88

Daimler Chrysler, 234–35
Dalai Lama, 152, 177
dams, 132, 134
Daniels, Mitch, 144–45
debt, national
  amount of, 186
  China and, 187, 189
  demographics and, 171
  education and, 87–88
  elections of 2012 and, 16
  elections of 2014 and, 23
  facts about, 31
  GDP ratio to, 187
  increase in, 16, 186–87
  leadership failings and, 7–8, 128
  as legacy for children, 69
  in 1972, 179–80
  Obama administration and, 115, 186
  opportunity gap and, 129
  rationalization of, 8
debt, subprime, 60
Defense Department, U.S., 105, 116, 190
deficits, budget. See debt, national
Delahunt, William D., 39–40

INDEX

Democratic National Committee, 230
Democratic Party
  as functioning coalition, 22
  See also specific person, administration, election, or topic
demographics
  abortion and, 157, 158, 159
  Baby Boomers and, 160
  birth control and, 152, 157, 159
  birth rate and, 154, 155, 156, 161, 162–63, 165, 166
  class issues and, 166
  and cost of raising children, 167–69
  culture and, 165–66
  definition of, 150
  education and, 166, 167, 171
  elderly and, 154–56, 157, 158, 163, 164, 169, 170
  entitlements and, 155, 160, 161, 163, 164–65, 171
  ethnicity and, 162
  family and, 165–66, 167, 169, 170, 171–73
  fertility rates and, 150, 154, 156–57, 159, 161–62, 165, 167–69
  financial crisis of 2008 and, 160–61
  food supply and, 151
  global economy and, 159
  health care and, 154, 157, 158, 161
  ignoring of crisis in, 169–71
  immigration and, 162, 172
  income and, 167–69
  infrastructure and, 171
  jobs and, 160–61, 165, 166, 171
  leadership and, 159, 173
  media and, 159, 170
  median age and, 163
  middle class and, 163, 167, 168–69
  national debt and, 171
  political correctness and, 157, 166, 170
  politics and, 169–70
  religion and, 166–67
  retirement and, 158, 160, 169
  solutions to crisis in, 171–73
  standard of living and, 165
  sterilization and, 159
  taxes and, 161, 163–64, 171
  unemployment and, 155, 157, 158, 166
  welfare programs and, 157–58, 160, 161, 164, 169
  women and, 165–66, 172

  workforce and, 155, 160–61, 163, 164, 165–66, 172
  See also population; *specific nation*
derivatives, 60, 67
Detroit, Michigan: construction industry in, 48
Deutschebank, 66
Dimon, Jamie, 61–62
Dinkins, David, 1
Disney Corporation, 152, 236
diversity/differences
  definition of, 223–24
  E Pluribus Unum and, 223–43
  election campaigns and, 224–26
  enforcement of, 224
  and English as the official language, 242
  political campaigns and, 224–26
  in Republican Party, 29–31, 32–34
  and U.S. as divided nation, 4, 225–43
  See also melting pot; multiculturalism
divorce, 33
Dodd, Christopher, 40–41, 42
Dodd-Frank Act, 56, 62
Dooley, Cal, 42
Dow Chemical, 42
drilling, oil and gas, 98–99, 102, 107
Dubai Ports World, 145, 146
DuPont, 42

E Pluribus Unum, 221, 222–43
economy, U.S.
  banks as threat to U.S., 56
  decline in U.S., 185
  facts and, 31
  government influence on, 10
  1990s expansion of, 63
  Obama administration and, 15, 176
  post-2008 growth in, 53
  Reagan administration and, 219
  and U.S. as economic superpower, 62–63
  See also debt, national; financial collapse of 2008; global economy; taxes
education
  American dream/values and, 70–71
  and college enrollment, 224
  cost of, 167, 171
  demographics and, 166, 167, 171
  devolution of, 87–88
  elections of 2012 and, 71

education (*cont.*)
federal government and, 86
funding for, 72, 75, 76, 80–81, 86,
87–88
gap in, 128
global economy and, 71, 86
graduation rates and, 166
as great equalizer, 70–71
ignorance/cluelessness about crisis in,
74
importance of, 70–71
labor unions and, 51, 70, 75, 76–88
and No Child Left Behind Act, 74–75,
76
Obama administration and, 71, 75
parents' role in, 87
politics and, 71–72, 87
private, 83
quality of, 72–73
Raza Studies and, 236
space program and, 121
union dominated, 70
and U.S. as divided nation, 243
women and, 224, 230
world rankings of, 72–73
See also mathematics; reading; schools;
science; teachers
Education, U.S. Department of, 94, 116
Egypt
economy in, 204, 205
elections of 2011 in, 203
media and, 199–200, 201
military in, 200, 203–4, 205
Obama administration and, 197–99,
200, 204–5, 206, 211
and Obama's Cairo speech, 197–98
popular protests in, 205
presidential election of 2012 in, 203
revolution in, 199–204, 206
terrorism and, 205
transition to democracy in, 204, 205
unemployment in, 204
Ehrlich, Paul, 151–52, 153, 156, 159
Eisenhower, Dwight D., 8, 141, 243
El Abidine Ben Ali, Zine, 206
el-Sisi, Abdel Fattah, 205
elderly, 11, 154–56, 157, 158, 163, 164,
169, 170
elections
campaign costs for, 43–44
campaigning during, 224–26
diversity/differences and, 224–26

importance of midterm, 15
labor unions and, 78, 79, 83
and re-election rates, 43
selection of Republican candidates for,
19–20
elections of 2008
energy issues and, 93, 100
labor unions and, 78
McCain and, 17, 19, 30
Obama and, 4, 20, 104
Republican funding for, 20
Romney and, 20
space program and, 117
elections of 2010, 15
elections of 2012
campaign discussions during, 32
comparison of Democratic and
Republican campaigns in, 17
Congress and, 16
cultural values and, 165–66
as dirty campaign, 22
education as issue in, 71
energy program and, 108
ideas and, 22
importance of, 16
infrastructure and, 142
labor unions and, 79
middle class and, 26–27
Obama administration and, 4, 15–17,
21, 22, 26, 28–29, 79, 165, 225, 226
reasons for Republicans' poor showing
in, 24
Republican "autopsy" of, 25
Republican campaign staff for, 19, 24
Republican disbelief about, 25
Republican failures and, 18, 26
Republican funding for, 20, 21–22,
24, 27
Romney and, 16, 19, 20, 21–22, 24,
25, 26, 27, 29, 30, 122, 142, 225,
226–27
selection of Republican candidates for,
19–20
slogans in, 28–29
space program and, 122
and U.S. as divided nation, 226–27
elections of 2014
grassroots campaigning in, 26
infrastructure and, 143, 147
need for change among Republicans
for, 17–18, 23
and Obama campaign staff, 225

and Obama goal as transformation of America, 10
as opportunity for Republicans, 25, 26
and Republican opposition to Obama, 23
Republican role in, 243
Republican strategies for, 17–18
suggested rules for Republicans for, 19–34
voter registration/turnout for, 34
elections of 2016, 18, 228
electoral system, 13
electrical grids, 132, 134–35, 143, 146
elites: in Washington, D.C., 51–52
Emanuel, Rahm, 27, 81–82
emerging nations: and U.S. as economic superpower, 62–63
Emerson, Ralph Waldo, 222
Ener1, 103
EnerDel, 103
energy
  axis of upheaval and, 12
  bank scandals and, 66–67
  Bush (George W.) administration and, 101, 102
  cap-and-trade legislation and, 101
  in China, 185–86
  consumption of, 90, 95
  cost of, 90, 91, 101, 107
  effective uses of, 91–92
  elections of 2008 and, 93, 100
  elections of 2012 and, 108
  growth in demand for, 91
  independence, 100, 107
  jobs and, 93–96, 98, 99, 100, 101, 102, 106–7, 108
  Keystone XL pipeline and, 99–100
  and leadership failings, 128
  long-term strategy for, 108
  Obama administration and, 10, 28, 92–95, 96, 99–101, 102, 104, 105, 106, 108–9, 186
  political promises about, 90–91, 92–93, 108
  prairie chickens and, 99–100
  regulation of, 101, 102
  subsidies for, 96, 97, 101, 102–6
  taxes and, 97, 98, 101
  technology and, 91–92, 107–8, 109
  U.S. dependence on foreign, 96

See also coal; electrical grids; gas; green energy; oil; renewable sources; solar energy; wind energy
Energy Conversion Devices, 103
Energy Department, U.S., 90, 104, 105, 106
energy grids. See electrical grids
English: as official language, 241–43
"enthusiasm gap," 17
entitlements, 155, 160, 161, 163, 164–65, 171, 194
Environmental Protection Agency, U.S. (EPA), 101, 102
espionage/cyberworld program: of China, 178–79, 182–83, 193
ethnicity, 162, 230
Europe
  "child-free movement" in, 152–53
  demographics in, 152–53, 157–58, 159, 170, 171–72
  economic crisis in, 159
  education in, 88
  family in, 170, 171–72
  infrastructure in, 136
  space program and, 115
  and U.S. as economic superpower, 62–63
  welfare systems in, 157–58
  See also European Union
European Space Agency, 115
European Union, 13, 155, 158, 176
evaluation: of teachers, 79, 81, 82–83, 86, 87
Export-Import Bank, 28
ExxonMobil, 97, 98, 234

Factor, Mallory, 77
facts: importance of, 31–34
failure
  of banks, 59, 64
  of business/corporate leadership, 8–10
  and energy issues, 128
  of leadership, 6–10, 127–28
  of media, 10–14
  parents as, 69
  political parties' acknowledgement of, 4
  of politicians/political leadership, 6–8
  of Republicans in elections of 2012, 18, 26
  schools as, 71–72, 73, 74
Fair Labor Standards Act, 37

Falcon 9 rocket, 123
family
  as central to American dream/values,
    166, 170
  culture and, 165–66
  decline of, 170
  demographics and, 165–66, 167, 169,
    170, 171–73
  impact of decaying infrastructure on,
    137
  and leadership failings, 128
  leave policies for, 37, 171–72
Family and Medical Leave Act, 37
Fannie Mae, 60
Federal-Aid Highway Act, 141
Federal Deposit Insurance Corporation
  (FDIC), 58
Federal Energy Regulatory Commission,
  66–67
federal government
  contractors/consultants for, 47
  dependency on, 127
  education and, 86
  expansion of role/powers of, 7–8, 10,
    16, 35, 129, 242
  salaries of employees of, 47
  size of, 16, 18, 46–47, 63–64
Federal Reserve, 54, 55–56, 65, 178,
  181
FedEx, 235
Fenty, Adrian, 78
fertility rates, 150, 154, 156–57, 159,
  161–62, 165, 167–69
financial crisis of 2008
  banks and, 53, 60–61, 67–68
  demographics and, 160–61
  housing and, 52, 56, 61
  impact of, 54
  and insider trading by congressmen,
    37–38
  and moral hazard, 56
  and net worth of congressmen, 45
  regulation and, 67–68
  and world economy, 61
financial disclosure forms: for
  congressmen, 39
"Financial Services Modernization Act"
  (1999). See Modernization Act
First Solar, 104
fishermen: and Delahunt as lobbyist, 40
Fisker, 106
flood insurance, 139

food manufacturers: Dooley as lobbyist
  for, 42
food stamps, 161
food supply: demographics and, 151
Ford, Henry, 68, 91
foreign aid, 199, 204
foreign policy
  Bush (George W.) administration and,
    204
  Obama administration and, 15, 176,
    197–99, 204, 206
  See also specific nation
Fort Hood shootings, 212
47 percent remark, Romney's, 30, 226–27
fossil fuels, 109
Fox News, 10–11, 77
France, 187, 192, 207
Freddie Mac, 60
free enterprise, 16, 57, 61, 62
Freedom of Information Act, 37
freedom of religion, 213–14
freedom of speech, 213–14, 215, 240
Friedman, Thomas, 183
Frum, David, 226
Furchtgott-Roth, Diana, 94

Gaddafi, Muammar, 206–7, 209
Gagarin, Yuri, 112
gas/natural gas, 89, 95, 96, 97–98, 100,
  101–2, 107–8, 109
gay marriage, 33–34, 170
Gay Pride, 221
Gaza, 202–3, 204
GDP (gross domestic product)
  impact of infrastructure on, 137
  national debt ratio to, 187
  oil and natural gas industry and, 97–98
Geithner, Timothy, 38
Gemini astronauts, 112
gender
  college enrollment and, 224
  diversity and, 223, 224–25
  and U.S. as divided nation, 226, 227,
    228–31
  See also homosexuality; women
General Dynamics, 114
General Motors, 234
generators, 134–35
Georgetown (Washington, D.C.), 49
geothermal energy, 95, 106
Germany, 156, 157, 163–64, 169
Ghosh, Anup, 193

Gingrich, Newt and Callista, 49
Glass-Steagall Act, 58, 59, 63
Glenn, John, 112
Glickman, Dan, 42
global economy
    China as largest in, 176–77
    demographics and, 159
    derivative market and, 67
    education and, 71, 86
    and financial crisis of 2008, 61
    U.S. as largest in, 176, 177
global warming, 89
Goldman Sachs, 231
Goldwater, Barry, 227
Goodlatte, Bob, 20, 24
government
    American dreams/values and, 5–6
    See also federal government; state/local
        government
Gowdy, Trey, 20, 24
GPS system, 133
graduation rates, 166
Graham, Lindsey, 20, 214, 219
Gramm-Leach-Bliley Act. See
    Modernization Act
grassroots politics, 26
Great Depression, 35, 48, 58, 59,
    141
Great Recession. See financial crisis of
    2008
Greece, 156, 157–58, 163, 164, 187
green energy, 10, 28, 89–90, 92, 93–94,
    98, 102–5, 183, 186
green jobs, 94, 106–7
Green Revolution (Iran), 182
greenhouse gases, 100
Greenwood, Lee, 3
Grocery Manufacturers Association
    (GMA), 42
group politics, 221, 243
Guantanamo, 212
Gulf War, 1–2

Halliburton, 49, 102
Hamas, 202, 204, 209, 218, 237
Hariri, Rafik, 209
Hasan, Nidal, 212
health care, 36, 154, 157, 158, 161,
    232. See also Medicaid; Medicare;
    Obamacare
Health and Human Services, U.S.
    Department of, 116

health insurance: prevalence in
    Washington area of, 50
Heritage Foundation, 79, 101, 102, 142
heroes, 111–12
Hezbollah, 209, 210, 211
Higginbotham, John, 125
Hispanics/Latinos, 17, 162, 225, 241, 243
Homeland Security, U.S. Department
    of, 238
homosexuality, 33–34, 166, 217, 225, 226,
    230, 243
House of Representatives, U.S.
    campaign costs for election to, 43–44
    elections of 2012 and, 17
    insider trading by members of, 38–39
    workweek of, 36
housing
    bank bailouts and, 56
    financial crisis of 2008 and, 53, 56,
        60–61
    foreclosures, 52
    middle class questions about, 52
    mortgages for, 59–61
    in Washington, D.C., 35
Housing and Urban Development, U.S.
    Department of, 116
HSBC, 66
hurricanes, 23, 134, 135
Hussein, Saddam, 1
hydraulic fracturing "fracking," 107
hydropower, 95

ideas: and suggested rules for
    Republicans, 21–23
identity politics, 221, 230, 243
Illinois: teacher compensation in, 80
Immelt, Jeffrey, 9
immigration/immigrants, 24, 162, 172,
    222, 223, 230, 232, 236, 240–41,
    242
income, 36, 128, 137, 167–69. See also
    salaries
India, 13, 73, 88, 136, 153, 176
Indiana
    infrastructure in, 144–45
    schools in, 78–79
infrastructure
    Bush (George W.) administration and,
        143–44, 145
    business/corporations and, 132–33,
        137
    in China, 136

INDEX

infrastructure (*cont.*)
and comparison of U.S. with other
nations, 132–33
and compensation for natural disaster
losses, 139
degradation of American, 130–47
demographics and, 171
elections of 2012 and, 142
elections of 2014 and, 143, 147
funding for, 135–36, 138, 139, 140,
141, 146
impact on GDP of, 137
importance of, 129–30, 136–37
jobs and, 133, 141, 142
and labor unions, 133, 142
media coverage about, 130, 138–39
and national security, 145–46
and natural disasters, 134–35, 139
Obama administration and, 141, 142,
146–47
as patronage and pork barrel projects,
138, 142
and private sector, 144–45
and public-private partnership, 140,
146
role of government and, 129
selling off to foreign nations of,
145–46
terrorism and, 145
and U.S. funding for infrastructure in
other nations, 143
*See also specific nation or type of
infrastructure*
Innocence of Muslims (video), 214–15
innovation/inventions, 10, 117, 119, 121,
186, 189, 194, 195
insider trading, 37–39
Institute for Energy Research, 98
integrity, 4, 31, 61
Intel, 114
interest rates, 60, 61, 64–66
Internal Revenue Service (IRS), 11, 235
International Space Station, 113, 117,
119, 123
interstate highway system, 140–41
investment banks, 57–59
Invincea, 193
Iran, 73, 145, 182, 209
Iraq, 1–2, 143, 209
Islam
and Islamic lobbyists, 217–19
Obama views about, 197–99, 215

radical, 13, 198, 207, 211–12, 218, 237
stereotypes of, 198
talking about, 211–13
terrorism and, 212
use of word, 211–12
See also Muslims; *specific person,
organization, or nation*
Islamiyya, Gamaa, 204
Israel, 176, 202, 211
Issa, Darrell, 44
Italy, 155, 156, 157, 187

Jabhat al-Nusra group, 209–10
Jackson, Jesse, 233–34, 240
Japan, 153–56, 163, 176, 179, 191, 198
jobs
Chamber of Commerce and, 231–32
China and, 183–84, 188, 194
Chinese currency manipulation and,
187
in construction industry, 48
demographics and, 160–61, 165, 166,
171
energy and, 93–96, 98, 99, 100, 101,
102, 106–7, 108
exporting to Mexico of, 144, 231–32
green, 94, 106–7
health care and, 161
and indifference to unemployment, 35
infrastructure and, 133, 141, 142
in manufacturing, 188
in 1990s, 63
Obama administration and, 35, 93–94,
161, 176
in oil industry, 98
outsourcing of, 35, 183–84, 231–32
part-time, 54, 161
post-2008, 53–54
as priority, 9–10
and shrinking middle class, 35
space program and, 114, 115, 118–19,
121
taxes and, 194
for teenagers, 165
and U.S. as divided nation, 243
See also unemployment
Jobs, Steve, 188
Johnson & Johnson, 235
Johnson, Lyndon, 114
J.P. Morgan Chase, 61–62, 66, 67
Judiciary Committee, House, 24
July 4 parades, 2

266

Kaiser, George, 104–5
Kellogg, 42
Kennedy, John F., 114, 125
Kennedy Space Center, 118–19
Keystone XL pipeline, 99–100
Khayat, Adel el-, 204
King, Martin Luther Jr., 151, 235
Kissinger, Henry, 180
Klein, Joe, 230
Korean War, 2, 112
Kotkin, Joel, 164
Krumholz, Sheila, 44
Ku Klux Klan, 227
Kuwait: Iraq invasion of, 1–2
Kyl, Jon, 239

La Raza, 221, 236
labor unions
    China relations and, 188
    as dominant force in Democratic
        Party, 77, 78
    education and, 51, 70, 75, 76–88
    elections and, 78, 79, 83
    fees and dues for, 77, 79
    infrastructure and, 133, 142
    political power of, 77–80, 87–88
    for teachers, 70, 75, 76–88
Latinos. See Hispanics/Latinos
Le Chateau de Lumiere (northern
    Virginia mansion), 51
leadership
    business/corporate, 8–10
    China relations and, 194–95
    demographics and, 159, 173
    diversity and, 224–25
    flaws and failings of, 6–10, 127–28
    global, 12–14, 62
    political, 6–8, 224–25
Lebanon, 73, 211, 219
legal system, 12
Lehman Brothers, 38
levees, 132
LG Chem, 104
LIBOR interest rate scandal, 64–66
Libya, 206–8, 211
Lincoln, Blanche, 41
Lincoln Policy Group, 41
Lindbergh, Charles, 111
Live Earth concert, 90
lobbyists
    as former public service employees,
        39–43

Islamic, 217–19
    salaries of, 41–42
    Washington area homes and offices
        of, 45
    See also specific person or organization
Lowes, 241
Luxor, 204–5

Macy's, 235
Mannock, Edward, 111
Mansour, Adly, 205–6
manufacturing, 185–86, 187, 188, 189,
    194
Mao Tse-Tung, 180, 183
market integrity, 61
marriage
    American values and, 166, 170
    gay, 33–34, 170
Mars space program, 113, 114–15, 121
Mashpee Wampanoag tribe: and
    Delahunt as lobbyist, 40
mathematics
    and education of children, 72, 73–74,
        75, 81, 121
    space program and, 121
    world rankings of education in, 72, 73
McCain, John, 17, 19, 20, 30, 214, 219
McCaul, Michael, 44
McDonald's, 107, 195
McLean, Virginia: affluence of, 48–49
media
    CAIR and, 218–19, 237
    China and, 183
    demographics coverage by, 159, 170
    Egyptian revolution and, 199–200, 201
    and English as official language,
        241–42
    failure of, 10–14
    immigration and, 240–41
    infrastructure coverage by, 130,
        138–39
    Obama administration and, 10–11
    political correctness and, 240
    traditional role of, 10
median age: in U.S., 163
Medicaid, 160
Medicare, 41, 69, 160, 164–65, 169, 170
melting pot, 222–23, 243
Mercury space program, 112
merit pay: for teachers, 78, 79, 83–84, 87
Merrill Lynch, 67
message: of Republican Party, 28–29

INDEX

Mexico, 66, 143–44, 231–32, 236
middle class
American values and, 35
cost of raising children in, 167, 168–69
demographics and, 163, 167, 168–69
and gasoline prices, 109
jobs and, 35
Obama's use of Dobbs's references to, 26–27
questions of, 52
Republican views about, 26, 27
as shrinking, 35
Middle East
Bush (George W.) administration and, 204
Obama administration and, 176, 199
popular protests in, 206
U.S. nation-building projects in, 190
See also specific nation
military
in China, 12–13, 176, 177, 178, 190, 191, 192–93, 194
in Egypt, 200, 203–4, 205
military, U.S.
celebrations for, 1–2
China and, 12–13, 178, 192–93
cyberattacks on, 193
funding for, 12–13, 189–90, 220
as global military power, 220
and Iraq-Kuwait war, 1–2
Obama administration and, 189–90, 219–20
political correctness and, 216–17
reduction in size of, 189–90, 192–93, 194
space program and, 124
vulnerability of, 189
Minneapolis, Minnesota
and I-35 bridge collapse, 130, 131
Somali cabdrivers in, 215
minority groups: political campaigning and, 225–26
Mitchell, Billy, 111
Modernization Act (1999), 59, 62, 63
Moe, Terry, 79
Mollenkamp, Carrick, 65
moon space program, 112, 118, 121, 122, 125
moral hazard, 53, 56
Morsi, Mohamed, 202, 203, 204, 205
mortgages, 59–61, 116

Motion Picture Association of America, 41, 42
Mountain Plaza Inc., 103
movie industry: Dodd as lobbyist for, 42
movies, 179
Mubarak, Hosni, 199, 200, 201, 202, 205, 206
multiculturalism, 221, 223, 240, 241, 242, 243
Murray, Charles, 166
Musk, Elon, 124
Muslim Brotherhood, 199, 200–204, 205
Muslim countries, space program and, 121
Muslims
as extremists, 198, 205, 210–11
political campaigning and, 225
on US Airways flight, 237–38
See also CAIR; Islam; Muslim Brotherhood

NASA (National Aeronautical and Space Agency), 112–19, 121, 122, 124, 125, 127
nation-building projects, U.S., 190
National Action Network (NAN), 232–33, 234–35
National Assessment of Educational Progress, 72
National Association for the Advancement of Colored People (NAACP), 221, 227–28
National Center for Health Statistics, 150
National Defense University, 190
National Education Association (NEA), 77, 78, 79
National Intelligence Council, 176
National Organization for Women (NOW), 228–31
National Post, 218
National Review, 218, 236
national security, 124, 145–46
National Security Agency (NSA), 178
National System of Interstate and Defense Highways, 141
National Transition Council, 207
Native American groups, 239–40
Native Hawaiian Federal Recognition Act, 239–40
NATO (North Atlantic Treaty Organization), 175–76, 206–7, 208

INDEX

natural disasters, 134–35, 139
natural gas. *See* gas/natural gas
Nelson, Ben, 38
Nevada
  elections of 2012 in, 17
  green jobs in, 106–7
New Deal, 141
New Jersey
  green jobs in, 94
  Muslim domestic disputes in, 215–16
New Orleans, Louisiana, 134
New York City
  blackout in, 135
  decline of jobs in, 47
  and Occupy Wall Street, 77
  parades in, 1, 2
  schools in, 70, 85–86
  teachers' unions in, 77
New York Post, 234
New York Times, 38, 39–40, 49, 183
Newquist, H. P., 124
Nixon, Richard, 90, 180, 184
No Child Left Behind Act, 74–75, 76
Noble Corporation, 102
nonprofit organizations, 232, 235. *See also*
  specific organization
Nordic Windpower, 104
North Africa, 208
North American Free Trade Agreement
  (NAFTA), 143–44, 231
North Dakota: oil and gas production
  in, 107
nuclear energy, 91, 95, 106
nuclear weapons, 190, 191–92
nurses: prostitutes as, 169

Obama, Barack
  and American exceptionalism,
    175–76
  and axis of upheaval, 14
  Benghazi video and, 214–15
  Cairo 2009 speech of, 197–98
  elections of 2008 and, 4, 20, 104
  as failure, 176
  goal of, 10, 14
  Islam and, 197–99, 215
  middle class and, 26–27
  at NATO 2009 Summit, 175–76
  and political climate, 5
  promises of, 4
  Quran burning and, 214
  wealth of, 50

Obama (Barack) administration
  banks and, 53, 57, 68
  business/corporations and, 9, 29
  characteristics of, 15, 61
  China and, 176, 178, 182, 184, 186
  economy and, 15, 176
  education and, 71, 75
  Egypt and, 197–99, 200, 204–5, 206,
    211
  elections of 2012 and, 4, 15–17, 21, 22,
    28–29, 79, 165, 225, 226
  and elections of 2014 as Republican
    opportunity, 25
  energy and, 10, 28, 92–95, 96, 99–101,
    102, 104, 105, 106, 108–9, 186
  flaws and failings of, 127–28, 179,
    198–99
  foreign policy and, 15, 176, 197–99,
    204, 206
  Fox News report about "nudge squad"
    of, 10–11
  impact of Sharia Spring and, 214–15
  India and, 176
  infrastructure and, 141, 142, 146–47
  innovation and invention and, 10
  Islam and, 211–12
  Israel and, 176
  jobs and, 35, 93–94, 161, 176
  labor unions and, 79
  Libya and, 206, 207–8, 211, 214–15
  Luxor and, 205
  media and, 10–11
  Middle East and, 176, 199
  military and, 189–90, 219–20
  Muslim Brotherhood and, 202, 203
  national debt and, 115, 186
  nuclear weapons and, 190
  Republican opposition to, 21, 23, 28
  Russia and, 176
  and salaries of federal employees, 47
  and size and power of federal
    government, 16, 46–47
  space program and, 113–19, 121,
    122–23, 127
  Syrian civil war and, 209, 211
  taxes and, 97
  terrorism and, 198
  and U.S. as divided nation, 225, 226,
    228, 242
Obama, Michelle: wealth of, 50
Obamacare, 16, 54, 154, 161, 164, 232
Occupy Wall Street, 77

269

oil, 89, 94, 95, 96–99, 101–2, 104, 107, 108
Olsen's Crop Service, 103
Olsen's Mills Acquisition Company, 103
One-Child Policy (China), 158–59, 184–85
opportunity gap, 128–29
Organization for Economic Cooperation and Development (OECD), 73–74
Overseas Private Investment Corporation, 28

Panetta, Leon, 211
parades, patriotic, 1–3
parents
  and devolution of education, 87
  as failures, 69
  unwed, 166
Pasker, Terry, 216
Pathfinder space program, 122
patriotism, 1–4
patronage/pork barrel, 138, 142, 235
Patterson, Anne, 205
Paul, Rand, 20
Paulson, Hank, 37, 38
Peabody Coal, 97
Pelosi, Nancy, 96, 99, 130
Penn, Sean, 97
pensions/retirement, 36, 86, 158, 160, 169
PepsiCo, 232–33
Petraeus, David, 214
Pfizer, 235
PhRMA, 41–42
Ping Cheng, 38–39
Pioneer Aerospace Corporation, 114
Planned Parenthood, 225
Pledge of Allegiance, 75–76
Plouffe, David, 17
political correctness
  axis of upheaval and, 12
  contraception and, 157
  culture and, 166
  demographics and, 157, 166, 170
  exclusion and, 224
  and impact of Sharia Spring, 213
  media and, 170, 240
  military and, 216–17
  multiculturalism and, 240
  patriotism and, 2, 3
  talking about Islam and, 212–13
  and U.S. as a divided nation, 240

politics/politicians
  banks and, 63
  China and, 177, 179, 188
  climate of, 4–5
  demographics and, 169–70
  diversity and, 224–25
  education and, 71–72, 87
  energy and, 90–91, 92–93, 99, 108
  failure of, 4, 6–8
  grassroots, 26
  group/identity, 221, 230, 243
  as indifferent to unemployment, 35
  infrastructure and, 137–38, 139
  labor unions and, 77–80
population
  decline in, 165–66
  food supply and, 151
  growth in, 149–50, 151–52
  over, 152–53
  world, 149–50, 151–52
  See also specific nation
Population Matters, 152
poverty, 50–51, 128, 243
Powell, Colin, 1
prairie chickens, 99–100
prescription drug plan: former congressmen/lobbyists and, 41–42
private sector
  decline in investment in, 129
  infrastructure and, 144–45
  space program and, 114, 118, 122–25
property taxes, 51, 75
prostitutes: as nurses, 169
public-private partnership, 114, 125, 140, 146
public service
  employment after, 39–43
  as lifetime occupation, 39–40
  as part-time occupation, 39
  See also politics/politicians
PUSH, 234, 235
Putin, Vladimir, 158, 169

Qatar, 73, 210
Quincy, Massachusetts: and Delahunt as lobbyist, 40
Quran, burning of, 213–14
Qutb, Sayyid, 201

race, 223, 226, 227–28, 230, 232–40, 243. See also African Americans; Hispanics/Latinos; Muslims

INDEX

radical Islamists, 13, 198, 207, 211–12,
218, 237
railroads, 134, 140, 144
Rainbow Coalition, 234
RAND Corporation, 190
Range Fuels, 103
Raser Technologies, 103
reading: and education of children, 73,
74, 75, 76, 81
Reagan, Ronald, 30, 31, 160, 181, 219,
220, 243
recycling: of Republicans, 19
Regan, Don, 67
regulation
of banks, 7, 54, 56, 57–58, 62, 63, 64,
66, 67–68
of business/corporations, 18
and comparison of China and U.S.,
194
energy and, 101, 102
Reid, Harry, 96, 106, 130, 214
religion, 11, 213–14, 166–67, 226. *See also*
Islam
renewable energy, 107, 108–9
Republican National Committee, 25
Republican Party
diversity/differences within, 29–31,
32–34
ideas of, 22–23
integrity of, 31
message of, 28–29
need for vision/renewal for, 23,
243
as party of American dream/values,
26–28, 31
as party of big business, 23
recycling of, 19
Ryan's role in, 24
suggested rules for, 19–34
visitors to, 22–23
*See also specific person, administration,
election, or topic*
retirement. *See* pensions/retirement
rewards: and suggested rules for
Republicans, 19–20
Rhee, Michelle, 78
Rice, Condoleezza, 204
Richtofen, Manfred von, 111
Rickenbacker, Eddie, 111
roads/highways, 131, 132, 134, 138,
140–41, 143, 146
Rockefeller, Jay, 44

Romney, Mitt
campaign staff for, 19
and China, 188
as divisive figure, 226–27
education and, 71
elections of 2008 and, 20
elections of 2012 and, 16, 19, 20,
21–22, 24, 25, 26, 27, 29, 30, 71, 122,
142, 188, 225, 226–27
47 percent remark of, 30, 226–27
infrastructure and, 142
middle class and, 27
Planned Parenthood and, 225
space program and, 122
taxes and, 23
Roosevelt, Franklin D., 17, 140–41,
197–98
Rove, Karl, 25
Royal Bank of Scotland, 66
rubber rooms: teachers in, 70, 85–86, 87
Rubin, Robert, 59
Rubio, Marco, 20
rules: for Republicans, 19–34
Russia/Soviet Union
Afghanistan invasion by, 180
China and, 180
in Cold War, 191
collapse of, 2
demographics in, 156, 158, 169
economy of, 13
largest world economy and, 176
nuclear weapons and, 192
Obama administration and, 176
Reagan administration and, 219
space program and, 112, 113, 115, 117,
119
submarines and, 191
Syrian civil war and, 209
and U.S. as economic superpower,
62–63
as world leader, 13
Ryan, Paul, 23, 24, 122

S&L crisis, 55
Sadat, Anwar, 202
salaries
of federal employees, 47
median U.S., 47
for teachers, 77, 80–81, 82, 86, 87
See also income
Sandhills (Nebraska): prairie chickens
in, 99

INDEX

Sarbanes-Oxley Act (1989), 37
Satcon, 104
satellites, 112, 133, 178
Saudi Arabia: Syrian civil war and, 210
Sawyer, Diane, 228
Schiff, Adam, 115
schools
  as failures, 71–72, 73, 74
  length of day for, 87
  and parents as failures, 69
  Pledge of Allegiance and, 75–76
  and school boards, 76
  in Washington, D.C., 50
Schwarzkopf, Norman, 1
science
  and education of children, 73–74, 121
  space program and, 121
  world rankings of education in, 72, 73
seaports: selling of, 145–46
Senate, U.S.
  campaign costs for election to, 44
  elections of 2012 and, 17
September 11, 63, 208, 215, 218
sequestration, 189
7 Up, 234
sexual orientation, 230. *See also*
  homosexuality
shale gas, 107–8
Sharia Spring, 213–16. *See also specific
  nation*
Sharpton, Al, 232–33, 234–35, 240
Sheffield, Horace, 235
Shell Oil, 97
Shepard, Alan, 112
Sierra Club, 89–90
Singapore, 72, 132
Social Security, 69, 160, 163, 169, 170,
  171
solar energy, 89, 92, 93, 94–95, 96,
  106
solid waste treatment, 132
Solyndra, 10, 28, 104–6, 108
Soros, George, 77
South Korea, 132–33
Soviet Union. *See* Russia/Soviet Union
Space: The Next Business Frontier (Dobbs
  and Newquist), 124
Space Command, U.S., 124
Space Foundation, 116
space program
  accomplishments/benefits of, 112,
    116–17, 122, 125–26

Bush (George W.) administration and,
  117, 121–22
China and, 113, 117, 178, 189
and commercial space flights, 124
and discovery of flight, 111–12
and dreams about space, 112
education and, 121
elections of 2012 and, 122
Europeans and, 115
funding for, 114–19, 121–23, 127
heroes of, 111–12
importance of, 122, 127
innovation/inventions and, 117, 119,
  121
jobs and, 114, 115, 118–19, 121
and list of first orbital launches, 120
manned flights and, 123
military and, 124
Muslim countries and, 121
national security and, 124
Obama administration and, 113–19,
  121, 122–23, 127
private sector and, 114, 118, 122–25
public-private partnership and, 114,
  125
Russia/Soviet Union and, 112, 113,
  115, 117, 119
technology and, 112, 114
See also specific program
space shuttle, 118, 121, 124
SpaceVest, 125
SpaceX, 123, 124
special interest groups, 223, 226, 227,
  230, 231, 232, 234. *See also specific
  group*
SpectraWatt, 103
spending
  and failure of politicians/political
    leadership, 7–8
  Republican views about, 23
  See also type of program
standard of living, 11, 165
State Department, U.S., 208, 215
state/local government, 16, 75
sterilization, 159
Stevens, Ted, 139
Steyn, Mark, 164
stimulus, 54, 138, 140, 141
Stirling Energy Systems, 103
stress tests: for banks, 55–56
Stumpf, John, 61–62
submarines, 191

subprime debt, 60, 61
subsidies, 27, 28, 96, 97, 101, 102–6
Sussex Rural Electric Cooperative, 135
Syria, 208–11, 219

takfiri ideology, 201
Taliban, 217
TARP, 116
Tauzin, Billy, 41–42
Tax Foundation, 45
taxes
    For business/corporations, 23, 27, 97,
        98, 194
    and comparison of China and U.S.,
        194
    Democrats views about, 18
    demographics and, 161, 163–64, 171
    energy and, 97, 98, 101
    jobs and, 194
    Obama administration and, 97
    Republican views about, 18, 23
    sequestration and, 189
    as solution to almost everything, 23
    and U.S. as divided nation, 231
    workforce and, 164
Tea Party, 15, 235
teachers
    accusations of misconduct against, 70
    bonuses and promotion for, 75
    certifications and degrees for, 84
    criticisms of, 75
    evaluation of, 79, 81, 82–83, 86, 87
    firing of, 75, 84–85
    labor unions for, 70, 75, 76–87
    layoffs of, 82, 85–86
    merit pay for, 78, 79, 83–84, 87
    paid leave for, 70
    protection of bad, 76–87
    in rubber rooms, 70, 85–86, 87
    salaries and benefit packages for, 77,
        80–81, 82, 86, 87
    seniority of, 84
    tenure of, 84–85
technology
    China and, 181, 188–89
    energy, 91–92, 107–8, 109
    Japan demographics and, 153
    space program and, 112, 114
teenagers: jobs for, 165
terrorism
    Bush (George W.) administration and,
        198

CAIR and, 237
Egypt and, 205
Gaddafi and, 206
infrastructure and, 145
Islam and, 212
Libya and, 206, 207
in North Africa, 208
Obama administration and, 198
Syrian civil war and, 209
and U.S. as divided nation, 2
See also specific attack
Tesla, Nikola, 91
Texaco, 231
Thompson River Power, 103
Tiananmen Square, 181–82
Time magazine, 51, 200, 230
toll roads: private sector operated,
    144–45
"too big to fail" banks, 53, 56–58, 66
Tracinski, Robert, 51
trade
    Chamber of Commerce and, 231–32
    China and, 177, 181, 185, 187, 188,
        190, 194
transit systems, 132, 134. *See also*
    railroads
Transocean, 102
Treasury Department, U.S., 56, 187–88
Truman, Harry S., 198
Tucson Unified School District (TUSD),
    Raza Studies and, 236

UBS, 66
unemployment
    and China, 184
    in construction industry, 48
    demographics and, 155, 157, 158, 166
    in Egypt, 204
    leadership failings and, 128
    national rate of, 46
    in 1972, 179
    politicians as indifferent to, 35
    post-2008, 54
    space program and, 118–19
    in Washington, D.C., area, 46
United Arab Emirates, 145
United Kingdom, 192, 207
United Nations, 152, 206, 215
United States
    and definition of Americans, 222
    as divided nation, 4, 225–43
    English as official language of, 241–43

INDEX

United States (*cont.*)
  Obama goal as transformation of, 10,
    14
  as world power, 2
  as world's largest economy, 176,
    177
  See also specific person or topic
universal banks, 67
unwed parents, 166
upheaval, axis of
  definition of, 6, 11–12
  examples of, 6–14
  external forces and, 12–13
  importance of, 6
  internal forces and, 13–14
  Obama and, 14
US Airways flight: Muslims on, 237–38
Utility MACT rule, 102

Van Roekel, Dennis, 77
Vietnam War, 2, 150–51
Virgin Airlines, 124
Virgin Galactic, 124
Virginia
  elections of 2012 in, 17
  stimulus grants and contracts awarded
    to, 45
Volcker Rule, 56
von Braun, Wernher, 119

Wal-Mart, 235
walk in space, 112
Wall Street Journal, 65, 67, 85, 190
The War on the Middle Class (Dobbs),
  26–27, 71
Warner, Mark, 44
Washington, D.C.
  affluent counties surrounding, 48–49
  African Americans in, 50, 51
  construction industry in, 48
  crime in, 46, 50–51
  elites in, 50, 51–52
  have-nots in, 50–51
  housing in, 35
  jobs in, 35, 46
  optimism in, 50
  poverty in, 50–51
  prevalence of health insurance in, 50
  prosperity in, 35, 45, 46
  schools in, 75, 78

stimulus grants and contracts awarded
  in region of, 45–46
Washington Post, 38, 48–49, 51
Washington Times, 218
water systems, 131, 132, 133–34, 135–36,
  143, 146
Weill, Sandy, 59
Weingarten, Randi, 77
welfare
  for business/corporations, 7, 27, 28
  Clinton reform of, 27–28
  demographics and, 157–58, 160, 161,
    164, 169
  in Europe, 157–58
  leadership failings and, 128
  spending for, 128
Well-Being Index, Gallup, 50
Wells Fargo, 61–62
White, Ed, 112
White House computer systems, 193
wind energy, 39–40, 89, 92, 93, 94–95,
  96, 106
Winning Our Future, 21
women
  Clinton (Bill) and, 229
  college enrollment of, 224, 230
  demographics and, 165–66, 172
  in Egypt, 203
  as election campaign targets, 225
  NOW and, 228–31
  and U.S. as a divided nation, 243
  in workforce, 165–66, 172
work ethic, 9–10, 153, 194
workforce: demographics and, 155,
  160–61, 163, 164, 165–66, 172
  Works Progress Administration
    (WPA), 141
World Bank, 181
World Economic Forum, 72, 132
World Trade Organization, 188
World War I: aviation in, 111
World War II: and veterans as heroes,
  112
Wright Brothers, 91, 227

Yeager, Chuck, 111–12

Ziobrowski, Alan J., 38–39
Ziobrowski, Brigette J., 38–39
Zuckerberg, Mark, 165